THE BAZ-NAMA-YI NASIRI
A PERSIAN TREATISE
ON FALCONRY

THE BAZ-NAMA-YI NASIRI A PERSIAN TREATISE ON FALCONRY

TRANSLATOR

DOUGLAS CRAVEN PHILLOTT

Published by

Isha Books
B-63, Ist Floor
New Gupta Colony
Near DDA Market
Delhi - 110009

Distribution Network
gyanbooks.com
India, USA, Canada, UK, Australia

ISBN: 978-93-6896-403-2 (PB)

First Published, 1908

2nd Impression 2025

Printed at: Gyan Press, Delhi.

THE BAZ-NAMA-YI NASIRI
A PERSIAN TREATISE ON FALCONRY
Translator: DOUGLAS CRAVEN PHILLOTT

THE

BĀZ-NĀMA-YI NĀṢIRĪ

A PERSIAN TREATISE ON FALCONRY

I

HUNTING AND HAWKING SCENE

(FROM A PAINTING IN AN ANCIENT PERSIAN MS.)

THE

BĀZ-NĀMA-YI NĀṢIRĪ

A PERSIAN TREATISE ON FALCONRY

TRANSLATED BY

LIEUT.-COLONEL D. C. PHILLOTT

SECRETARY, BOARD OF EXAMINERS, CALCUTTA,
GENERAL SECRETARY AND PHILOLOGICAL SECRETARY, ASIATIC SOCIETY OF BENGAL,
FELLOW OF THE CALCUTTA UNIVERSITY, EDITOR OF THE PERSIAN
TEXT OF THE *QAWĀNĪN[u] 'Ṣ-ṢAYYĀD*
ETC. ETC.

LONDON
BERNARD QUARITCH
1908

TO

HIS EXCELLENCY

THE 'ALĀ[u] 'L-MULK

FORMERLY

GOVERNOR-GENERAL OF KIRMĀN

AND

PERSIAN BALUCHISTAN

THIS TRANSLATION IS AFFECTIONATELY DEDICATED

IN MEMORY

OF

CERTAIN DAYS NOT UNPLEASANT WHEN WE MET IN THE

BĀGH

AND MINGLED OUR TEARS OVER OUR

EXILE

بیادگاری

آن ایامی که تماماً غیر مرغوب نبود که با

جناب جلالتمآب علاء الملک دام اجلاله

فرمانفرمای سابق کرمان و بلوچستان ایران در باغ کرمان

از دوری دیار و یار اشک حسرت از دیدها فرو میریختیم این

ترجمهٔ محقر باکمال خلوص بنام معظم له

معنون گردید

TRANSLATOR'S INTRODUCTION

THE author of this work was *Ḥusām*[u] *'d-Dawlah* Taymūr Mīrzā,[1] one of the nineteen sons of Ḥusayn 'Alī Mīrzā,[1] *Farmān-Farmā*, the Governor of the Province of Fārs, and one of the sons of Fatḥ 'Alī Shāh, Qājār.

On the death of Fatḥ 'Alī Shāh, in A.H. 1250 (A.D. 1834), general confusion prevailed: the claimants to the Crown were many. The details of these claims and the actions of the various aspirants to establish them are exceedingly complicated and difficult to follow. The old *Ẓill*[u] *'s-Sulṭān* first mounted the throne at Teheran. His nephew the young Muḥammad Mīrzā was then Governor of Tabrīz, and his troops had not been paid for some time. However, receiving pecuniary support from the English ambassador, and moral support from the Russian, he marched on Teheran (putting out the eyes of a brother or two *en route*), and was met by the army (hastily paid up to date, and even in advance), of the *Ẓill*[u] *'s-Sulṭān*. The moving spirit in Muḥammad Mīrzā's army appears to have been an Englishman named Lynch, who, nominally in command of the artillery, virtually managed what cannot be better described than as "the whole show." The camp of the *Ẓill*[u] *'s-Sulṭān* awoke in the morning to discover that, during the night, their General had gone over to the enemy; and that Mr. Lynch, having pointed four big guns at their camp, was haranguing them from his position, and exhorting them to go home. His arguments appeared reasonable. Part of the *Ẓill*[u] *'s-Sulṭān's* army crossed over to Mr. Lynch, and part returned home. "In a moment, this fine army was disbanded, scattered like the stars of the Great Bear, every man going to his own place."

Muḥammed Mīrzā now entered Teheran without the slightest opposition, and his uncle the *Ẓill*[u] *'s-Sulṭān*, "in the greatest despondency," placed the crown on his head and handed him the state jewels. Muḥammad Shāh (no longer Mīrzā) then proceeded to

[1] *Mīrzā* after (not before) a name signifies Prince.

despatch the *Ẓill*[u] *'s-Sulṭān* and most of his uncles and brothers to the dreaded fortress of Ardabīl.

Shaykh 'Alī Mīrzā, *Shaykh*[u] *'l-Mulūk,* "though he had none of the requisites of sovereignty except a band of music," was another prince that made an even more feeble bid for the throne. He was then Governor of Tūy Sarkān. Royal governors, in Persia, have bands that play in the evening; but a morning band is a prerogative of the Shah. Shaykh 'Alī Mīrzā ordered his band to play in the morning as well as in the evening, and thought that by so doing he had become Shah. However, on receiving the unexpected news that Muḥammad Shāh was in Teheran, he tendered his submission. and was soon packed off to join the "caravan" at Ardabīl.

Ḥaydar Qulī Mīrzā, *Ṣāḥib Ikhtiyār,* another royal prince, also made a burlesque attempt to obtain sovereignty. His own adherents split into two parties, quarrelled amongst themselves, and then at a moment's notice turned him out of the city of which he was Governor. On his way to Isfahan he fell off his horse, and was carried into that city in a prostrate condition. Once or twice, after this, he flits across the page of history as a fugitive from the wrath of Muḥammad Shāh.

It must not be supposed that all this time the *Farmān-Farmā,* the father of our author and the eldest living son of the late Fatḥ 'Alī Shāh, was idle. He seems to have been popular in Fārs, for Shīrāz was kind enough to offer him the crown of Persia. He induced his brother the *Shujā'*[u] *'s-Salṭanah,* the Governor of Kirman, to have coins struck in his name there, and also the *Khuṭbah* read in his name at the Friday prayers. He further sat on a throne in Shīrāz. A few days later, news of the arrival of Muḥammad Shāh in Teheran and of the abdication of the *Zill*[u] *'s-Sulṭān,* reached him. The *Shujā'*[u] *'s-Salṭanah,* who had arrived at Shīrāz from Kirmān, was then placed in command of an army, and under him were two of the *Farmān-Farmā's* sons, Najaf Qulī Mīrzā in command of the Cavalry, and Rizā Qulī Mīrzā in command of the Infantry. The destination of the army appears to have been Isfahan, the inhabitants of which, it was hoped, would declare for the *Farmān-Farmā.* The season was winter. The second march was commenced in a storm of snow and rain. The plains became a lake: the hill passes were blocked by snow: men and horses died: guns sank in the mud: property was lost. Rations, too, ran short, and the country had lately been visited by locusts. Even proper guides were wanting. But worst of all, one march from Isfahan, Mr. Lynch was discovered blocking the way. In the night, three of Mr. Lynch's artillerymen "deserted" to the Shīrāz camp, and tampered with its artillery. In the skirmish next morning, all the artillery horses of the Shīrāz camp went bodily over to Mr. Lynch. The remainder of the Shīrāz army scattered and disappeared, got entangled in the mountains, and retraced its steps to find Mr. Lynch with some artillery blocking one path, and a Mr. "Shir"—apparently another Englishman—blocking another.

The Shīrāz Commander-in-Chief, with his two nephews, and presumably a remnant of the army, eventually slunk back into Shīrāz, in a miserable plight from hunger and exhaustion. A grand Council was then held, and everybody talked, and the *Farmān-Farmā* listened to all in turn. One thing seems quite certain, no one *did* anything. Strange rumours now began to reach Shīrāz of weird Turkish troops that spoke no Persian, and were commanded by an ubiquitous Englishman. The merchants, panic-stricken, fled with their property. The city people revolted, and seized some towers; while the troops, of course, deserted to the other side. A faithful eunuch then informed the *Farmān-Farmā* that he had met some of the city people on their way to seize the gates, and that a plan had been concocted for capturing the *Farmān-Farmā* with all his relations, adding that the delay of *one minute* meant the loss of everything. Still the *Farmān-Farmā* shilly-shallied: still he maintained his attitude of keeping "one foot in the stirrup and one on the ground," giving ear, first to the advice of his son to flee, and then to the advice of his brother the *Shujā'u s-Salṭanah* to stay. The result was, that the two elder princes were taken. The *Farmān-Farmā* was deported to Teheran, where he was honourably treated but speedily died. The *Shujā'u s-Salṭanah* was carried to Teheran, deprived of his sight *en route*, and then sent to enliven the family party at Ardabīl. The princes, Najaf Qulī Mīrzā, Riẓā Qulī Mīrzā, Taymūr Mīrzā the author of this Bāz-Nāma, with Nawāb Ḥājiya the mother of Najaf Qulī Mīrzā, and three more princes, brothers or half-brothers, narrowly effected their escape, and a month later reached Baghdād in safety.

At that time relations between the English and Persian Courts were extremely friendly. The eldest prince, Riẓā Qulī Mīrzā, with his brothers Najaf Qulī Mīrzā, and Taymūr Mīrzā our author, started for England to obtain the mediation of William IV., reaching London *viâ* Damascus and Beyrout in the summer of 1836. Their journey from Damascus to Beyrout was as feckless and mismanaged as their expedition to Isfahan.

For four months the princes were a popular feature of London Society, and during that time succeeded in losing their hearts several times. Then, as they had obtained the object of their journey, Lord Palmerston having arranged matters to their satisfaction, they returned to Bag̲h̲dād and exile.

Najaf Qulī Mīrzā wrote an account in Persian of the events that occurred on the death of their grandfather Fatḥ 'Alī Shāh, and of their own adventures in consequence, and he also kept a diary of their tour to England and back.

As'ad Ya'qūb K̲h̲ayyāṭ,[1] a Syrian Christian who had accompanied the princes to Europe as Dragoman, secured this MS. in Bag̲h̲dād; but on his journey back to Syria he was held up by Bedouins and deprived of that portion of the MS. that treated of the actual flight of the princes from Shīrāz and of the arrest of their father—the illiterate Arabs mistaking these pages for the Holy Qur'an. The remainder of the journal was translated by him into English, and under the title of a "Journal of a Residence in England and of a Journey from and to Syria, of their Royal Highnesses Reeza Koolee Meerza, Najaf Koolee Meerza, and Taymoor Meerza of Persia," was printed in London for private circulation only. The present tragi-comic page of Persian history has been compiled, partly from this narrative, and partly from Persian sources.

Some twenty-eight years after the bid for sovereignty, and fourteen years after the death of their cousin Muḥammad Shāh, the two princes Riẓā Qulī Mīrzā and Taymūr Mīrzā started from Bag̲h̲dād to revisit their native land. Who knows what secret hopes they cherished, what dreams they dreamt of royal favour? In a few pathetic words, our author, in his Preface, informs us that, at the second stage of their journey, the truth of the sacred text, 'And ye know not in what land death shall overtake you,' was forcibly revealed to him: his brother suddenly sickened and died.

---

[1] In his translation of the Journal he transliterates his name Asaad Y. Kayat. *K̲h̲ayyāṭ* is a common family name amongst Syrian Christians.

Taymūr Mīrzā was well received by Nāṣir[u] 'd-Dīn Shāh, whose constant companion he became in all sporting expeditions. He died in A.H. 1291 (A.D. 1874); I am told, in Teheran.

In Persia, and round Baghdād, Taymūr Mīrzā's name is still a household word. "Ah," exclaim the Persians when hawking is mentioned, "if Taymūr Mīrzā were only here."

His treatise on Falconry, of which the present book is a translation, was composed in A.H. 1285 (A.D. 1868) and was originally lithographed in Teheran. A second, and perhaps a third, edition was lithographed in Bombay, a few pages on pigeons and game-fowl, apparently written in India, being added as an Appendix.

The present translation has been made from a copy of the original Teheran edition to which marginal notes have been added by a former owner. For the versification I am indebted to the assistance of poetical friends.

D. C. P.

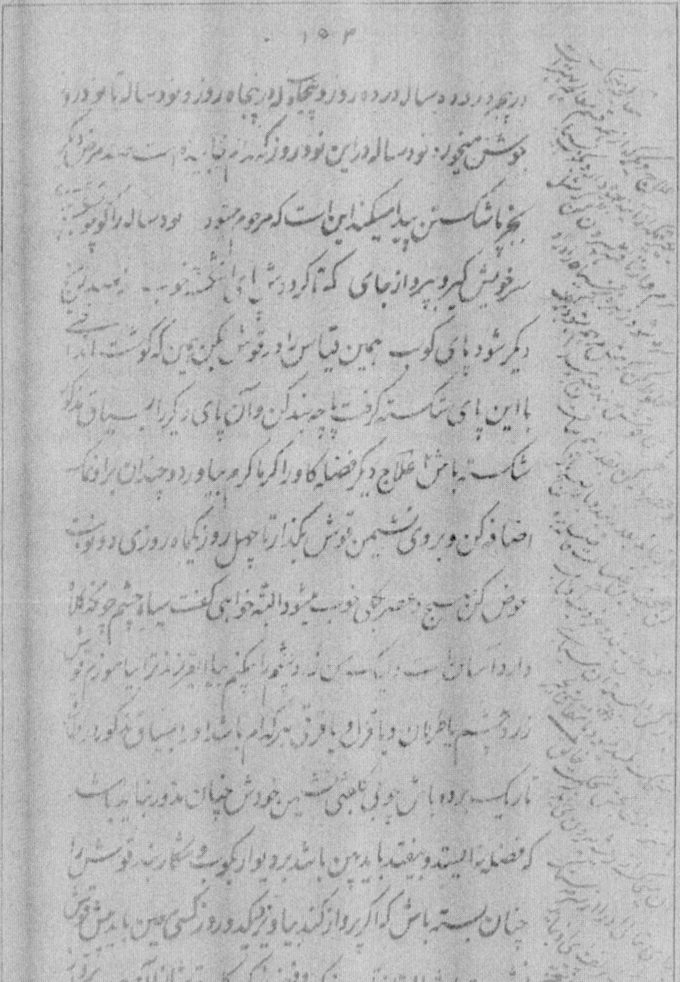

II

FACSIMILE OF A PAGE OF THE TEHERAN LITHOGRAPHED EDITION

THE

"BĀZ-NĀMA-YI NĀṢIRĪ"

A TREATISE ON FALCONRY DEDICATED TO NĀṢIRᵁ 'D-DĪN SHĀH OF PERSIA

IN THE NAME OF GOD, THE MERCIFUL, THE COMPASSIONATE

LET us embroider this Treatise on Falconry with the design of the Praise of the All-Sufficient; and let us exalt our Pen by a votive offering of praise to the Great Fashioner, in the path of whose worship the wings of those falcon-like Pure Spirits of the Saints are spread wide open,[1] like as the portals of His Mercy are opened wide in the faces of those that truly love Him. Let us also praise the matchless beauty and grandeur and perfection of that high-soaring Bird,[2] the robe of whose being God adorned with this sacred verse: "And was at the distance of two bow-strings, or even less."[3]

We further extol the Family, the *Humā*[4] of whose noble spirit soars aloft on the pinions of sure belief and true knowledge, winging its way to the eyrie of union with the Eternal Phœnix:—

Falcons thrice four and twain,[5] that on the wing
Of Unity soar ever hovering
Round Caucasus (within whose rocky caves
Dwells the *Sīmurgh*); while ever on their graves
The clouds of God's Grace every moment pour
Unnumbered blessings from His bounteous store.

[1] *Tajnīs:* a play upon the words *bāz*, "a goshawk," and *bāz*, "open."

[2] *i.e., Muḥammad.*

[3] Qurān, liii, 9.

[4] *Humā*, the Lammergeyer; *vide* Journal and Proceedings Asiatic Society of Bengal, Vol. II, No. 10, 1906.

[5] *i.e.*, the 14 *Ma'ṣūms*, which are *Muḥammad*, *Fāṭimah*, and his descendants the 12 Imāms.

Thus says this writer, His Royal Highness Prince *Taymūr Mīrzā*,[1] son of the Blessed[2] *Ḥusayn 'Alī Mīrzā, Farmān-Farmā*,[3] and grandson of the Blessed[2] King *Fāth 'Alī Shah, Qājār* (whom Allah has clothed in the Robes of Light) :—"At the beginning of the reign of King *Muḥammad Shāh* (the Receiver of God's Pardon[4] and a Dweller in Paradise), in the year of the Flight 1250 (a thousand blessings and praises on Him that performed it[5]) I with my brothers *Riẓā Qulī Mīrzā*,[1] *Nāqib*[u] *'l-Iyāla*, and *Najaf Qulī Mīrzā, Wālī*, both my elders, and *Shāh-rukh Mīrzā*, and *Iskandar Mīrzā*, younger than the writer, departed from the Province of *Fārs* on a pilgrimage to the Sacred *Karbalā*[6]—best of blessings and perfect benedictions on its silent[7] inmates! After a residence of some months in that Celestial City, I, as God and Fate decreed, with my brother *Riẓā Qulī Mīrzā* and *Najaf Qulī Mīrzā* took a journey to Europe, returning to the Holy Places[8] after the space of a year and a half. By the grace of God we spent the long space of thirty years, in peace and freedom, in those Abodes of Peace, visiting the Holy Shrines and hawking and hunting in their environs.

When the throne of the Kingdom of *Īrān*—which God protect from the changes and vicissitudes of Time—was adorned and illuminated by the splendour of the auspicious accession of His

---

[1] *Mīrzā* after a name signifies Prince: Mīrzā before a name signifies one whose mother is a Sayyida. But *Mirzā* (with short i) before a name signifies a "clerk, writer, etc."

[2] *Marḥūm*, "blessed" (usually only of Muslims by Muslims), signifies "dead and pardoned by God," *i.e.*, "late."

[3] *Farmān-Farmā*—a title, and also a Governor or Viceroy. Ḥuṣayn 'Alī Mīrzā, much lauded by the Poet Qā,ānī, was Governor of Fārs.

[4] *i.e.*, "deceased;" *vide* note 2.

[5] *i.e.*, on the Prophet.

[6] *'Atabāt-i 'Alīyāt*, the "Exalted Thresholds," is a Shī'ah term for the city of Kerbalā, the burial place of the martyrs Imām Huṣayn, his family and his followers; sometimes Najaf and Kāẓimayn are included.

[7] *i.e.*, those buried in those sacred spots.

[8] *Amākin-i Musharrafa*.

Majesty *Shāh Nāṣir*[u] *'d-Dīn*, a *Jamshīd* in rank, the shade of God's Grace and His Blessing to men, the Divinely-aided, a King and the son of Kings; and when the fame of the Justice and the echo of the Clemency of this peerless Monarch spread and re-sounded throughout the world, nay reached even to the high oratories of Heaven's Dome, I, your humble slave, with *Riẓa Qulī Mīrzā*, left Baghdad, the Abode of Peace,[1] in the year of the Flight 1279, on a pilgrimage to Holy Meshed, in order to kiss the sacred shrine of the Eighth Imām,—the blessings of God Almighty on him, his honoured forefathers, and his descendants the Leaders of men!

In *Kirmānshāh* his pre-destined death overtook *Riẓa Qulī Mīrzā*, in the Fort known as *Ḥājī Karīm*, one of the stages on our journey; and in accordance with the passage, "All that breathes shall taste of death," he passed away, and the hidden mystery of, "No living thing knoweth in what land it shall die" was manifested to us.

When the bird of his spirit spread its wings and soared to the eyrie of Rest we despatched his bier to the Holy City of *Najaf*[2] (thousands of blessings on him that has sanctified it) where was his dwelling-place and ancestral home, so that he might there be buried with his fathers, while I, alone, with my burden of grief continued on my way to the most Sacred City.[3]

When I was blessed by the pilgrimage to *Haẓrat-i 'Abd*[u] *'l-'Aẓīm*[4]—Peace and Honour be to him—the intense heat had already set in, and His Majesty and his Court were moving to the summer residence at *Shimrānāt*. Certain well-wishers of His

---

[1] *Dār*[u]*'s-Salām* is an epithet or a name of Baghdad.

[2] *Najaf-i Ashraf;* near Kerbalā and the burial place of *'Alí*.

[3] *Arẓ-i Aqdas* is *Mash,had-i Muqaddas*.

[4] Probably the place of this name near Teheran, the burial place of the saint from which the place takes its name.

Majesty and of the State informed him of my circumstances. Since the Creator of Existence, He who has made the heights and the depths, has decreed for every low estate a high estate, and for every grief a joy, and for every disgrace an honour, and for every pain a cure, the Royal mind was inspired to appoint *Dūst 'Alī Khān*, the Minister of Public Works, to summon this attached slave to the Presence. So, according to Royal Mandate, I drove with the Minister in his carriage to *Nayāvarān*,[1] where the Royal Camp then was. After a short wait in the shade of the tent we were honoured by admittance to the sun-like Presence of the King—May our souls be his sacrifice! Such kindness he showed and so wide did he open the doors of his favour and kingly condescension, that what I had heard was but a thousandth part of the reality—as it were but a handful as a sample of an ass-load. I exclaimed :—

> When the poor traveller's glance on thee alight,
> Thy beauty charms his vision with its sight.
> No longer wishful through the world to roam,
> His heart but seeks to find with thee a home.

He spoke on various topics and strung the pearls of kingly words—and kings' words are the kings of words—on the string of discourse. I too, his slave, according to my mean ability, presented my poor contribution to the conversation, which at last turned on sport. The Shadow of God (may our souls be his sacrifice) is an expert of experts in all sports, but especially in shooting. I have never seen or heard of his equal in shooting, either on foot, or off a galloping horse. For example, one day in the *Kūh-i Shahristānak*, I and *Mahdī Qulī Khān* the *Ghulām bachcha-bāshī*, and *Āqā Kushī Khān* the gun-keeper, were sitting with him behind a stone—*Muṣṭafā Qulī Khān* the *Mīrshikār*[2] with several other

[1] Near *Shimrānāt*.

[2] *Mīr-shikār*; in Persia a head game-keeper, but in India a title of any bird-catcher, assistant falconer, etc.

rifles having made a circuit to drive the herd of wild sheep within range of the king's rifle—when the herd suddenly turned aside and made off. Five three-year old rams that had not scented the danger came fearlessly on towards the stone behind which His Majesty and the rest of us were crouching. His Majesty had with him a double-barrelled gun for slugs, and three rifles. When the rams arrived within forty paces, His Majesty fired the gun and brought down one with one barrel, and a second with the second barrel. The three remaining rushed down the hill. His Majesty seized the rifles with his auspicious hand, and by the will of the One God brought down all three head one after the other:—

> The Heavens exclaimed "Bravo!"
> The Angels cried "Well-done!"[1]

Now only an expert shot knows at what ranges to fire five successive and successful shots at a fleeing herd.

> No sport is this but miracle and wonder!

True it is that kings are the shadow of God and able to accomplish all by the help of their Master.

> As long as in the heavens the Lord shall reign,
> May our King's rule upon the earth remain;
> For surely so long will a shadow last
> As He by whom the shadow's self is cast.[2]

Many other feats, too, like this I've seen, up till now, the year 1285[3] (of the Flight).

Sixty-four years of my life have now passed, all spent in hunting and shooting. I have had no hobby but sport, no recreation but it.

This slave of the King's Court, *Taymūr*, desired that like the ant he should present his offering to the Court of the Solomon of the

---

[1] From the *Shāh-Nāma*.
[2] The Shah, and in fact all kings, are styled "The Shadow of God."
[3] A.D. 1868.

Age,[1] that is, compose a treatise on Falconry and its branches, and on the various species of hawks and their treatment in health and disease.

Although the old Falconers have written treatises on this subject, still in my humble opinion those old writers were by no means experts in their science and should not be classed as masters in their art. I, therefore, thought of myself writing on the subject and leaving a memento for all lovers of the sport, whether tyros or experts. When these are seated by a stream, refreshed and rested after the morning's sport, I hope they will recall the writer in their prayers and pass over the shortcomings of his work.

I have honoured my book with the auspicious name of His Majesty the King, and have named it the *Bāz-Nāma-yi Nāṣirī* and have divided it into several *bābs*.[2]

---

[1] The allusion is to some story of the ant presenting Solomon with the leg of a locust.

[2] The book, however, contains only two numbered *bābs*; the first, pages 1 to 26 (1st Edition) on "The species of Hunting-birds;" and the second, the remaining 157 pages of the book on other subjects. The 2nd *bāb*, however, commences with: "On the black-eyed birds of prey that have at various times of my life come into my possession and which . . . ."

CONTENTS

ILLUSTRATIONS

Part I

THE YELLOW-EYED BIRDS OF PREY

CHAPTER I

ON THE SHORT-WINGED HAWKS USED IN FALCONRY

THE Birds of Prey are divided into two great divisions, the "Yellow-eyed" and the "Black-eyed," these being again subdivided into numerous species.

We will first treat of the Yellow-eyed Division.

Ṭughral [CRESTED GOSHAWK ?]—The first species worthy of note is the *Ṭughral*.[1] During my many wanderings I have searched diligently for this species, but in vain, and am, therefore, unable to describe it from personal knowledge. There is a current tradition, that a single specimen was once brought to Persia from China,[2] and presented as a curiosity to King *Bahrām-i Gūr*,[3] who treasured it greatly and guarded it jealously. One sad day, when the king was out hawking, the *ṭughral* suddenly took to "soaring" and was quickly lost to the sight of the disconsolate monarch. His retinue were soon scattered in every direction in search of the

---

[1] *Ṭughral*; a species frequently mentioned in old Persian MSS. on falconry. It is probably the "Crested Goshawk" (*Astur trivirgatus*) which is said to have been formerly trained in India. Jerdon, quoting Layard, says it is trained in Ceylon. The *Ṭughral* is confused by Indian falconers with the *Shāh-bāz*, or "Royal Goshawk" which, according to Jerdon, is the name given by native falconers of Southern India to the Crested Hawk-Eagle (*Limnætus cristatellus*). The same author also quotes Major Pearse as his informant that the Rufous-bellied Hawk-Eagle (*L. kienierii*) is, "Very rarely procured from the N.W. Himalayas and trained for hunting and is known as the *Shāh-bāz*."

[2] *Chīn*; under this name are included Yarkand, Khutan, Mongolia, Manchuria, etc.

[3] *Bahrām* was surnamed *Gūr*, from his passion for hunting the *gūr* or wild ass. He belonged to the Sassanian dynasty of Persian kings and his name frequently occurs in Persian poetry. The Greek Varanes is said to be a corruption of *Bahrām*.

III

PERSIAN CARPET DEPICTING HAWKING SCENE

missing hawk, and the king was left almost alone, being attended by a few only of the royal favourites. *Bahrām-i Gūr* and his party also took up the search; and wandering far and wide, at length happened on a large and shady garden, where they alighted. The bewildered owner of the garden advanced exclaiming:—

> "The simple peasant on whose '*kulāhed*'[1] head
> The Sultan, Phoebus-like, his grandeur shed,
> Trembles within his soul and well nigh dies,
> That on him shines the Sultan's kindly eyes."

On being questioned about the lost hawk he replied, "What a *Ṭughral* may be, I know not, but not two hours since a hawk with bells and a jewelled 'halsband,'[2] took stand in a tree of this very garden; but taking fright at my attempt to secure it, it flew off and settled in that grove yonder." Bahram was overjoyed at this clue, which enabled him to recover his lost favourite.[3]

From this reference to a "halsband" and bells, and to the *ṭughral's* habit of sitting on trees, the author concludes that this unknown species belongs to the yellow-eyed division of the birds of prey.

CHAPTER II

THE GOSHAWKS

THREE SPECIES.—[The author now describes three races of goshawk, which he distinguishes by the names of *Tīqūn*; *Ṭarlān*; and *Qizil*:[4] each of these three he sub-divides into varieties, only distinguishable from each other by slight differences in colouring, in marking, or in size. The first-named species is the white

[1] *Kulāh* is the felt hat worn by Muslims.

[2] *Jalqū*; "Halsband, *lit.* neck-band; a contrivance of soft twisted silk, placed like a collar round the hawk's neck and the end held in the hand; . . ."—*Harting*. The object of the halsband is to steady the hawk and enable it to start collectedly when the falconer casts it at the quarry. In the East it is considered an indispensable portion of the equipment of every Sparrow-Hawk. It is also very frequently attached to the Goshawk, but is not, however, used with the *Shikra*. *Zang* "bell."

[3] This anecdote is from the *Shāh-Nāma*.

[4] The *Ṭarlān* and the *Qizil* are the same species; the latter is the local race that breeds in Persia.

goshawk; the second is that variety or race of the common goshawk that is caught after migration into Persia; while the third is the local race that breeds in the country.

After hazarding a conjecture that the white goshawks[1] are not a true species like the *Ṭarlān* and *Qizil*, but are either albinos, or else accidental varieties produced by the pairing, for one or more generations, of two exceptionally light specimens of the common goshawk, the author proceeds to describe a pure white variety of the *Tīqūn*, which, he says, is known to the people of Turkistan by the name of *Kāfūrī*.[2] He remarks that he has caught albino specimens of the Saker Falcon, and has further observed albinos of the *Shāhīn*, "pie-bald crow,"[3] peacock, sparrow, sparrow-hawk, pin-tailed sand-grouse, chukor, hoopoe, English merlin, *kākul* lark, and common crane. As regards the *Kāfūrī*, he states his opinion that it is the offspring of albino *Ṭarlāns* that happen to have paired for two generations. He continues :—]

WHITE GOSHAWK OR *Tīqūn-i kāfūrī*.—The female of this variety of *Tīqūn* is noted for its large size, the male on the contrary for being extremely small. The head, neck, back, and breast are totally devoid of markings, the plumage being white as driven snow.[4] In the immature bird the eyes have only a slightly reddish tinge, but after the first moult their hue generally deepens and turns to a ruby-red.[5] The claws and beak, though frequently white, are more often a light grey, while the cere is greenish.

E'en such the noble thorough-bred *Tīqūn*;
May God in mercy grant us such a boon!

---

[1] In Blandford's *Zoology of Eastern Persia* the author states his opinion that the white goshawk is merely a variety of the common goshawk.

[2] *Kāfūrī*; adj. from *kāfūr*, "camphor," an emblem of whiteness.

[3] *Kulāgh-i pīsa* "the pied crow"; *qil-i quiruq* T. "the pin-tailed sand-grouse"; *hudhud* "hoopoe"; *kākulī*, *vide* page 24, note 4, "a species of crested lark"; *durnā* "common crane."

[4] Jerdon mentions a pure white goshawk as being found in New Holland, and states that Pallas notices a white goshawk from the extreme north-east part of Asia. Some Afghan falconers call albinos of any species *taighūn* (*tīqūn*).

[5] In the adult *shikra* (wild caught), the iris is sometimes a deep red and sometimes a bright yellow. In "eyess" *shikras*, even after the moult, the iris is frequently almost colourless, the result perhaps of confinement in dark native houses.

IV

FROM AN OLD PERSIAN PAINTING, INDIAN, PROBABLY OF THE MUGHAL PERIOD

I remember having once seen a "cast"[1] of this variety—male and female—in the possession of *Fatḥ 'Alī Shāh*[2] (now a resident of Paradise), both of which were exceptionally fine performers in the field.

The people of Turkistan, who are highly skilled in the art of training goshawks, call this variety *lāziqī*.[3]

It is commonly believed by falconers and bird-catchers, that in the early spring, when the female goshawk is desirous of the attentions of a male, she utters loud and plaintive cries, which attract to her many species of birds. From these she selects a male of a species different from herself,[4] and the result of this union is a diversiform progeny. However, the *kāfūrī* or *lāziqī* variety is the offspring of two white parents.

The following circumstance lends some colouring of truth to this quaint belief:—

Some years ago a hawk of this species was brought from Russia and presented as a curiosity to the late Shah, who, in turn, bestowed it on *Ḥusayn 'Alī Mīrzā*,[5] Governor of the Province of Fārs. The Governor (now in the abode of the Blessed) forwarded it to me—the contemptible. It must have been a bird of four or five moults, when it came into the possession of this slave. After infinite pains I succeeded in taking with it one solitary *chukor*,[6] and that, too, a bird harried and worn out by another hawk. It had a very villainous and scurvy disposition. The plumage of this hawk, an unusually large female, was peculiar, in that its feathers were alternately snow-white and raven-black; the claws and beak were of the colour of mother-of-pearl, and the eyes were

---

1 "Cast of hawks, *i.e.*, two; not necessarily a pair."—*Harting*.

2 A contemporary of Napoleon.

3 *Lāziqī* T., is said to be the name of a white flower: this is said to be the same as the *gul-i rāziqī* P., a kind of jasmine (the *bel phul* of the Hindus).

4 A similar belief is current in parts of England with regard to the cuckoo, which, by some country people, is supposed to mate with the wryneck or "cuckoo's mate."

5 This *Ḥusayn 'Alī Mīrzā* was apparently the father of the author.

6 The *chukor* (Caccabis chukor) of India and *kabk* of Persia, with its "joyous laughter," enters largely into Oriental fable. On account of its cheery cry, it is a favourite cage-bird with both Hindus and Muslims. The male is also trained to fight. It is not an uncommon sight to see a man strolling along the road with a *chukor*, or a grey partridge, trotting behind him like a little fox terrier.

a reddish yellow. I feel confident her albino mother had mated with a raven, and that this spurious half-caste was the result of the union. There *is* some truth in the statements of the bird-catchers.

The above description is given, as it seems in some measure to support the stories of the bird-catchers. Sure and certain knowledge, however, rests with God.

V

FROM A PAINTING IN AN ANCIENT PERSIAN MS. WRITTEN IN INDIA

GOSHAWK (*Ṭarlān*).—There are three varieties of *Ṭarlān*, the dark, the light, and the tawny. The last two are common, but though tractable and easily reclaimed,[1] they are not good at large quarry. The dark variety that has a reddish tinge, is universally acknowledged to be the best, and I have myself taken with it

1 "'Reclaim,' *v.* Fr. *reclamer*, to make a hawk tame, gentle, and familiar."—*Harting*.

common crane and great bustard.[1] The colouring should be very dark, with a tinge of red in it; though this variety may be sullen and self-willed, it is also hardy and keen, and, once thoroughly reclaimed, will be as docile and obedient as any falconer could desire.

LOCAL RACE OF GOSHAWK (*Qizil*).—The third species, the *Qizil*,[2] breeds in Māzenderān,[3] and in many other parts of Persia, and a fair number are captured in nets, each Autumn, together with the *Ṭarlāns*. Like the last-described species, this also contains three varieties, the dark, the light, and the tawny. The dark variety with the cheek-stripe[4] is the best, and the darker this marking —with a tinge of red in it—the better the bird. With a "passage-bird"[5] of this last variety, the author has himself taken common cranes, great bustards, and "ravine-deer"[6] fawns. The difference between the wild caught *Qizil* and the *Ṭarlān* is in reality very small. The latter has a somewhat finer presence, a more noble disposition, and is rather faster in flight; also from its habit of mounting higher and thus commanding a more extensive view, it is better able to mark down or "put in"[7] its quarry. It is for these reasons only that the *Ṭarlān* has a higher value than the *Qizil*.[8]

---

[1] *Mīsh-murgh*, *lit.* "sheep-bird" (*Otis tarda*). In Albin's *Natural History of Birds*, it is stated that the goshawk used to be flown at geese and cranes as well as at partridges and pheasants. In Hume's *Rough Notes*, there is an account by Mr. R. Thompson of hawking with the goshawk in the forests of Gurhwal and the Terai, the quarry killed being jungle fowl, *kālij* pheasants, hares, peacocks, ducks and teal. The peacock knows well how to use its formidable feet and legs as weapons of defence, and is a more dangerous quarry than even the common crane.

[2] *Qizil* T., means "red."

[3] Māzenderān, a hilly province on the south coast of the Caspian.

[4] *Madāmiʻ* Pl. Ar. The author explains this to mean "having black under the eyes and under the chin." *Vide* also note 2, page 50.

[5] "'Passage-Hawk,' a wild hawk caught upon the passage or migration."—*Harting*.

[6] *Āhū*; the Persian gazelle (*Gazella subgutterosa*). Unlike its congener, the Indian gazelle (the well-known *chikāra* or "ravine-deer" of the Panjab), the female of this species is hornless. A full-grown Indian gazelle weighs about thirty-six pounds, and stands a little over two feet high at the shoulder. "It [the goshawk] takes not only partridges and pheasants but also greater fowls as geese and cranes."—Albin's *Nat. Hist. of Birds*.

[7] "'Put in,' to drive the quarry into covert."—*Harting*.

[8] A Persian falconer informed me that the *Qizil* is smaller, slower, and inferior in courage to the other races, and that it can readily be

VI

PERSIAN CARPET DEPICTING THE COURT OF A SIKH MAHARAJA

Eyess of *Qizil*.—The eyess[1] of the *Qizil* is more courageous than the "passage hawk,"[2] for it has the courage of inexperience. Reared with fostering care from its nestling days, what recks it of the frowns of Fortune? Untaught by Time, what knows it of the spoiling Eagle's might? Though the eyess may at first excel the passage-hawk in courage, it is inferior to it in powers of flight. With increased knowledge, comes decreased courage. In a word, the nestling bears the same relation to the passage-hawk that the town-bred man does to the desert tentman.

Passage and Eyess *Qizil* compared with *Ṯarlān*.—Compared with the eyess, the passage *Qizil* is the better, especially that variety which has the reddish-black cheek-stripe.[3] Although inferior in powers of flight to the *Ṯarlān*, it is better at taking large quarry, and in this quality, as well in affection for its master, it improves moult by moult. The *Ṯarlān*, on the contrary, with increasing age becomes a regular old soldier: it wastes the day excusing itself and shirking its duty and saying: "Oh! an eagle put me off that time;" or "Why! I didn't see the partridge;" or else, "How clumsily you cast me! You hurt my back." When the sun is near sinking, the cunning truant will suddenly rouse itself, and by a grand effort kill in the finest style. Well it knows that at that late hour, a full crop and no more work must needs be the reward of its single exertion. With hopes excited, its gulled master will rise early next day,

---

distinguished while in the immature plumage, but not after the first moult. I was shown a moulted *qizil* and a moulted *bāz* side by side; except that the former was slightly smaller, there was no outward difference between the two.

[1] "'Eyess;' a nestling or young hawk taken from the 'eyrie' or nest; from the Fr. *Niais* . . ."—*Harting*.

[2] *Vide* page 8, note 5. Chapter V of Bert's treatise is headed: "*Of the* Eyas *Hawke*, [Goshawk] *upon whom I can faſten no affection, for the multitude of her follies and faults*." The following quaint derivation is from the *Boke of St. Albans*:—"An hawke is called an Eyes of hir Eyghen, for an hauke that is broght up under a Buſſard or a Puttocke: as mony be: hath Wateri Eghen. For Whan thay be diſcloſed and kepit in ferme tyll thay be full ſummyd. ye shall knawe theym by theyr Wateri Eyghen. And alſo hir looke Will not be ſo quycke as a Brawncheris is. and ſo be cauſe the beſt knawlege is by the Eygh. they be calde Eyeſes." "Now to ſpeke of hawkys. firſt thay ben Egges. and afterwarde they bene diſcloſed hawkys . . ."

[3] *Siyāh-yashmāghlī* T.; *yashmāghlī* T., is a black handkerchief worn by women round the head. Perhaps in the text it means "black-headed."

and start off to make a big bag. Alas for the fair promise of last night!

> Like yestere'en, to-day she fails to kill,
> The truant bird, blaming her master's skill.

The *Ṭarlān,* however, brings luck to its owner. Besides it has a nature sweet, and docile, and loyal, and true. Hence of the *Ṭarlān* it has been said:—

> One day a Knight in splendour bright
> His Hawk at quarry flew.
> The Royal Bird, soon lost to sight,
> Soared high into the blue,
> When lo! mid-air she meets a mate,
> Who says in tones imploring,
> "Return no more to leash or cage
> But stay in freedom soaring."
> The Hawk replied:—"True friends are rare;
> I cannot break my oath;
> To stop with thee I do not dare;
> To lose man's love, I'm loth."

CHAPTER III

THE SPARROW-HAWK

MUCH that has been written of the *Ṭarlān* Goshawk is also applicable to the Common Sparrow-hawk.[1] There are four varieties, the light, the dark, the khaki, and the tawny. Of these four, the khaki has the best heart. The eyes in this variety are small; and the smaller the markings on the breast, the more the hawk will be esteemed, for the more courageous it will prove: it is the opposite of the *Qizil.*

> Into the azure vault of Heaven, my hawk I flew,
> Whispering to it a prayer, "Oh Bird of Mine be true;
> Come back to me!" But my foolish heart did not discern
> That a hawk mid-air, well on the wing, could not return.
> O Fate, whose face is veiled to me!
> Return my hawk—propitious be!

With the Sparrow-hawk, I have myself taken teal, *chukor,* stone-

---

[1] *Bāsha* P.; *qirghī, qirqī,* etc. T. (Accipiter nisus).

plover,[1] black-bellied sand-grouse[2] and short-eared owl.[3] Considering its size, the Sparrow-hawk is the boldest as well as the most powerful of all the short-winged hawks used in falconry.[4] I have frequently seen sparrow-hawks (especially eyesses) "bate"[5] at hares, but I could never muster up courage to let one go, to see the result.

YOUNG PASSAGE SPARROW-HAWK.—Should a very good young sparrow-hawk be brought to you about the time of year that the Sun first enters into Virgo,[6] which is about the time the Sparrow-hawks first arrive in the country, nurse her carefully, for she is well worth keeping. At this time she will be a mere nestling, scarcely in fact more than seven weeks old. Her bones will not be properly set and her whole appearance will be spare and weakly. Now, don't be in a hurry to fly her, unless indeed you wish to spoil her. If you destine her for large quarry, such as *chukor, see-see,*[7] black-bellied sand-grouse, and the like, "man" her very carefully, and let her take no fright at dogs or water, etc. Next train her to come to the lure, or fist. When she will fly readily to the fist, kill a small chicken under her daily,[8] and gorge her on it,—day by day increasing the size of the chicken, till she will fly readily to it,

---

[1] *Chākhrūq*, also called *bachcha hubāra*, the common stone-plover (*Œdicnemus crepitans*).

[2] *Pterocles arenarius.* The common Persian name is *siyāh sīna* or "black breast." The author, however, invariably gives it its Turki name *bāqir-qara* or *bāghir qara*, a word having the same signification. The Pin-tailed Sand-grouse is called *qil-i quiruq* T.: it is the *qaṭā* of the Arabs.

[3] *Yāplāq*, T.; *vide* under short-eared owl.

[4] The late Sir Henry Lumsden (who used to hawk "ravine deer" with *charghs* in Hoti Mardan), told the translator in Scotland that he had frequently seen wild sparrow-hawks kill wood-pigeons, and that he had that very morning seen a sparrow-hawk *knock over* an old cock pheasant on the lawn, which it was of course unable to hold. Hume, in *My Scrap Book* (page 132), under the description of his "Dove Hawk" expresses a doubt whether the "true nisus" would kill a bird as large as a dove: *vide* note 2, page 15.

[5] *Ṭapīdan*, "to bate." "'Bate, bating;' fluttering or flying off the fist. . . . Literally to beat the air with the wings, from the French *battre.*"—*Harting.*

[6] *i.e.*, about the middle of September.

[7] *Tīhū* or *tayhū;* the desert or sand-partridge, called in the Panjab *sī-sī* or *sū-sū* from its cry. It is not such a favourite cage-bird as the black partridge or the *chukor*. It is not used for fighting: both sexes are spurless. In Oudh the sparrow-hawk is flown at grey partridges without the assistance of dogs.

[8] The value of a fowl is about four pence.

and seize it in your hand, the moment that you present it held firmly by both its legs. Proud of the progress made by your pupil, you may feel inclined to release your grasp of the chicken's legs, in order to allow her to kill it unaided; but on no account must this fatal inclination be yielded to.

Now, after the hawk has been called to, and gorged on, two or three chickens given in the hand, she must be entered to two or three flying pigeons; the pigeons, with shortened wings, being released before her, in such a manner that she may take them. Each time she takes the pigeon, kill it cautiously, and let her take her pleasure on it.

When she has taken a few pigeons in this manner, call her as before to a live fowl held by the legs, but this time call her to it from some distance. As soon as she comes and seizes it, which she ought to without hesitation, kill it, and gorge her on it.

As soon as her training reaches this point, she should be confined in a cupboard, some seven feet long by three and a half broad. The cupboard, which should first be thoroughly swept and cleaned, must be kept to such a pitch of darkness, that it will be impossible for its occupant to distinguish the day from the night. If much more light be admitted, the hawk, by bating against the door or wall, will probably do herself some irremediable injury. She should be fed every evening, three or four hours after dark, by the light of a lamp, being taken on the fist for the purpose, and allowed to eat her fill. Her principal food should be sparrows and young pigeons, but in any case she must have constant change of diet. When so gorged that she can eat no more, offer her water in a cup, flicking the water with the finger to attract her attention to it. If she drink, so much the better, let her drink her fill: but if she evince no inclination to drink, remove the water and replace her in her prison. This treatment must be continued for at least forty days.

After the expiration of forty days, reduce the quantity of her food for four or five nights, and carry her by lamp light; in fact treat her in every respect like a wild-caught hawk. Evening by evening, the amount of carriage must be increased, until she is thoroughly "manned,"[1] when she will be ready to obey her master's every behest.

[1] "'Manning, manned'; making a hawk tame by accustoming her to man's presence'."—*Harting.*

The above method has certain special advantages. During the rest in confinement, the hawk's bones will become thoroughly hard and set;[1] and from the high feeding during that forty days, she will attain the growth and strength of a twelvemonth; and her toes will be long and thick; and even large quarry, such as *chukor*, pigeons, and black-bellied sand-grouse, will stand a poor chance of breaking away from her clutches.

It is of course understood that, if destined for large quarry, she must never have been flown at sparrows nor even given any small bagged bird whole, from the day you first get her till the present. She must be made to forget that there is such a thing as small quarry in existence, or that any bird is fit for food except partridge, and sand-grouse, or such large game.

Eyess Sparrow-hawk.—I will now instruct you in another method of training the Sparrow-hawk, by which, in the field, it will be no whit inferior to the goshawks of most falconers. In the early Spring, get some trusty fowler to mark down a tree, in which a pair of Sparrow-hawks are "timbering."[2] A strict watch must be kept on the nest, and the first time the parent birds are observed carrying food to their young, the tree must be scaled, and all the nestlings, except the largest female, removed. The nest will contain from three to five nestlings. The whole attention of the parent birds will now be bestowed on the solitary occupant, which, by thriving apace, will fully repay the care lavished on it. The nestling must be inspected by the fowler almost daily, until the whole of the quill feathers of the tail and wings are out.[3] Then four or five days before it is ready to fly, he must "seel"[4] its eyes while it is still in the nest and remove it, substituting for it, one of the nestlings originally

[1] *Maghz-i ustukhwān-ash siyāh mī-shavad, lit.* "the marrow of her bones becomes black."

[2] "And we ſhall ſay that hawkys doon draw When they bere tymbering to their nestes."—*Boke of St. Albans.* ["To timber," in old English, is "to build a nest."]

[3] *Parhā-yi ḥalāl, lit.* "lawful feathers." There is a belief that until the quills of the tail and wings are produced a bird is not 'lawful' for food.

[4] "To seel," is to sew up the eyes: a thread is passed through the centre of each lower eye-lid, near its edge; the two threads are then knotted together on the top of the head, being drawn so tight that the lower eye-lids cover and close the eyes. Wild birds so treated sit quite still and do not injure themselves.

abducted. The nest will not then be forsaken: the parent birds will rear the restored substitute, and will year after year build in the same tree.

The nestling, its eyes "seeled," must be conveyed carefully home, and its education conducted in precisely the same manner as already described. When taken up at the end of the forty days of confinement, your friends will probably delight you by mistaking her for a male goshawk,[1] so great will be her size. What a goshawk will do, she will do.

The author has also adopted the above plan with nestlings of the *Shāhīn*, the Saker and the *Qizil* Goshawk, with eminently satisfactory results. He humbly begs leave to add that the idea is an original one.

CHAPTER IV

THE *PĪQŪ*[2] SPARROW-HAWK

THE *Pīqū* (*Shikra*).—The next hawk to be described is the *Pīqū*. There are two varieties. The first, or tawny variety, has the markings on the breast large and distinct. The second, or dark variety, has a reddish tinge running through the darker colour of its plumage.

These hawks arrive in the country about the beginning of September, some twenty days before the advent of the Sparrow-hawks.

INFERIORITY OF EYESS *Pīqū*.—Unlike the Sparrow-hawk, the eyess of the *Pīqū* is much inferior to the passage-hawk; the eyess, from its craven spirit, being with difficulty entered to quarry.

---

[1] *Jurra-bāz.* A "tiercel" goshawk: *vide* page 25, note 3.

[2] The *Pīqū* is merely the common *Shikra* of India (Astur badius—*Blan.*). In a wild state this hawk preys on lizards, small birds, rats, mice, locusts, and occasionally doves. I have once or twice seen it chase the common Indian ground squirrel round and round a tree, hovering in the air close to the tree and making sudden darts to the opposite side, the squirrel all the time keeping the trunk between it and its pursuer and chattering shrilly. I once caught a "haggard" *shikra* in a *do-gaza*, with a very large homing pigeon—a cock Antwerp—as a bait. The net had been set up for an eagle. *Vide* note 4, page 12.

For this reason it is little esteemed. The eyess of the Sparrow-hawk, on the contrary, surpasses the passage-hawk.

Of the two varieties, the tawny is the better, surpassing, as it does, the Sparrow-hawk in appearance, more especially so after the first or second moult.

The dark variety, however, is sulky and runaway.

Though slower on the wing than the Sparrow-hawk, the tawny variety can take with success any quarry that the former can In fact, from a working point of view, there is little to choose between them. The *Pīqū* is, however, by far the hardier of the two, enduring with indifference the extremes of heat and cold. Flown in the hot weather from morning till night, it shows no signs of distress, but rather seems to get brisker and brisker after each successive flight: it is impervious to fatigue. It is certainly quite ten times hardier than the Sparrow-hawk.

In affection for its master, it also surpasses the Sparrow-hawk, but as before stated, it is slow on the wing, and to be flown with success, requires to be thrown skilfully.[1] If unskilfully thrown, the quarry will get a start, and the hawk will meet with nothing but disappointment. The *Pīqū* must take its quarry right off or not at all.

In appearance the *Pīqū* very nearly resembles the Sparrow-hawk, but its feet are stouter, its "arms"[2] more powerful, and its wings shorter: it has also a conspicuous dark line under the chin. The larger this chin-line, the better the bird.[3]

---

[1] The *Shikra*, held in the right hand protected by a pad or glove, the breast lying in the palm of the hand held upwards, and the tail, legs, and points of the wings coming out between the forefinger and thumb, is thrown at the quarry while the quarry is still on the ground, or else the moment it rises. The Sparrow-hawk being a bird of swift flight is carried on the fist in the usual manner, a "halsband" being used to steady it. It must be a very poor and badly trained Sparrow-hawk that requires to be thrown from the hand. The Sparrow-hawk, being a bird of nervous disposition, is hooded only when carried by rail, or on other necessary occasions: not so the *Shikra*.

[2] "'Arms;' the legs of a hawk from the thigh to the foot."—*Harting*.

[3] The chin-stripe is not always present. The author describes its eyes as "*Chashm-ash qarīb bi-zāq ast.*" The meaning of *bi-zāq* I am unable to discover.

CHAPTER V

THE *SHIKRA*

The *Shikra*[1] is said to be of stouter and finer appearance than either the *Pīqū* or the Sparrow-hawk and to be trained in India to take the pied crow.[2] It is rarely found in Persia. I have never come across it. God alone knows the facts of the case.[3]

CHAPTER VI

THE SERPENT EAGLE

We now come to the Serpent Eagle,[4] so well known to every fowler. Should one be desired as a pet, it can either be captured by any of the ordinary fowler's devices, or else taken with a *charkh* trained to eagles.[5] It must be fed principally on snakes, as it will not thrive on any other food.

---

[1] The author, writing from hearsay, has imagined the *Shikra* (Astur badius) to be a separate species from the *Piqū*. In India, *shikras* are flown, or rather cast, at partridges, quails, *mainās*, and common crows. *Vide* also note to scavenger vulture.

[2] *Kulāgh-i ablaq*; the Royston crow, the common crow of Persia, is a different species from the common crow of India. The Royston or Hooked Crow is, for a falcon, a far easier quarry than the rook.

[3] Muhammadans frequently qualify their statements by some such expression, the inference being that men are prone to err and that exact knowledge lies with God alone. It is related of the Prophet that once, on being asked how many legs his horse had, he dismounted, counted with care, and then said, "Four." Had he made a positive statement from memory, the Almighty might have altered the number to two, or to three, and so convicted him of error.

[4] *Sanj*. Perhaps the Common Serpent Eagle (*Circaëtus gallicus*). The author in two lines of imperfect description—omitted in the translation—also states that in size and appearance it so nearly resembles the buzzard (*sār*), *vide* p. 32, note 7, that even an experienced falconer might easily mistake the two. The author does not include this amongst the *'Uqāb* or Eagles, *vide* Chapter XII.

[5] For this poaching flight, *vide* pages 113-114.

CHAPTER VII

THE EAGLE OWL

We now come to the owls, of which there are eight or nine species, the most magnificent of them all being the Great Eagle Owl.[1]

Great Eagle Owl.—Nestlings of this species are frequently taken by fowlers, reared by hand, and then trained[2] for the sport of "owling." When first taken from the nest, they must be well and frequently fed, and be kept in as high condition as possible; for if at all neglected at this age, the immature feathers become "strangled" and fall out.

As soon as Autumn commences and the weather begins to cool, *i.e.*, as soon as the birds of prey and other birds have commenced their in-migration from the hills and other summer-quarters, the nestling owl is taken up, fitted with jesses,[3] carried on the fist, sparely dieted, and "manned," just like a young hawk in training. When thoroughly "manned," a stick is procured about twenty inches long: to one end of this a circular piece of black horse-blanket, or felt, is securely fastened. To this again a twist of black goat-hair rope[4] is attached, so that by its means the owl's meat may be tied on to the black felt.

The fowler, in the morning, places the stick, garnished with meat, about two paces from him on the ground. He then takes the owl on his fist and shows it the meat on the stick. The owl will leave the fowler's fist and fly to the meat. It is allowed to eat a little only of the meat, being taken up and flown at this lure a second, and a third time. It is then permitted to make a light meal and is removed.

---

[1] *Shāh-būf.*

[2] *Rasānīdan*, "to train."

[3] *Pācha-band.* "Jesses, the short narrow straps of leather fastened round a hawk's legs to hold her by."—*Harting.* The jesses are never removed from the hawk's legs. In the East the jesses are frequently made of woven silk or cotton, with small rings or "varvels" attached to their ends: with the short-winged hawks, the use of leather jesses is the exception. The "leash" is a long narrow thong (or in the East a silk or cotton cord) that is attached to the end of the "jesses" by means of a swivel, or otherwise, and is used for tying up a hawk to a perch or block. *Vide* also page 78, note 2.

[4] *Qātima*, a word used by the E. Turks and Kurds for a rope of goat hair. In India gut, or the sinews of cranes, are used for binding lures, etc.

In the late afternoon the lesson of the morning is repeated, the distance from which the owl is flown being slightly increased.

The above training is continued daily, the distance being increased step by step, till the owl will fly a good long way to the garnished stick laid on the ground. When this stage of the owl's education is reached, the stick is no longer laid down, but, felt-side upwards, is planted *lightly* in the ground, in such a manner that the moment the owl settles on the felt to feed, the stick collapses. If the stick is planted too firmly, it will not fall flat to the ground, the result being that the owl remains suspended half-way. As soon as the owl will fly readily to the upright stick, from a distance of five- or six-hundred paces,[1] its education may be considered complete.

Now, if accidents are to be avoided, the owl, during the whole of its training, must have been fed on nothing but red meat, meat without the vestige of a feather. If fed on pigeons or fowls, or any kind of "feather," it may learn the fatal vice of bird-killing, a vice that will be fully appreciated by the fowler the first time a fine falcon becomes entangled in his net; for seeing the falcon struggling in the net, that dog-begotten owl will abandon the lure, and fastening on to the captive, will by a single squeeze of its deadly feet deprive her of life. Before the fowler can arrive, the murder is done, and his regrets—of what avail are they?

In addition to the owl, the fowler must procure a fine silk net. The silk thread from which it is made should be woven of six or seven fibres and should be dyed to match the ground where the net will eventually be set up. When in position, the net should be invisible. In size it should be about ten feet long by sixteen to eighteen feet broad.[2] A very long fine silk cord of the same colour as the net is threaded through its top meshes, and the net (erected much in the same manner as an ordinary *du-gaza*[3] for

---

[1] *Qadam;* a short pace of about twenty inches.

[2] *Ẕira'*. "Three *ẕira'* long, by five or six *ẕira'* broad." The Persian *ẕira'* is variously stated to be a measure of forty, and forty-two inches in length.

[3] *Du-gaza;* a light, large-meshed net, six feet or more long, by four and a half feet or more broad, and suspended between two light bamboos or sticks, which are shod with iron spikes. This net is planted upright, twenty yards or more away from a resting hawk, while a live bird is pegged down in the centre of the net, a few feet from it, and on the side opposite to the hawk. A certain amount of spare net is gathered

catching sparrow-hawks), is supported in an upright position by two very light poles[1] as long as the breadth of the net, and these are placed under the cord, at fourteen to fifteen paces distance from the ends of the net. The ends of the cord are made fast to pegs driven into the ground at a good distance from the ends of the net. The poles must be so erected that, at any slight shock to the net, they will collapse suddenly.

The "luring-stick," garnished with a shank of sheep or goat securely tied to the black felt, is now erected exactly in the centre of the net, and about five feet[2] from it. The net so arranged is in position for use.

The fowler now takes the owl on his fist, shows it the garnished "luring-stick," and then turns about and walks off in the opposite direction for a distance of five- or six-hundred paces: he then halts, turns about again, and casting off the owl into the air, quickly conceals himself.

The owl, in accordance with its previous training, flies straight for the lure, and is soon closely mobbed by all the birds of the neighbourhood. Do not leave your ambush; watch. If you are near the hills, perhaps a goshawk, *qizil* or *ṭarlān*, or else a saker falcon will come down and join the crowd. The owl, however, having no other object but to reach its goal, ignores the clamouring presence of its pursuers and continues on its straight course. The first bird to buffet the owl, on its alighting on the lure, is a fast prisoner in the net.

Let us suppose a noble saker falcon has thus fallen a victim to your fowler toils. Leave your ambush, and, cautiously and gently, I adjure thee by God, go and secure thy prisoner, treating her with all honour and respect.

The eyes of a newly-caught hawk should be "seeled" on the spot, and if a fine needle and fine thread (not silk) be used for the purpose,

---

towards its centre and allowed to rest loose on the ground. The hawk makes straight for the fluttering bait, through the invisible net; the loose portion on the ground permits the net to "belly" like a sail, while the shock given causes the light uprights to collapse inwards, thus effectually enveloping the hawk.

[1] Presumably the length of these poles should be somewhat less than the breadth of the net.

[2] "One and a half *ẕira'*." The old English name for hawk-catching nets was "urines" or "uraynes."

the falconer into whose hands the hawk eventually falls, will call down blessings, not curses, on the operator's head.

Nestling of Eagle-Owl Preferred.—For the above sport, the nestling is preferred to the wild caught bird. Being ignorant and inexperienced, and consequently more courageous, it treats eagles and other unknown dangers, with contempt. The nestling has also greater staying power.[1] The hours it should be flown are from early morning till about eleven o'clock, and from three in the afternoon till within half an hour of sunset. A hundred flights in the day are not too much for a really good bird.[2]

Disadvantages of wild-caught Owl.—The wild-caught owl soon gets done up, and after a few flights gets sulky and flies off aimlessly and settles on the ground.

Arab Name for Eagle Owl.—The Arabs call the Eagle Owl *Fahdu 'l-Layl*, or "Panther[3] of the Night." What the Golden Eagle is to the day, the Eagle-Owl is to the night. Hares and foxes fall an easy prey to it.[4]

Riding Down Eagle-Owl.—Should you, by chance, when riding out in the open country, put up an Eagle-Owl, set your horse into a gallop and start in hot chase. If closely pressed, the owl will not rise more than thrice; after that it may be easily captured.[5]

Treatment of newly caught Eagle-Owl.—It is not at all necessary to "seel" the eyes of an owl captured in the above manner. It should at once be placed on the fist and "carried" like a short-winged hawk; if it declines to sit up, duck its head under water three or four times in rapid succession. This will

---

[1] Perhaps it can be kept in higher condition.

[2] It must not be supposed from this description that hawk-catching is by any means an easy business. In India, in the course of two or three weeks, the fowler *may* not catch more than three hawks worth keeping, and that, too, at the season the birds are migrating into the country.

[3] Apparently a slip on the author's part. *Fahd* is properly the *cheeta* or hunting-leopard and not the panther. In Persian the former is called *yūz* and sometimes *yūz-palang*, while the latter is called *palang* only.

[4] In *Seebohm's British Birds*, it is stated that the eagle owl preys on capercailzie and fawns, besides hares and other game.

[5] Partridges are caught in this manner by the Baluchis round Dera Ghazi Khan. *Vide* also Shaw's *High Tartary, Yarkand and Kashgar.*

soon bring it to its senses and send away its perversity: plunging its head in cold water extinguishes the fire of pride in its heart and makes it steady as a rock.[1]

CHAPTER VIII

OTHER SPECIES OF OWLS

[SHORT-EARED OWL; LONG-EARED OWL.—The author now imperfectly describes five or six species of owl, which the translator is unable with any certainty to identify. The first species mentioned by him is the *Yāplāgh* or *Yāplāq*, and this species he again divides into two sub-species or races, viz., the "Desert or Plain *Yāplāq*," and the "Garden or Grove *Yāplāq*." The colour of the latter is said to be somewhat darker than that of the former. The first species is probably the Short-eared Owl (*Otus brachyotus*); while the second is probably either the Common Long-eared Owl (*Otus vulgaris*), or the Tawny Wood-Owl. The author also states that

---

[1] The following description of owling is taken from Blaine's *Encyclopedia of Rural Sports*. It is stated there that any owl may be used, but that the great horned owl is the usual bait:—"The owl, confined between two wooden stands or rests, is taught to fly from one rest to the other without touching the ground. Between the rests, a cord is stretched, on which a ring plays, and to which another slacker cord is attached by one end, the other being fastened to the jesses on the legs of the owl, whose movements are thus confined to flying from one block or rest to the other. To this change of posture he is accustomed by presenting him with food on the opposite side to that on which he may happen to be resting, until he becomes completely habituated to this method of exercising himself. A saloon is now formed in the midst of a copse, of boughs, in the centre of which a log or stand rests, and without the saloon a similar one is placed about a hundred paces distant, the intermediate space on which the owl is placed being cleared away. It is necessary that the top and sides of this saloon should be covered with boughs in such a manner that although the outside is distinctly seen there is no opening that will admit any bird to enter with unfolded wings. Nets are placed against the top and sides, leaving open that part only opposite to the resting place of the owl. The fowler, now concealing himself, keeps watch, and when he observes the owl lower his head and turn it on one side, he becomes certain that some bird of prey is in the air. The hawk, now marking the owl for his own, follows him into his retreat; when, becoming hampered in the meshes of the net, he is easily secured." *Vide* also *History of Fowling*, by the Rev. H. A. Macpherson: Edinburgh: David Douglas, 1896.

the former species, once it has successfully shifted from the first stoop of the falcon and has begun to "tower,"[1] is an exceedingly difficult quarry, and that only a passage *Shahīn* or Peregrine is equal to the flight, the Saker not being swift enough.[2] The latter species of owl, he adds, is a poor performer and unable to "ring up"[1] to any great distance without being overtaken and killed.

INDIAN GRASS-OWL.—The Short-eared Owl is, however, an easier quarry than the Indian Grass-Owl (*Strix candida*), which in India is taken both with Sakers and Peregrines. If, however, the Saker is not in high condition (in much higher condition than it is usually kept by natives of India), both hawk and quarry will soon be lost to view, ringing up, on a calm day completely out of sight and almost perpendicularly into the sky. In this species the iris is dark; it is therefore presumed that neither it nor any nearly allied species can be included under the name *yāplāq*.

Indian falconers, however, in the Panjab, have only one name for both the Short-eared and the Grass-Owl.

Afghan falconers state that, in their country, the Short-eared Owl is a common quarry for the Saker, as well as for the Peregrine.

The author continues:]—

BRIDE OF THE WELL.—The next species of owl is smaller than the *Yāplāq*, and is hornless. Its prevailing colour is a yellowish white, something like that of the *Tīqūn* Goshawk. This species is especially common in Baghdad and other sacred places.[3] It is known to the Arabs by the name of the "Bride of the Well."[4] It preys principally on the pigeons of the "Sacred Precincts;"[5] for that cuckoldy pimp, lacking regard and consideration, has settled that the pigeons of the precincts[5] are its proper prey, so it hunts

[1] "'Tower;' 'ring up;' to rise spirally to a height."—*Harting*.

[2] The Indian grass-owl, *Strix candida*, though a much more difficult quarry than the short-eared owl, can be successfully flown by a trained saker, provided the latter is in high condition: a saker is not fit for this flight unless she weighs *at least* 2 lbs. 4 oz., better 2 lbs. 6 oz.

[3] Such as Kāẓimayn, Najaf, Karbalā, etc.

[4] *'Arūs-i chāh*; *'arūs* is the Arabic for "bride," but *chāh*, "well," is Persian.

[5] *Ḥaram*: the sacred precincts round both Mecca and Medina are known as *ḥaram*, and certain acts such as slaying game are forbidden within the boundaries. *Ḥaram* is also a name for the women's apartments. The author by *ḥaram* probably means the sacred precincts of Mecca, but from the context his meaning is not clear.

them in the night-watches. In the Spring the attendants pull out the young owls from their holes in the walls, or from the interiors of the domes, and slay them. This species is smaller than the *Yāplāq*.

LITTLE OWL (SPOTTED OWLET ?).—[The author next mentions a small owl that he styles *Bāya-qūsh* or *Chughd*. In the Panjab, the spotted owlet (*Athene Brama*) is known by the latter name.[1] The author says of this species:]—It frequents old ruins. A young *shāhīn*, intended for the flight of the stone-plover, should first be given two or three pigeons from the hand, and then flown at a wild *chughd* or two. After that it may be entered to stone-plover. The *chughd* is useful for no other purpose but this.

"BIRD OF NIGHT-MELODY"[2] OR "BIRD OF TESTIMONY."[3]—The next species we come to is the "Bird of Night-melody,"[2] better known under its popular name of "The Bird of Testimony."[3] The male of this beautifully marked little owlet is scarcely larger than a lark.[4]

All the above species of owl are strictly nocturnal in their habits.

Too whit, too whoo! The helpless owl,
In evening shades alone can prowl;
To find its food, to chase its prey,
'Tis helpless quite in light of day.

[1] In the Derajat this owlet, called there *chhapākī*, is a quarry for the *shikra*, and also for the common and the red-headed merlin. Its blood is supposed to be a cure for prickly heat, hence its local name. (*Chhapākī* is a corruption of *shapākī*, "prickly heat"). In some parts of India it is used as a decoy for small birds.

[2] *Murgh-i shab-āhang*.

[3] *Murgh-i Ḥaqq*. *Ḥaqq* means the "Truth" or "God." This little owl, which is probably the Persian owlet (*Athene Persica*), is reverenced by Muhammadans: it clings to walls and cries "*Ḥaqq*, *Ḥaqq*," after the manner of the dervishes.

[4] *Kākulī*. Elsewhere the author states that the Arabs call this lark *qumburah*, which is an Arab name for the Crested Lark (*Alauda cristata*).

CHAPTER IX

THE HARRIERS

HARRIERS.—[The author next proceeds to describe what appear to be two species of harriers. He says :]—

We now come to the *Bayl-bāqilī*, called by the Kurds, *Dasht-māla*,[1] and by the Arabs, *Abū-ḥikb*. There are two species, one yellow-eyed, and one dark-eyed.[2]

YELLOW-EYED SPECIES.—In the yellow-eyed species, the plumage of the young bird is henna-coloured [chestnut brown], but after its first moult, some white feathers make their appearance. After the second or third moult, the plumage is very like that of the *Tīqūn* Goshawk, the back turning a bluish grey and the breast becoming white. The female is about the size of a small *Qizil* "tiercel."[3] Only a falconer could distinguish the adult female from a *Tīqūn* tiercel. The "stalke" of this species is long and slender.

DARK-EYED SPECIES.—In the dark-eyed species, there is no material difference between the plumage of the young and the adult bird. In the latter, however, the markings on the breast are larger. The general colouring of the dark-eyed species is darker than that of the yellow-eyed.

In habits, both species are similar; they haunt open plains, preying on mice and sparrows, and occasionally on quails. They are mean-spirited, ignoble birds, with poor and weakly frames.

WAGER WITH THE SHAH.—When in attendance on the Shah (may our souls be sacrificed for him!) I once made a bet with some

---

[1] *Dasht-māla* may be translated "desert-quarterer." In the Panjab this is the name of the Pale Harrier (*Circus Swainsonii*) and probably also of Montague's Harrier (*Circus cineraceus*).

[2] In the young of the Marsh Harrier, the iris is hazel. The iris of the female of Montague's Harrier is also said to be hazel.

[3] "'Tiercel, Tercel, Tassel' (Shakespeare) and 'Tarsell' (Bert), the male of any species of hawk, the female being termed a falcon. The tiercel is said by some to be so called from being about one-third smaller in size than the falcon; by others it is derived from the old belief that each nest contained three young birds, of which two were females and the third and smallest a male. Note the familiar line in *Romeo and Juliet*: 'Oh! for a falconer's voice to lure this tassel gentle back again.'"—*Harting.*

fellow sportsmen that I would catch a harrier [1] and train it to take *chukor*. I made no idle boast. Praise be to God, I won my bet and proved myself a man of my word, for I trained it and took a *chukor* with it. The puissant King of Kings, who has surpassed in renown even Jamshed and Cyrus, regarded me with extreme condescension, and in just appreciation of my skill bestowed on me lavish commendation and a rich robe of honour.

On a second occasion, in Baghdad, I laid a wager of a Nejd mare with some sportsmen of that city, that within a space of fifty days I would "reclaim" [2] one of these hawks and successfully fly it at wild quarry. I flew it in the presence of my friends, and took with it one black partridge,[3] one quail, and one rail.[4]

As previously stated, it is quite possible to train these hawks, as indeed it is possible to train many other useless birds of prey: even—

> The Bird whose Soul Delights the night
> With care and trouble you can train,
> To use its senses, use its sight,
> In flying quarry on the plain.

The harrier is an ill-tempered bird with no great powers of flight. To train it is a matter of extreme difficulty, and the result by no means repays the labour. However, give the devil his due: it is very long-winded.

---

[1] It is not clear which of the two species the author trained, but apparently the "black-eyed."

[2] "Reclaim;" Fr. *reclamer*, to make a hawk tame, gentle and familiar."—*Harting*.

[3] *Durrāj*; the Common Francolin (*F. vulgaris*). It is a favourite cage-bird in India, especially with the Muhammadans, who liken its call to the words *Subhān Teri Qudrat* "Oh Lord! Thy Power" (*i.e.*, who can fathom it?). The practical Hindus say its call is, *Chha ser kī kacharī*, "Twelve pounds of *kacharī*."

[4] *Yalva* is a name incorrectly applied to several species of bird with long beaks, as the woodcock and snipe, etc. I am told that in Teheran it is applied to a rail.

CHAPTER X

THE LAMMERGEYER OR BEARDED VULTURE

[THE description of the Bearded Vulture[1] as given by the author is sufficiently accurate for identification. He, however, adorns it with "two horns or ears like those of the horned owls." He then continues :]—

The Lammergeyer is noted for its wondrous powers of flight. It soars aloft, bearing with ease a bone as large as the bleached thigh-bone of a donkey. This it drops on a rock, and then descends to eat the shattered fragments.[2] The Poet has said of it:—

> "The *Humā* o'er other birds has flown
> Because its food is only bone."[3]

POPULAR SUPERSTITION.—It is a popular superstition that any one wilfully slaying a Lammergeyer will meet his death within

---

[1] *Humā*; the Lammergeyer, Bearded Vulture, or Ossifrage. Translators, imagining the *Humā* to be a fabulous creature, have identified it with the Phœnix. It was a popular Persian superstition that the shadow of a *Humā* falling on a person's head predicted his rise to sovereignty. The adjective (and proper name) *humāyūn*, signifying "august," "fortunate," and "royal," is derived from this bird. In the Panjab, the Lammergeyer, common as it is, seems to have no special native name.

[2] It is well-known that the Lammergeyer does not confine itself to dry bones. I once saw one shot in the Tochi valley over a dead fowl laid out as a bait. When shot it was carrying off the fowl in its beak and not in its feet. The most contradictory statements exist regarding its habits. As it sweeps round the hill side, the fowls in the compounds show no alarm and will let it pass within a very few yards of them. At Kingri, in Baluchistan, I saw one stoop at a flock of *chukor* and sent a sowar to the spot to see what had happened: the man returned with a *chukor*, unbroken and still warm. Some years ago at Sheikh-budin, the hill station near Dera Ismail Khan, I saw one stoop repeatedly at a *mārkhor* kid, on a narrow ledge on the cliff-face below me. At each stoop the plucky mother lowered her horns to the "charge," and effectually repulsed the attacks of the assailant. Whether the Lammergeyer was really trying to brush the kid off the cliff, with intent to feed on its mangled remains, or whether it was merely animated by that spirit of mischief that enters into birds as well as beasts, I cannot say. The Pathan shikaris with me stated that they knew from experience that the former was the case. A shot Lammergeyer shown to a tame monkey will drive it into a paroxysm of terror. Can it be that the latter recognizes in it a natural enemy, or does it mistake it for an eagle?

[3] *Ṣa'dī*: Gulistan, Chap. I, St. 3.

forty days. Once, when out hawking, I saw one of these fateful birds seated on a stone a short distance from me. With me was a servant, a sturdy villain fearing nothing. Gun in hand he approached the Lammergeyer, bent on slaughter. Do all I could, I failed to dissuade him. I told him the popular superstition, but he laughed and said, "Oh! that's an old woman's story." Heedless of my advice he shot the Lammergeyer, and died himself on the fortieth day. This is a fact: I myself was an eye-witness. Was his death a mere coincidence, or is there truth in the vulgar belief? God knows.

TAKING A LAMMERGEYER WITH A *Charkh*.—I was once hawking in *Sulaymānīya Shahrzūr*[1] and saw what I took to be an eagle,[2] seated on a stone some little way off. I had with me a very fine *charkh*[3] trained to eagles.[4] To unhood and cast it off was the work of a moment, and it was not till I had actually secured the quarry, that I discovered it was no eagle but a Lammergeyer. I recollected the fate of my servant, and hastily released it. [By a play on the words *humā* and *humāyūn*, the author here pays the Shah a flowery and far-fetched compliment, difficult to render in English. He pretends that the popular belief mentioned in the first note on the previous page was certainly fulfilled in his case, since the King of Kings had always distinguished him by his especial friendship and bounty, and thus raised him to the dignity of ordinary kingship. He adds:]—

Through the lucky shadow of the Humā's wing
Am I thus highly honoured by the King.
Honoured of him, Lord of my fate I stand,
And rich as Korah, through his bounteous hand.

---

[1] In *Kurdistān*, and a little over a hundred miles south of Lake Urūmiah.

[2] *'Uqāb*. The author uses this word as a generic term. By falconers of certain parts of the Panjab the name is specially applied to the Tawny Eagle.

[3] The author applies the name *charkh* only to nestlings of the Saker Falcon: passage falcons he calls *bālābān*. In the Panjab, and in Kabul, the species is termed respectively *chargh* and *charkh*, the word *bālābān* being unknown except to a travelled few.

[4] *Qara-qūsh*. Any eagle, but specially the golden eagle. For a description of this "flight" see pages 113-114.

CHAPTER XI

THE OSPREY [1]

[The author gives only a very brief description of the Osprey and its habits, mentioning the peculiar structure of its feet, and its habit of hovering over water. He also mentions that like the *Shikra* Sparrow-hawk (*Pīghū*), and the *Sangak*, the iris is sometimes dark and sometimes yellow.[2] He adds :]—

I once took one alive with a *charkh* and kept it in confinement for some little time. It could not be induced to eat meat, refusing all food except fish. It is with reference to the osprey that the poet has said :—

> "Thro' the mercy of God and His tender care
> The sea yields her fish to the fowl of the air."

[1] *Damirdizināq* T. Another name is *damir-qaynāgh* T., from *damir* T. "iron" and *qaynāgh* T. "claws" (*nākhun* P.). The author does not include this amongst the *'Uqāb* or Eagles. According to F. O. Morris, the osprey in olden times was occasionally trained for falconry.

[2] In the only living specimen examined by me, the iris was light brown, possibly a mark of nonage. In several standard works consulted, the iris is stated to be yellow.

Part II

THE DARK-EYED BIRDS OF PREY

CHAPTER XII

THE EAGLES[1] AND BUZZARDS[2]

[The author commences this chapter with the statement that it is his intention to describe those species of the black-eyed birds of prey that have at different times come into his possession, or that have been trained by him "according to their several capabilities." His descriptions of the eagles are too vague for identification. All the eagles, he says, are migratory, with the exception of the *'Uqāb-i māh-dum* or "Moon-tailed eagle,"[3] which he describes as follows:]—

'Uqāb-i māh-dum, "The Moon-tailed Eagle."—The whole of the tail of this eagle is white, with the exception of the end, which is black. The plumage of the breast, back, and head, is uniformly dark, without markings of any description. Its powers of fasting are extraordinary: it can endure seven or eight days without food and yet be not one whit the worse. Migration, too, is not a necessity for it. Even in the depth of Winter I have observed it high up in the snows. It seldom descends into the plains. The fierce rays of the sun and the bitter blasts of the snows are all one to its proud, enduring nature. I have observed it in the hills, preying on partridges, hares, and "lambs."[4] It is the most daring and powerful of all the eagles.

---

[1] *'Uqāb* Ar., or *qara-qush* T. The latter word properly means "black bird of prey," and is a term specially applied to the Golden Eagle.

[2] *Sār*, *vide* note 7, page 32.

[3] *'Uqāb-i māh-dum*, "moon-tailed eagle." Can this be Pallas's sea eagle? The author does not mention that it is found in the vicinity of water.

[4] *Barra;* properly a lamb. The author elsewhere uses this word for the fawn of the "ravine-deer."

'Uqāb-i kūchigān [White-tailed Sea Eagle?].—The next species is the *'Uqāb-i kūchigān*. In this species the whole of the tail (which is rather short) is white. The wings are long, and the flight is exceedingly swift. The plumage of the back and breast is dark. The beak, which is large and powerful as a vulture's, is of the colour of amber. This eagle always hunts and feeds in couples, preying chiefly on water-fowl; hence it is seldom found far from water.

'Uqāb-i ā,īna-lī [Imperial Eagle?].—In this eagle, which is smaller than either of the preceding, the back, breast, claws and beak are all uniformly dark; the colouring of the head is a dark reddish brown. Fowlers have named it *Ā,īna-lī*[1] from the fact of its having a few white feathers in its back.

Karlak.—This eagle equals the first-named species, *i.e.*, the *Māh-dum*, in size. The beak and claws are black and extraordinarily powerful. The plumage is generally brown, and covered with markings. The head and back are, however, one uniform colour. In habits it resembles all the eagles.

Black Eagle.—Another species is black without markings, but the colour of the head is slightly different from that of the body. It is not a very noble species.

'Uqāb-i zard ("Yellow Eagle.")—Description. The plumage of the back is very dark, with a tinge of yellow in it, while that of the breast is tawny (yellow), and marked with longitudinal black drops. The head and neck are very handsome, and somewhat like a goshawk's. This eagle, in the immature plumage, is called the *'Uqāb-i sīna-bāzī*.

Once, when in attendance on the Shah, I trained a single specimen of this species, and took a certain amount of quarry with it.

Būq-khura; The "Frog-eater" [Spotted Eagle?].—Another species of eagle is the *'Uqāb-i qurbāqa-chi*[2] ("Frog-eater"), called by the people of Kurdistan Sulemāniya, *Būq-khura*.[2] The plumage of the head, neck, back, and breast is blackish yellow. This eagle frequents marshes and reed beds, preying on wounded or dead

---

[1] *'Uqāb-i ā,īna-lī. Ā,ina* means "mirror."

[2] *'Uqāb-i qurbāqa-chī; būq-khura. Qurbāqa* and *bāqa* are both Turki names for a frog. *Būq* T. is "ordure," and figuratively anything filthy. The Spotted Eagle (*Aquila nævia*) feeds largely on frogs.

water-fowl. Failing these, it contents itself with frogs, dead fish, or other stranded material. It is from this habit of eating frogs that it has earned its names of "Frog-eagle" and "Frog-eater."

Dūbarār [A HAWK EAGLE ?].—In habits the *Dūbarār* resembles the eagles, but not in size, the male being scarcely larger than a female goshawk.[1] This species always hunts in couples and is very daring and bold by nature. In the immature bird, the plumage of the back is a yellowish black, while that of the breast is a dark red without spot or marking. After the moult, the plumage of the breast assumes a deeper and brighter hue. The "pendant"[2] feathers of the thigh hang down to the tarsus.

When in *'Arabistān*,[3] I once took one with a *charkh* I had trained to eagles. I succeeded in training it in the space of about forty days and flew it successfully at black partridge, *parah malā*,[4] hare, and common heron.[5] A friend of mine then took it from me.

Large numbers of these eagles breed in the vicinity of *Hamadān*.[6] I have trained nestlings, but never with success: they are poor performers on the wing. The wild-caught bird is superior in every way. Still I found this species swifter and more tractable than any other kind of eagle.

THE *Sār* (OR BUZZARD).—Another kind of eagle is the buzzard,[7] of which there are two common species. In the first the general

---

1 The length of the female goshawk is said to be 22 to 26 inches: of the male 18 to 21 inches. There is in Persia a species of small eagle or hawk-eagle that always hunts in pairs and that is known to Persians by the name of *Du-Barādarān* or "The Two Brothers." The *Dūbarār* of the author is perhaps a corruption of *Du-Barādarān*. In the *Ḥāyat[u] 'l-Ḥaywān*, the Arab name of the latter is said to be *Zumaj*, a word that occurs in old Arabic and Persian MSS. on falconry.

2 *Parhā-yi rān-ash tā pācha rīkhta.* Possibly by this expression the author means that the whole of the tarsus is feathered. "'Pendant Feathers,' those behind the thighs of a hawk."—*Harting.*

3 *'Arabistān* or *Khuzistān*: its capital Shuster is about 130 miles north of the head of the Persian Gulf.

4 *Parah malā* (?); possibly for *Parlā* T., which is said to be the name of a "black water-bird with a white beak." The coot?

5 *Ḥaqar*: variously spelt in old Persian MSS. on falconry *awqār*, *aqār* and *'uqār*; latter correct.

6 *Hamadān*: about 100 miles North-East of Kirmānshāh.

7 *Sār* (for *sā ?*): Apparently two species of large buzzard are so-called by the author. This word must not be confused with *sār* the common Persian word for starling. In Dr. Scully's list of the Turkish names of birds, *sā* is said to be the name applied to Buzzards, Harriers, and Kites.

colouring of the plumage is very dark without spot or marking: the feet and cere are a deep orange yellow. The plumage of the second is tawny. Both species are ill-conditioned and villainous by nature. Their prey is rats, mice, frogs, lizards, and wounded or sickly birds. When they dare, they rob their more weakly neighbours. They are too mean-spirited for the purposes of falconry.

CHAPTER XIII

KITES AND HARRIERS

KITES [AND HARRIERS].—There are three common species of kites.[1] In the first, the two centre tail-feathers, called by the Arabs *'amūd*,[2] and by Persian and Turkish[3] falconers *qāpāq*,[4] are shorter than the rest, the outer feathers being longer. The general colouring of the plumage is a dirty brown with dark coloured drops on the breast. The feet are small and the tarsi[5] short.

2ND SPECIES [MARSH HARRIER ?].—The second species haunts marshes and reedy pools in quest of frogs and rats. In this species the tarsus is long[6] and unfeathered, and the feet are small, ill-looking, and black. There is also a certain amount of white on the head.

3RD SPECIES.—In the third species the general colouring of the

[1] *Chīlāq* T. The kite is rare in Persia. It is, however, fairly common near Bushire.

[2] *'Amūd* Ar., "a prop, a pillar."

[3] Turk. This word properly includes Turks, Tartars, and all who claim their descent from Turk the son of Japhet. A large proportion of the population of Persia is Turkish.

[4] *Qāpāq*, the "deck-feathers" of old English falconers. According to the *Boke of St. Albans* the centre or uppermost tail feather was called *the beme feder of the tayle*, the flight feathers being called *the beme federes of the wyng*.

[5] *Sāq*, properly the shin or shank of a man, animal, or bird. Elsewhere the author, with one other exception, uses the word *qalam*, "a pen, etc.," for "tarsus."

[6] The Kites have short tarsi, the Harriers, long. In the adult Harriers the iris is yellow, but in the immature birds, of several species at any rate, the iris is brown. The iris of the common Pariah Kite (*Milvus govinda*) is brown, while that of the "Common Kite" of England (*M. regalis*) is said to be yellow.

plumage—with the exception of the head, which is reddish—is very dark. In habits it resembles the two preceding.

All three species are cowardly and mean-spirited. A good *Ṭarlān*, trained to large quarry, will generally take them.[1]

Should the fork-tailed kite[2] see a sparrow-hawk or merlin with a bird in its feet, it will fuss round it, doing its utmost to steal it from the lucky possessor. If unsuccessful, it returns to its quest of mice and garbage.

These above-described species are related to the eagles. Under this head, too, I have even included the Carrion Vulture[3] and the Scavenger Vulture.[4]

CHAPTER XIV

THE VULTURES

VULTURE.—[The author now briefly describes a species of bare-necked vulture that he calls *Dāl*, apparently the only species of true vulture known to him. The description contains nothing of interest. He continues:]—

SCAVENGER OR EGYPTIAN VULTURE.—Before the first moult the plumage of the Scavenger Vulture is dark, with a few small light-coloured spots on the back and breast. The head is nude and yellow. After the first moult, a certain number of white feathers make their appearance. After the second, the bird becomes quite white, with the exception of the ends of the flight-feathers, which remain black.

The gut[5] of this vulture, which is at the end of the sternum,[6] applied as a poultice, fresh and warm, for three consecutive days,

---

1 Haggard Sakers will generally fly at harriers, refusing to give up the chase and so getting lost. A haggard peregrine I had killed a harrier.

2 *Chīlāq-i qāpāq-i kūtāh.*

3 *Dāl*; elsewhere *dāl-i murdār-khur.*

4 *Kachal charkas*; the Egyptian Vulture: *kachal* means "scald-headed;" *charkas* is corrupted form of *karkas*, a common term for a vulture. The Egyptian vulture feeds largely on human ordure, a habit that can be traced in the popular name given to it by soldiers in India.

5 *Khazīna*, *khazāna*, "the gut." This word does not mean the "crop."

6 *'Azm-i zawraqī*, *lit.* "boat-bone."

is a certain cure for scabbed eyes that water, and from which the lashes have dropped off, or for fistulous sores that will yield to no ointment. The poultices should not be removed for twelve hours: it will then be noticed that numerous minute worms have been drawn by them from the wound. At the third application, if it please God, a cure will be effected. The author can testify to the efficacy of this remedy.

USE AS A "TRAIN."—If it is intended to train a *charkh* to take eagles, it should first be given the necessary "trains" by hand, and then entered to wild quarry by being flown a few times at young scavenger vultures in the dark immature plumage. As they are slow on the wing and show no fight,[1] the young *charkh* can take them with ease.

Though purely carrion feeders, the Vultures (as also the Raven described in the next chapter) are generally included amongst the Rapacious Birds: these huge birds, with beaks powerful enough to tear open the skin of a dead camel or ass, are unable to catch and kill even a helpless partridge.

CHAPTER XV

THE RAVEN

RAVEN.—The Raven,[2] though a carrion feeder, has just claims to be considered a Bird of Prey. I recollect once seeing a raven in the

---

1 Some thirty odd years ago the *shikra* used to be trained in the Kapurthala State to take the Egyptian Vulture. The young *shikra* was entered by being fed on a live vulture with seeled eyes, meat being tied on the back or head. The Egyptian Vulture is slow in taking flight, and when on the ground will let a man approach to within a few feet of it. The falconer, *shikra* in hand, has only to walk up to within a few feet of the unsuspecting vulture while it is resting on the ground, throw the *shikra*, and secure the quarry before it has even got so far as to spread its wings for flight. It is probably this "flight" that is referred to by old travellers who state that the *shikra* is flown at eagles. The Egyptian Vulture is also a quarry easily taken by a trained lynx. The lynx simply bounds quietly and quickly up to it, and springs as the vulture prepares to spread its wings. Partridges and such quarry are, however, scientifically stalked by it.

2 *Kulāgh-i siyāh-i quzqūn.* I once saw a pair of ravens harassing a wild hare by pulling tufts of hair and skin out of it. Had I not interfered they would have killed it. Wild ravens in India will chase house-pigeons and occasionally enter the dovecot and kill them.

jungle seize a wild *chukor;* I eventually succeeded in releasing the bird from its clutches.

It is a peculiarity of the Raven that if it is deprived of sight by having its eyeballs pierced with a needle, it may, by confinement in darkness for the space of twenty-four hours, be completely restored to sight.

In *'Arabistān* it is caught in traps and trained for fowling in the same manner that the Kestril[1] is trained in the *Dashtistān*[2] of *Fārs,* and the eagle-owl in *Kirmānshāh*[3] and elsewhere.

CHAPTER XVI

THE *SHUNQĀR* OR JERFALCON

SHUNQĀR OR JERFALCON.—The Jerfalcon[4] is a species known to me only by description. During the whole of my sporting career,

---

[1] *Vide* chapter XXV, page 69 for method of training for fowling purposes. I heard of the raven being thus trained and used as a "lure" for charg͟hs, in Baghdad, Basra, and Muhammara.

[2] *Dashtistān* of *Fārs*; a warm region fringing the west of the Persian Gulf: Bushire is nearly the centre of its coast line.

[3] *Kirmānshāh* is a district about 250 miles north of *Baṣrah* (Bussora): its capital is said to be locally called *Kirmānshāhān.*

[4] *Shunqār.* In old Persian MSS. on falconry, this disputed name is undoubtedly applied to a Jerfalcon, a species of which is said to exist in Northern Asia. The following is a footnote from *Falconry in the British Isles*:—

"We have been informed by travellers that some few *large white falcons,* which must be Greenland falcons, are caught annually on their passing over the Caspian Sea and that they are highly prized by the falconers of Syria and Persia."

The late Sirdar Sher 'Ali Khan, the exiled Wālī of Kandahar, told the translator that he kept *shunqārs* in Afghanistan, and that he once had one that was pure white. Jerdon, quoting Pallas, states that it is the Baschkir Tartar name of the Jerfalcon. Also in Courteille's *Dictionnaire Turk-Orientale* we find:—"*Shūnqār, faucon, proprement le gerfaut.*" Dr. Scully, however, in his Turki vocabulary of birds states that *shunqār* is the name of *Falco Hendersoni,* and *ītālgū* of its female. If the coloured illustration of F. Hendersoni (supposed by its describer to be identical with the *shunqār*) that was published in the account of the Government Mission to Yarkand be a correct representation of the original, then no falconer, however experienced, can discriminate between F. Hendersoni and many old *charg͟hs* (F. Cherrug or F. Sacer) caught annually in the Panjab. Further, the Turks of Persia call the charg͟h *Itālgū, Aitalgu,* etc.

I have neither come across it myself, nor known a falconer to whom it was more than a name.

SPECIMEN BROUGHT FROM RUSSIA.—In the year of the Flight 1284[1] a strange falcon which I take to be a *Shunqār* was bought in Russia for a great price, and presented as a curiosity to His Lofty and Imperial Highness, the Shah of Shahs, the Shadow of God. Out of the plenitude of his bounty and the immensity of his condescension, His Most Noble and Exalted Majesty delivered it into the humble keeping of his servant [*i.e.*, the author], decreeing that it should be trained to the flight of the Common Crane. The Royal Gift was accepted by this slave, with due tokens of humility: he kissed the falcon's jesses and then placed it on his obedient head:—

> I stood before the King as might a slave;
> The Royal hand to me the falcon gave.
> I placed it on my head in fashion meet
> When I'd imprinted kisses on its feet.

Scanning the bird with a falconer's eye, I saw that three flight-feathers of each wing were old and unshed. It was evident it had been taken up while still in the moult, so I had it replaced in the mew[2] and fed on fresh birds, with frequent changes of diet. Three months later it was taken up clean moulted, not a single old feather remaining.

As it may interest falconers, I append a description of this particular falcon.

DESCRIPTION.—In size it was about half as large again as a fine female Saker Falcon.[3] The plumage of the back and head was a brown ash colour, and each feather of the back and tail was marked with two tiny white spots. From the back of the neck to the rump, the plumage was ash-coloured, and covered with small yellowish-white spots. The breast was white, each breast feather being

---

[1] A.D. 1867.

[2] *Qūsh-khāna.*

[3] The average length of some living specimens of the female immature saker measured by the translator was 22 inches. The average weight of young passage sakers, caught in the Panjab in October, is 2 lbs. 5 oz. Haggards very seldom exceed 2 lbs. 10 oz. An exceptionally fine *chargh* in the translator's possession in 1892 weighed, when in flying condition, 2 lbs. 13⅓ oz.; while a second bird received in April, 1897, weighed 3 lbs. when fattened up for the moult. Both these last were young passage hawks. All weights were taken with the crop and stomach empty.

tipped with one small black spot and margined with black marks interlacing each other like the links of a chain. The tarsi[1] were robust and short; the feet small in proportion to its size, but stout and powerful; the claws and beak black; the iris dark, and the thighs[2] as thick as those of a male eagle.[3] The wing in length was something betwixt that of the long-winged and short-winged hawks, longer than that of a *qizil* or *ṭarlān*, and shorter than that of a *shāhīn* or a saker. The tail was broad and full of spots and markings. Like the *Qara-qūsh-i ā,īna-lī*,[4] it had a few stiff white feathers in the back, whether a mark of the species or merely a sign of old age, I am unable to say. (White feathers do occasionally make their appearance in aged sakers.) In weight it equalled nearly three sakers.[5] From my experience of hawks I should say that, when it reached me, it was in its tenth or twelfth moult. What its immature plumage may have been like, I cannot even guess.

TEACHING THE FALCON TO KNOW ITS NAME.—After removing this falcon from the mew,[6] I commenced her training with the utmost care. I named her "*Shunqār*." By feeding her through the hood, calling her by name the while, she quickly learnt to recognize her name and associate it with a good meal.[7]

When she had somewhat abated her high condition and had begun to show a proper inclination for food, I attached a strong "creance"[8] to her jesses and carried her out into the field to lure her to a lure of crane's wings. Unhooded by my falconer she

---

1 *Sāq*, *vide* note 5 on page 33.

2 *Rān*.

3 *Qara qūsh*.

4 *Vide* page 31.

5 An unconscious exaggeration on the author's part. A mounted falconer, who will carry for six or seven hours at a stretch, without complaint, a hawk that weighs 2½ lbs., will tire at the end of an hour if this weight is exceeded by half a pound or even less. At such moments it is difficult to avoid forming an exaggerated estimate of the burden.

6 "'Mew;' the place where hawks are set down to moult . . . Mew, *v.* to moult, from the Fr. *muer*, to change the feathers."—*Harting*.

7 *Vide* Chapter on training the newly caught "passage" Saker Falcon. Neither English nor Indian falconers attempt to make hawks recognize their names. As, however, hawks are naturally very intelligent and can easily be trained to come to any distinct call, there would probably be no great difficulty in the matter. The idea seems novel.

8 "'Creance,' *s*, Fr. *créance*, Lat. *credentia*, a long line attached to the swivel, and used when 'calling off'; flying a hawk as it were on credit. . . ."—*Harting*.

started with eagerness, but had hardly flown a few feet before she subsided to the ground and attempted to finish the distance on foot. I examined her carefully. Her feathers were perfect, and she appeared sound in wind and limb. What could be the cause of her extraordinary behaviour? Puzzled and perplexed, I buried my head in the collar of reflection, determined to unravel the tangled skein of the difficulty. Still, ransack my brains as I might, the clue to the mystery eluded me. I then screwed up my courage, and putting my trust in God, removed the "creance" from her feet, and called her again. The result was much as before. I bit the finger of astonishment, and by reason of the falcon's great infirmity became plunged in the abyss of despondency. Burying my head in the collar of reflection my thoughts drifted to those animal-gardens in Europe, where people buy strange beasts and birds for ridiculous prices, and after turning them into a public show for a few years, tire of them and put them up to public auction. It then dawned on me that my falcon must have come from one of those very gardens, and that, like a long-caged parrot, which, wild defied the swiftness of the Sparrow Hawk,[1] can now flutter no higher than its own perch, it too from long imprisonment had grown stiff-jointed and wing-tied.

Daily Exercise.—That the falcon might recover her lost powers of flight, I set about exercising her daily. Morning and evening I used to bear her to the top of a high mound[2] and cast her off, giving her five flights at each exercise. On the sixteenth day, instead of, as usual, merely flying down to the level, she went off some distance and settled on a second mound. I decided this was sufficient and commenced calling her to the lure, luring her at first from high ground to a lower level.

"Trains."—When her powers of flight were fully recovered I gave her a certain number of "trains," and gradually succeeded in thoroughly entering her to common crane. At last one joyous day, on the auspicious occasion of the Royal return from a pilgrimage to *Qum*,[3] I unhooded her at a common crane near the caravan stage of

---

[1] For a straight short flight, Oriental falconers are generally agreed that the Sparrow Hawk is one of "the swiftest birds that fly."

[2] *Māhūr* prop. "up and down land" (whether sand hills or hard ground).

[3] *Qum* is about eighty miles south of Teheran.

Pul-i Dallāk,[1] and in the Imperial presence of the Shah—let our souls be sacrificed for him! Right nobly the falcon acquitted herself, "towering" up into the clouds, and striking a huge crane down to the dust of the earth.

And on the spot *Kāshānī's* spirit fled,
You might have said he ne'er was else than dead.

DISPOSITION OF THE "*Shunqār.*"—Judging from my small experience, I should say that the *Shunqār* Falcon has naturally a docile and fearless disposition. At the moment I write (*i.e.*, in the year of the Flight, 1285),[2] the bird I have described has been in my possession just two years. During this period she has twice moulted. This year, I rejoice to say, she was "full-summed"[3] quite three months earlier than last.

SUFFERS FROM HEAT.—Though kept on a damp bed of pebbles and sand, in the *Bāgh-i Raz-kanda,* in the cool region of *Shimrānāt,*[4] she yet feels the heat greatly, so that even in this cool climate of *Shimrān* she has to be well supplied with ice and snow, both of which she swallows freely.

HAGGARD TIERCEL.—This year—it being the Spring of A.H. 1286—owing to the high fortune of His Majesty (sacrificed be our souls for him!), and the kindly aid of Heaven, the royal trappers have snared a "tiercel" of this species. It was caught in the district of *Khār* and *Varamīn,*[5] and is a fully moulted "haggard."[6] It is now, in the beginning of this Spring, something less than two months since it first came into my hands; and I have now placed it in the mew. I have taken with it both purple[7] and common heron. This "tiercel" is a stout and heavy bird about as large as a female saker. Its flight is lofty and swift; its nature noble and

[1] *Pul-i Dallāk* or "Barber's Bridge" is N.E. of and close to *Qum*: it spans the *Qara-sū* or *Qara-chay.*

[2] A.D. 1868.

[3] "A hawk is said to be 'summed' or 'full summed' when, after moulting, she has got all her new feathers and is fit to be taken out of the mew."—*Harting.*

[4] *Shimrānāt,* a name given to the summer-quarters in the hills, near Teheran.

[5] *Khār* is a plain in *'Irāq-i 'Ajamī,* some thirty miles east of Teherān and separated from *Varamīn* by hills.

[6] "'Haggard,' a hawk that has been caught after assuming its adult plumage, that is, after having moulted in a wild state."—*Harting.*

[7] *Jarda.* I believe this is the purple heron.

generous. I have now set it down to moult and am anxious as to the result.

Of the *Shunqār* it is fabled that when flown at a flock[1] of cranes it does not act like ordinary falcons and single out and kill a solitary individual; that its lofty and imperious nature permits it to cease from slaughter only when every crane in the flock is a carcass on the ground. Now this is a superlative falsehood. My *shunqār*, like other hawks, kills only one. It has, indeed, chanced to me that, when flying a passage saker at a flock of cranes, the falcon, stooping from a height and dealing a crane a deadly blow, has then shot upwards by its impetus, and finding itself close to a second bird, has seized the unexpected opportunity, and "bound"[2] to the second crane's head and so added a second victim to the bag. Once indeed I saw three cranes killed in this manner by a single hawk. Such occurrences are, however, lucky accidents. No hawk that I ever knew *systematically* acted in this manner.[3]

It is also commonly believed that the *Shunqār* is the acknowledged sovereign of the hawk tribe, and that should one be placed in the mew, every hawk will step down from its perch in token of humble submission. This, too, is a falsehood, pure and simple,—or else my young man is not a *shunqār*. At the moment I write I have more than fifty hawks of various kinds in my mews, but not one of them has ever left its perch, or honoured this sovereign, or shown respect in any manner of way. What is more, my fine gentleman the *Shunqār* stands very much in awe of eagles. Of course I am assuming that this hawk *is* a "*shunqār;*" equally of course I may be mistaken. All I know is that neither have I, nor has the oldest falconer in Persia, ever seen a falcon like it. The manner it stoops and recovers[4] is unequalled, either by

[1] Under "the compaynys of beeftys and Fowlys" in the *Boke of St. Albans* we learn that it is correct to speak of "an Herde of Cranys" or of "swannys" but a "Gagle of Gees" or of "women."

[2] "'Bind,' to fasten to the quarry in the air."—*Harting.*

[3] It is, of course, not the habit of wild hawks to kill more than one bird at at a time. Major C. H. Fisher, commenting on this fact, writes (p. 140): "Nevertheless I have seen it done more than once by a wild falcon, and many times by my own trained birds—in the case of the wild falcon from having at her first stoop struck down her prey too close to a man; from over-keenness, I think, by the tame hawk."

[4] In this quality of shooting up and preparing for a second stoop the Saker excels the Peregrine. The stoop, however, of the Saker is not as quick and sudden as the Peregrine's.

the Shahin or the Saker. I have several times flown it at common crane with a good *shāhīn*[1] trained to this flight, and it has always reached the quarry and bound to it before the latter came up.[2] Every one says it is a *shunqār*. I say so, too. Of the "'tis" and the "'tisn't" of the case, God alone is the Judge.

CHAPTER XVII

THE *SHĀHĪN*[3]

THIS species is very widely distributed. It is divided into three varieties—namely, the dark, the light and the yellow.

The best *shāhīns* are procured from three districts: from *Urūm*[4]

---

[1] It must be recollected that the term *shāhīn* includes the peregrine.

[2] Good evidence, but not proof, since there is nothing to show that the "shāhīn" was flying its fastest, or that the condition of both birds was the same. *Vide* also note 4, page 56.

[3] Blanford (*Eastern Persia*, vol. II., page 103), writes:—"Persian falconers distinguished three varieties of Shahin, the Stambulī, Karabāghī and Fārsī, the first from Western Asia Minor, the second from Circassia, Georgia and Armenia, and the third from Southern Persia. The first has the darkest plumage, the last the lightest. . . . The Shahin is, however, not so much used in Persia as formerly; indeed, I have never seen it out of the royal mews, except when brought to Bushire, for sale to the Arabs of the opposite coast. The falcon described by Marco Polo as found in the mountains of Paríz near Karmán, can be no other than the *Sháhín*. The old traveller says, 'In the mountains of Paríz near Karmán are found the best falcons in the world. They are inferior in size to the peregrine, red on the breast, under the neck and between the thighs; their flight is so swift that no bird can escape them'."

Considerable confusion exists as to the term *Shāhīn*. Arab falconers in the Persian Gulf and the Persians of Bushire call the female peregrine *shāhīna*, and rarely *baḥrīya*. The *Shaykhs* of *Baḥrayn* Island procure peregrines from Bushire. The *shāhīn* (but not the peregrine) seems to be unknown in Baṣrah and Baghdād. An Arabic MS. composed in the tenth century says, "If you desire to possess a *shāhīn*, then procure one of the peregrine (*baḥrī*) kind, especially if it be black-backed, ugly-faced, narrow-bodied, short-tailed, large-headed, sunken-eyed, piercing-eyed, large-beaked, deep-mouthed, short-backed, with long flight-feathers, and wings far apart from the body." The peregrine (*baḥrī*) is unknown to the falconers of Kirman except by name. The *shāhīn*, however, is not uncommon in the district. The translator, who was for eighteen months in Kirman, found three nests of the *shāhīn* and one of the *chargh*. The shāhīns of *Pārīz* are, however, no longer famous.

[4] Is this meant for Ezerum?

VII

INTERMEWED PEREGRINE

in Ottoman territory, from *Ardabīl*[1] in Persia, and from the hills of *Shammar*[2] in Arabia on the road to the holy city of Mecca.

The *Urūm* shahin is particularly common in *Sīvās*,[3] which place may be described as the "mine" of this variety. My private opinion, however, is that this, the shahin of *Urūm*, is not a shahin at all, but the young of the Peregrine; *i.e.*, when snared it is a "peregrine," when taken from the nest a "shahin." My reason for forming this opinion is that I happened one Spring to be in Sīvās and called on the Governor. At my request he gave me a guide, who conducted me to a spot about two *farsakh* from the city, where there was a shahin's eyrie in the hill-side. I sat down to observe it. My patience was soon rewarded by the appearance of the parent birds, bringing food for their young. I observed the birds closely, and discovered that they were not shahins but peregrines. This strengthened my previous supposition that confusion existed between the nestling and the passage hawk of the same species.

On another occasion I met a *shikārchī*[4] in Sīvās, with a peregrine on his fist. "What have you there," I asked, "and what does it kill?" His reply was, "This is a shahin, which I took myself from the nest, and which I have trained to take eagles." I accompanied him to his house, where he showed me ten or fifteen live eagles with clipped wings, which he kept loose near the house. It appeared that they had all been taken with the falcon then on his fist. I was seized with a desire to possess her, and offered him a large price; but he declined to part with his treasure.

THE *Shāhīn* OF *Jabal Shammar*.—Although the shahin from the mountains of *Shammar* is small, the female not exceeding in size the male of the other two species, still it is swift, bold, and easily entered to quarry, small or great. One eyrie, known by the name *Jarāza*, is especially famous; eyesses obtained from it are better and bolder than all others.

Though the passage shahin has more pace and a better wind

---

[1] *Ardabīl* is East of *Tabrīz* and almost on the Caspian. It is a convict station.

[2] *Shammar* is a hilly district in Central Arabia.

[3] *Sīvās*. Is this the town in Asia Minor on the river Kizl Irmak and south of Trebizond?

[4] *Shikārchī* is the Turkish equivalent of the Hindustani *shikārī*. These words do not necessarily refer to professionals.

VIII

YOUNG PEREGRINE (INDIAN HOOD)

than the eyess, it is far less tractable, for it has preyed for itself in the jungle, and is filled with overweening pride of its powers of flight. Say you have, with infinite pains, succeeded in training one to large quarry, and have unhooded her at a common crane or a heron, and that suddenly, beneath her, she spies a wild duck, or a pigeon, or some other small quarry. What does she do? She "checks," forsaking the large quarry for the small, and fills you with bitter disappointment. Now an eyess shahin will not act in this scurvy manner.

Supposing a passage falcon, shahin or peregrine, comes into your possession and you have no choice but to enter her to large quarry, you should blind her in the left eye, for when her right eye is on the quarry she has no spare eye to cast elsewhere, and her whole attention is necessarily occupied with the quarry at which she has been unhooded. This is in accordance with the saying of the poet:—

> "My left eye I will darken to the light,[1]
> So that I view thee only with my right."

I have successfully made the experiment and speak from experience.

Should you, however, wish to keep her for small quarry, on no account blind her. For small quarry you will find her better than the eyess: she will ring up better, especially after Royston Crows[2] and those blackguardly *yāplāq* owls.[3]

As remarked previously, the passage shahin and the peregrine are one and the same, with this difference, that the peregrine is stronger and larger. The courage of the peregrine, too, is greater than that of the passage shahin.

Rūmalī[4] eyess shahins are bolder than all others—especially the dark variety.

---

[1] In Persian, "to regard with the left eye" is an idiom for "to gaze at with contempt; to regard as an enemy."

[2] *Kulāgh-i ablaq, lit.* "the piebald crow," is the Royston Crow or a species exactly like it; it is common round Baghdad and in Persia. (The English magpie is also common in Persia and may locally be so named).—*Vide* page 55, note 5.

[3] *Yāplāgh-i pidar-sag,* "the dog-fathered *yāplāq,*" is perhaps the Indian grass owl or a species like it. The Author also calls another species, probably the Short-eared Owl, *yāplāgh,* but omits the epithet "son of a dog" when mentioning it. The former is a difficult quarry, the latter an easy one.—*Vide* note 2, page 23.

[4] Apparently an adjective from *Urūm.*

CHAPTER XVIII

THE PEREGRINE (*BAḤRĪ*)

Baḥrī.—I have already stated my opinion that the Peregrine is merely the *Rūmalī Shāhīn* caught after it has left the nest.

At any rate the best variety of peregrine is the yellowish, almond[1]-coloured, variety.

I have trained peregrines[2] to gazelle. They are, however, delicate[3] birds, as well as bold and daring: they dash themselves impetuously against the gazelle's horns and thus frequently injure themselves fatally. This is the reason that falconers do not care to train them to gazelle. Further, on account of the flightiness[4] of their disposition they are not so very highly prized. When choosing a peregrine, select one with large feet, short legs, and long slender wings. Count the scales on the middle toe. Ordinarily there are only seventeen or eighteen.[5] If you find a bird

---

[1] *i.e.*, the colour of the *skin* of an almond. The yellow variety of peregrine is avoided by Panjab falconers.

[2] The only Englishman who attempted gazelle hawking in India was the late Sir Harry Lumsden who raised the Corps of Guides. He told the translator that the Amir used to send him from Kabul, at the beginning of the cold weather, trained hawks and greyhounds, as well as falconers. In an article in the *Badminton Magazine* on Sir Harry Lumsden's gazelle hawks, there is an illustration of a peregrine striking at a gazelle. This is an error. Sir Harry used only *charghs* for gazelle.

[3] Delicate compared to the saker, the falcon most prized by Orientals. In Baghdad (in 1900-01) the price of a peregrine had risen from three to ten rupees, whereas a saker was said to be worth as much as seventy rupees. In the Panjab, sakers range from Rs. 3 to Rs. 7. The Saker is, by most Easterns, preferred to the Peregrine, as it is hardier and can, to a certain extent, be fed on butcher's meat, and still work well; whereas it is impossible to keep a peregrine in first-class condition without a constant supply of doves and pigeons, or birds whose flesh is equally good. Further, in the desert, the crops are scanty, and in consequence the houbara cannot always be marked down in their feeding grounds, but have to be laboriously beaten for by a long line of mounted men in open order; even a *young* saker will sit barefaced on the rider's fist without bating, but keeping a sharp look out for the quarry, which, by running round the line or dodging through the intervals, may escape the keen sight of the beaters, but not the keener sight of the falcon.

[4] Hence the epithet *yāwā* applied to it and to the shahin, in the Kapurthala State.

[5] That is there are, in the female peregrine, seventeen or eighteen large scutæ (*pūlak*) that extend across the whole breadth of the toe. These scutæ vary greatly in size, and their number is no guide to the length of the toe: a hawk with a large number may have a short toe.

with twenty-one, you have a treasure. A good peregrine should have a fine full breast, a broad back, and toes that are long and lean; and its body should be round and compact. An old master has not without reason sung:—

If I could have my fancy free,
Goshawks like wagtails[1] all should be,
And Sparrow-hawks like Goshawks all;
But *Shāhīns* round and *Chargh*s tall.[2]
Should *Baḥrī*s too from faults be free,
In truth broad-shouldered they must be.

[1] *Ṣa'wa.* I believe this is properly a wagtail, but the term is by some Turks also applied to a species of sparrow. Miyān Maḥmūd Sāhibzāda, of Taunsa, a Muslim friend of mine, and a keen and successful falconer of considerable experience, is of opinion that though a goshawk should be long, it should have a short tail and a short tarsus. As a matter of course the hawk should be heavy and well furnished, the flesh being hard, not soft. "Never," said this authority, "buy a camel, a horse, or a goshawk, with a short neck. A long neck is a sign of staying power and vigour." The present Nawāb of Teri says that, in his experience, goshawks with sharp clean claws are inferior to those with worn and blunted nails, and this experience is confirmed by other Panjab falconers. Blunt and worn nails probably indicate that a hawk is keen and persevering; that after it "puts in" the partridge, it runs round and round the cover on foot and does not give up the chase. Indians, or rather Panjabis, object to light eyes in a goshawk. ". . .; the worſt you can ſay by an hawke for their ſhape is, that ſhee is a long ſlender and beeſome-tailed hawke."—*Bert.* "In yo[r] choice observe when yo buy, a larg beake, a larg foote, a short train, an upright stande, and all of a peece."—*Harting* (quoting a MS. in the British Museum): *vide* page ix, Introduction, *Booke for Keping of Sparchawkes.* In the latter work the "Tokens of a Good Hawke" are: "Large: heade ſlender: beake thick and greate like a parot: ſeare ſayre: nares wyde: ſtalke ſhort and bygg: foote large, wyde, and full of ſtrengeth: mail thick: wynges large w[t] narow fethers: heye of fleſhe and euer diſpoſed to feede egerly."

[2] Many Panjab falconers assert that long charghs are faster and stoop in better style. They are certainly not inferior to the shorter birds.

CHAPTER XIX

THE SAKER[1] FALCON (*F. Cherrug*)

[The author now mentions fourteen races and varieties of *bālābān*,[2] each of which he distinguishes by some special epithet.

[1] *Ṣaqar* (sometimes pronounced *ṣagar* or *ṣaghar*) is one of the names by which this falcon (*F. Sacer* of Jerdon and *F. cherrug* of Blanford) is known to the Arabs. Possibly the word *ṣaqar* is by Arabs applied to other falcons also.

[2] Considerable confusion exists with regard to the various names of this falcon. By Indians this species is called *chargh*, by Afghans *charkh*. By Persians the passage falcon is styled *bālābān* and the eyess *charkh*, while by the Turks of Persia the passage falcon and the eyess are often both called *aitālgī*. The Author, however, himself a Turk, states that the nestling of a particular variety is by Turkish falconers distinguished by the name *aitalgī*. In *Lahore to Yarkand*, a report on some of the scientific results of the expedition to Yarkand in 1870, there is a coloured figure of an old and not uncommon variety of the Saker, to which the scientific name of *Falco Hendersoni* is appended; and it is stated that Mr. Hume considered this falcon to be the *Shunqār* of Eastern falconers. Apparently following up this idea, Scully, in his vocabulary of the Turki names of birds, gives as the equivalent of the Turki *aitalgū*, "the female of the '*shunqār*,' *Falco Hendersoni*." There is, however, evidence to show that, in ancient times, *Shunqār* was a name given by Indian falconers to a species of Jerfalcon, *vide* page 36, note 4. Modern Indian falconers, proverbial for inaccuracy, have a habit of calling any Saker (*chargh*) that is unusual in size and markings a "*shunqār*," and so, by exciting emulation, obtain a fictitious price from some credulous native gentleman. Though seemingly only one species of *chargh* visits the Panjab, individuals so vary in size, shape, markings, and colouration, that it is at first sight difficult to believe that they are of the same species. Amongst young birds some are whole-coloured, others have some small white specks on the back, while others again have white heads with spotted tails. In some varieties the tail spots are barely visible; in others they are so white and numerous that the spread tail appears to be nearly all white. Peculiarities may disappear to a great extent in the first moult. The colouring of the "intermewed"* falcon depends, to a great extent, on feeding and exposure. "Haggards" vary, nearly, if not quite, as much as the immature hawks. A rare variety is said, by Panjabi falconers and others, to have the tarsus feathered "like certain breeds of pigeons." In the Derajat this variety is distinguished by the term *pā-moz* or "booted," while in the Pindi Gheb district it is considered a distinct species and called *Sang-sang*. The evidence of the existence of this peculiar variety (which is also supposed to be above the average in size) is detailed and corroborative. Arab falconers of *Baṣrah* have described this variety to the translator,

* "'Intermewed.' A hawk that has been moulted in confinement."—*Lascelles*.

Kabīdī (?).—The first race or variety described is apparently named *kabīdī*: [1]]—It has a white head, without any cheek-stripe or dark mark under the eyes.[2] With this exception the colouration is dark: the feathers of both the body and the tail[3] are without spots. It is large in size and bold in nature, and good for either crane[4] or gazelle, but, alas, it is scarce. In the whole of my experience I have met with only one.

Bālābān-i Fārsī.—Next is the *Bālābān-i Fārsī*, or "Saker of Fārs," which is subdivided into the red and the white varieties. Neither has cheek stripes. The back, from the neck to the oil-bottle,[5] is covered with spots and markings, and the redder these are in tint, the better the bird. The flight-feathers,[6] seven in each wing, are also covered with spots. The feet are a very light slate-colour. The darker and smaller the beak, tongue, and nails, the better. The feet are lean, the tarsi short, the thighs stout, the chest and back broad, the wings fine and pointed, the eyes sunken, the eyebrows prominent; the neck is long, the forehead broad, the "waist" small. If the hawk has all these points, it is incomparable.

Bālābān-i Aḥmar-i Shām.—Next is the *Bālābān-i aḥmar-i Shām* or the "Red Syrian Saker," of which there are two varieties, the red and the black. In a good bird of this race, the two centre tail-feathers, called by the Arabs *'amūd* or "props," and

---

and stated that it is known to them by the name of *Shunghār*. By the name *Sang-sang* some species of falcon (probably a *charkh*) is known to the Afghans. The Chargh breeds in Afghanistan, Persia, and elsewhere, but not in India. Apparently more than one race visits India. In the Panjab it is flown only at large quarry—kite, hare, houbara, and occasionally at black ibis and common heron. In Baghdad it is said to be flown at geese. Corballis, in *Forty-five Years of Sport*, says, "This falcon is good at smaller game, such as grouse, partridges, etc." Apparently he is speaking of Syria. The Saker is too slow for sand-grouse in ordinary circumstances.

[1] This word is perhaps a copyist's error.

[2] *Madma'* Ar. sing. "The place where the tears collect in the sides of the eye"; the pl. *madāmi'* comprises the inner and outer angles of the eyes, but is especially applied to the inner. *Vide* note 4, page 8.

[3] In India a hawk with a tail without marks is called *lagar-dum*, or "tailed like the Lagar Falcon."

[4] In Dresser's *Birds of Europe* it is stated that Jerdon once took a *Sārus* crane (*Grus Antigone*) with a Saker.

[5] *Mudhun* A. and *rūghan-dān* P.

[6] *Shāh-par*, "flight-feather."

IX

YOUNG PASSAGE SAKER [illegible]

by the Turks *qāpāq*,[1] as well as the two outer tail-feathers, one on each side,[2] should be without spot or marking.

Bālābān-i Badrī.—The next race is called *badrī.*[3] It has a white head and no cheek stripe. The general colouration is reddish, and the back and breast are without markings. The two centre tail-feathers are sometimes with spots and sometimes without: if with spots the smaller and redder they are the better.

These four races or varieties are by the Arabs styled *ḥurr ṣāfī.*[4]

Badū-pasand (?).—[A variety of the *Badrī* has a name[5] that cannot be deciphered with certainty.] This is a variety of the *Badrī*, but the whole of the tail is white without the admixture of any other colouring. It is uncommon, and though it belongs to the class of *ḥurr*,[4] it is poor-spirited and not prized.

Jibālī.—The next race is the Mountain[6] (?) Saker. It has a little black only, under the eye. It has on the back, two, four, or six white spots, called by the Arabs Pleiades (*Thurayyā*). The "prop" feathers have sometimes spots and sometimes none. In any case it is not styled by the Arabs *ḥurr ṣāfī*, for the *ḥurr ṣāfī* must not only be without cheek stripes, but must also have certain other points.

The first four described are, however, all included in the *ḥurr ṣāfī*. According to the idiom of Arab falconers, the *ḥurr ṣāfī* must have the back "free from Pleiades,"[7] the "prop" feathers "clear of marks,"[8] and the two outside feathers (one on each side) "void of stain."[9] Also it must have no cheek stripe, nor black under the eyes. Should the hawk not have these points, they class it as *jibālī* and not as *ḥurr ṣāfī*.

Bālābān-i Lafīf.—Next is the *bālābān-i lafīf*,[10] and of this there

---

[1] *Qāpāq*; derivation unknown.

[2] These two feathers are apparently called by the Arabs *rudāfa*. This word is the plural of *radīf*, which literally signifies "to ride pillion." In m. c. it is the name given by Persians and Turks to the "Army Reserve." *Vide* also page 73, note 2.

[3] Possibly from *badr*, "the full moon."

[4] *Ḥurr* Ar. "free-born"; hence "noble." The Saker and Goshawk are styled *ḥurr*, and also the young of certain animals. *Ṣāfī*, "pure, unmixed, etc."

[5] Apparently *Badū-pasand*, "liked by the Bedouins."

[6] *Jibālī*, adj. from *jibāl* "mountains," plural of *jabal*.

[7] *Sālim*[u] *Ṣurayyā*.

[8] *Muṭlaq*[u] *'l-'amūd*.

[9] *Māṣiḥ rudāfa*.

[10] *Lafīf*: meaning of *lafīf* obscure.

X

YOUNG PASSAGE SAKER (DARK VARIETY)

are three varieties, the yellowish, the dark, and the light. All three have cheek-stripes or dark feathers under the eyes. As in the case of the eyess *charkh*, if this race is taken from the nest it is called in Turki *aitālgī*, in Arabic *wacharī*,[1] and in Persian *charkh*. Should it have left the nest and be caught in a net, it is called (in Persian) *bālābān-i lafīf:*

Now as for those four races described above as *ḥurr ṣafī*, I have in my many travels and constant inquiries never met with any hawk-catcher or sportsman[2] who has taken a *ḥurr ṣāfī* from the nest. No one even knows in what country, birds of this race breed. All I know for certain is, that in the beginning of Autumn they come to us from across the sea, from the direction of Muscat and Bahreyn.[3] God knows where they breed and whence they travel. Those that I have seen in Persia, Turkey,[4] and Europe[5] have all been *lafīf* and have all had cheek stripes.

The *lafīf* is to the *ḥurr ṣāfī* what the *ṭarlān* is to the *qizil*, or what the Nejd[6] horse is to the Turkoman pony.[7] Moult after moult the *ḥurr ṣāfī* becomes better, whereas the *lafīf* flies well for not more than three seasons: after that it becomes cunning.[8] I have at present two *bālābān* of the *ḥurr ṣāfī* race, one of sixteen and one of seventeen moults; one is "Persian" and the other "Red

---

[1] There is no letter *ch* in Arabic. In 'Irāq, however, *k* is sometimes pronounced *ch*. *Wakr (wachr)* in Arabic is a nest, so "*wachrī*" *might* signify "nestling." An Arab gentleman in *Baṣrah* (a falconer) told me that the white Saker with drops on the back is called *Ḥurr Ṣāfī;* the same if of a reddish tinge *Ḥurr Shāmī;* and that these races are supposed to come from "Persia" and "Syria." The dark Saker with drops on the back is, he said, called *Wacharī Jarūdī*, and without drops *Wacharī*. The best for gazelle, he stated, was the "Persian" and "Syrian." The Baghdad Sakers are preferred to those of Baṣrah. Sakers are caught in Bushire and taken for sale to Baṣrah, where they fetch as much as seventy rupees. In the Panjab their price varies from three to ten rupees, according to locality and season.

[2] *Shikārchī*, a comprehensive term; "sportsman, fisherman, bird-catcher, etc., etc."

[3] The Sheikh of *Baḥrayn* keeps many sakers and peregrines which are flown at houbara on the opposite Persian Coast. The translator once travelled with the Sheikh's two sons in a B. I. boat: they had fifty or sixty falconers and as many peregrines and sakers, all, with one exception, young and newly trained.

[4] By Turkey, the Author probably means Asia Minor.

[5] Probably Turkey in Europe.

[6] The best bred Arab horses are from Nejd.

[7] *Yābū*, a pony of a coarse breed.

[8] *Duzd*, *lit.* "a thief."

Syrian."[1] Both are still excellent at common crane.[2] Birds of this race, while life lasts, year by year improve, for their nature is noble.

THE BĀLĀBĀN-I LAFĪF OF BAGHDAD.—A variety of the *Lafīf* that I have met with nowhere except in Baghdad, is called by Baghdad falconers *Wacharī*.[3] In general colouring, it is dark with a tinge of red on the head. The flight feathers are dark in colour and long, extending beyond the tail. It has small feet and the female is about the same size as the tiercel of the eyess *charkh*.[4] It is very swift, nearly as swift as the *shāhīn*. It takes the small piebald crow,[5] black partridge,[6] and stone plover, with ease. Some few I have seen that would take houbara.

It has a great outward resemblance to the Hobby which is found round Teheran.

CHAPTER XX

THE EYESS SAKER FALCON

THE eyess *charkh*[7] is of four kinds. First there is the variety that in the Spring[8] months breeds in the hills of Persia and Turkey.[9]

Another is found in Nejd[10] in Turkish territory, where it lays its

---

[1] *Fārsī* and *Aḥmar Shāmī*.

[2] The common crane is, in the air, an easier quarry than the heron. The struggle on the ground is, however, severe and highly dangerous, as the crane uses its sharp claw with great effect.

[3] *Vide* page 54, note 1.

[4] Some Indian and Persian falconers I questioned in Baghdad had never met with a falcon that answered this description. The *Lagar* falcon (*F. Jugger*) of India—a desert falcon—does not answer to the description. Also it does not appear to be found in Persia or Asia Minor.

[5] *Kulāgh-i kūchak u ablaq*, presumably "the hooded crow," common around Baghdad and in Persia. The author probably styles it "small" as compared to the raven, which is sometimes called by the same name. *Vide* page 46, note 2.

[6] *Durrāj*, "the francolin."

[7] *Charkh* is the eyess saker, and *bālābān* the passage saker.

[8] There are four distinct seasons of the year, in Persia. The Spring, unlike the Indian Spring, is long and cool. The Saker falcon migrates from the Panjab much earlier than the peregrine.

[9] *i.e.*, Turkish territory.

[10] Nejd, in central Arabia, directly west of Bahrayn Island.

eggs on the bare ground, like the black-breasted sand-grouse,[1] and the houbara bustard. This variety is called *charkh-i māniʿī*.[2]

Another kind nests in the hills and dry water-courses of Nejd. From thence nestlings are obtained by the Arabs who style them *Ḥijāzī*.[3]

All these kinds, if obtained from the nest, are *charkh*, and if snared after they have left the nest are *lafīf*.

The *charkh-i māniʿī* is exceptionally good, whether for gazelle, or common crane, or golden eagle: you can train it to anything. I am able to state that it is faster even than the *shāhīn*, for I have often flown one at crane in company with a *shāhīn*, and it has reached and "bound" to the crane a long way ahead of it.[4]

The colouration of the *māniʿī* varies, but that variety that has very red markings on the back, like a kestril,[5] is the best. Of all the *charkhs* of the world the *māniʿī* with red spots on the back is the best. Although it is an eyess (*charkh*) and is obtained from the nest, it is equal to any noble passage falcon (*bālābān*) of the *ḥurr ṣāfī* race. It is to be obtained only from the Arabs of *Unayza*.[6] In that waterless part of *'Arabistān* its chief prey is houbara and hare.[7]

---

[1] *Bāqir-qara* T. and *Siyāh-sīnah* P.: both words signify literally "black breast." The Arab gentleman mentioned in note 1, page 54, informed me that in certain localities the saker nests on the bare ground. *Vide* also page 115, note 3. An Englishman told me that he once, in Wales, found two peregrine's eggs laid on the bare open ground close to a cliff edge.

[2] Has *māniʿī* here the signification of "difficult of access"?

[3] *Ḥijāz*, a province on the Red Sea. It is not in Nejd.

[4] This is no sure test of swiftness, for a peregrine flown with a large and powerful saker often flies "cunning." *Vide* note 2, page 42.

[5] I have known a saker that in the immature plumage was white and covered with spots (such a saker is styled in the Kapurthala State *chītal chargh* and is there considered useless for anything except hare) assume this red kestril-like plumage on its first moult.

[6] *Unayza*, name of a tribe and of a place in West Nejd. The tribe is famous for a breed of horses, larger and coarser than the Nejd breed. The name is said to be the diminutive of either *anza*, a "she-goat" or of *anaza*, a "javelin."

[7] All sakers in a wild state occasionally prey on houbara. Trained haggards, but not young passage hawks, will as a rule take hare without being entered by a "train." Perhaps during the nesting season, the parent birds are driven to killing hare. I have seen a young passage hawk of mine, flying close to the ground, carry a hare for two or three hundred yards. The hare, a fine hill specimen, weighed 4½ lbs., while the saker weighed only 2 lbs. 4 oz. I have seen an "intermewed"

CHAPTER XXI

STRANGE ARAB DEVICES FOR CATCHING THE PASSAGE SAKER

THE Arabs have two strange devices for catching the *bālābān*. It chances sometimes that, while out hawking, a wild *bālābān* will suddenly drop from the sky, and seize a flushed houbara. The Arabs wait till the falcon has broken into the quàrry and has begun to eat. Then they go slowly towards the falcon, which, unable to carry off the heavy quarry, perforce abandons it: the falcon will retire to a distance of five- or six-hundred yards and regard her quarry with eyes of regret. Two *shikār-chīs* go up to the dead houbara and quickly and deftly dig a pit in the sand with their sticks. One of them stealthily gets into this pit and is completely covered with sand, his nose only being above ground. One arm is extended, but concealed by a light sprinkling of sand. The dead houbara is then placed on his open palm and the other men all withdraw to a distance. After a short time, the *bālābān*, seeing the coast clear, returns without suspicion to its prey. Poor thing, what knows it of what is underground? Slowly it returns to its quarry and re-settles on it. That cuckoldy pimp in his living grave feels the falcon settle; then slowly, very slowly, under cover of the houbara's feathers his hand searches for his victim's feet. The hapless falcon, in dread of a robber eagle, eagerly busies itself with pluming and eating: its whole attention is directed to its food. Sooner or later some part of its foot or leg touches the hidden hand, and the freedom of the noble bird is gone. The dead man then comes to life and rises from his sandy grave.[1]

---

saker stoop at, and strike, a large hare on the head, with such force that the hare never moved again. In Dresser's *Birds of Europe* it is stated on the authority of Colonel Przevalsky that in Mongolia, in Winter, the chief food of the saker is the Alpine hare.

[1] An Afghan acquaintance told the translator that he had seen demoiselle cranes (*khar-khare*) caught in the following manner at Kabul. Small boys were buried in the sand at intervals, their noses above ground and their arms extended—the arms carefully covered with sand and shingle. The unsuspecting cranes were then slowly driven towards the hidden children. Sometimes two or three birds are

Another Device.—There is another cunning device, which can be practised only during the season of the terrible east wind of Baghdad—" We take refuge in God from it."[1] This wind blows with incessant severity for two to nine days at a time. Day and night it rages, ceasing not for one minute. None dare venture out in it; everything comes to a standstill. All sorts of wild birds, fearing to be swept away far from their hunting and feeding grounds, take refuge from the force of the wind by settling on the ground. Perhaps some luckless sportsmen, when out hawking, get caught in this wind, and by chance spy a *bālābān* seated on the sandy gritty soil. One of the party will go directly up-wind of it, and raising all the dust and sand[2] he can with his hands and feet, will scatter it on the wind. Under cover of this cloud of dust, which is carried by the wind on to the falcon, he quickly advances, stirring up the while all the sand he can with his hands and feet. The falcon's eyes get filled with the sand: in vain it rubs them on its feathers: the sand-storm continues, while the man behind it ceases not advancing with rapidity. The falcon is first forced to close its eyes, but the sand stops up its nostrils, and it soon has no choice but to seek protection for its head under its wing. In this unsuspecting and helpless attitude it is secured by hand.

Author captures a Vulture.—Once I went on a pilgrimage

---

caught in this manner. The children are buried on the spot where the cranes rest at night. In Chitral, goshawks are said to be caught by the following device: The top of a bare hillock is selected, scooped out and roofed over, the chamber thus made being sufficiently large to conceal a man. The trapper enters the chamber from the side, and closes the entrance. He then puts through a hole in the roof a live *chukor* fitted with jesses, and with a leash five or six feet long. The hole in the roof is closed, and the partridge flutters at the extent of its leash. When the goshawk appears, the cries of the *chukor* warn the trapper. When the goshawk seizes the partridge, it is slowly drawn towards the hole by the trapper. The hawk, feeling resistance, only "binds" the tighter, till it is suddenly seized by the legs from within the hut. The chief places for catching goshawks near Chitral are said to be the *Singūr* forest; the *Bakamak* hill; the *Makhtāmābād* hill; and the *Urgutch* hill. These are the four *Mihtarī* places, *i.e.*, hawks caught there are the property of the *Mihtar*.

[1] A common exclamation amongst Muslims; used in time of danger, on hearing of an accident, and on seeing one afflicted with a horrible disease such as leprosy.

[2] *Shin va māssa.*

to *Hazrat-i Salmān-i Fārsī*,[1] and intending to kill two birds with one stone took with me four or five *charkhs* and *bālābāns* that were trained to gazelle, and nine or ten mounted falconers. I started early in the morning, and expected to secure during the day five or six gazelles at least. We had gone about two *farsakh*[2] when the east wind began to rise. It gradually increased in force till about two hours before noon, by which time we had reached the very "mine"[3] of gazelle. To the right and left of us there was nothing but gazelle, but, on account of the wind, it was impossible to fly the hawks. Soon the air became darkened, and so strong was the wind that it could have borne aloft a thousand thrones of Solomon.[4] We were nearly lifted off our horses to be hurled far into the desert. There was nothing for it but to "mail"[5] the *charkhs* and *bālābāns* and carry them under our arms, or in the skirts of our robes. We were now in ground that is called *Hawr Sa'da*[6]: it is low-lying ground, void of dust or sand, for when the Tigris overflows its banks in the Spring, the hollow retains water, and grass and reeds spring up. This hollow was about two *farsakh* broad by six or seven long, and was a favourite feeding-ground of gazelle. The well-known medicinal herb

---

[1] *Salmān-i Fārsī* was a Persian of Abyssinian extraction. He was one of the "Companions of the Prophet." His tomb, on a bank of the Tigris, not far from Baghdad, is close to the old ruined palace of Kisra, called by the Arabs *Tāq-Kisra* "The arch of Cyrus." Here, too, is the site of *Madā'in* or "The cities," the capital of Persia at the time of the Muslim conquest. Seven cities are said to have existed on this site, *Taysafūn* or Ctsesiphon being one of them. It was in the latter that the *Tāq-Kisra* existed, built, according to some accounts, by Nūshīravān the Just.

[2] A *farsakh* is about $3\frac{3}{4}$ miles.

[3] "Mine," an Arab idiom for any place where the game is found in abundance.

[4] *'Arsh-i Sulaymān*. The winds were subject to Solomon. His throne was placed on an immense carpet of green silk, and his forces, men on the right, *jinn* on the left, took their stand upon it, and the wind bore it aloft under Solomon's orders, while the army of birds formed a canopy above.

[5] *Qapāncha kardan*, "to mail" a hawk, *i.e.*, to wrap it up in a "sock" or cloth, so that it is in a kind of strait-jacket. Even on foot it is impossible to carry hawks in a strong desert wind.

[6] *Hawr* is low-lying ground or dried marsh land that is full of grass and reeds. *Sa'da* is an adjective from the grass *sa'd-i kūfī* mentioned later.

galingale[1] is produced here in abundance; hence the name of *Ḥawr Sa'da* given to the spot.

Well, as soon as we emerged from this *ḥawr*, we lost sight of the Arch of Ctsesiphon and the dome of *Haẓrat-i Sulaymān.* Though we knew the ground thoroughly, having hawked gazelle there hundreds of times, we completely lost our bearings and wandered about aimlessly and perplexedly, we knew not whither. At last we emerged on to the sandy desert, and realized that we had left the shrine of *Sulaymān* on our left. Our horses were unable to proceed, for their eyes and nostrils were soon choked with sand.

Suddenly a huge carrion vulture[2] dropped to earth and settled before us. I told my attendants to stop still while I circumvented it by the Arab method. I made a circuit and got up-wind of it, and assisted the wind in covering it with sand and dust. At last I reached the vulture and saw that the poor thing had tucked away its head, and was to all appearance asleep. I cast myself on it and secured it, and saw that its eyes and nostrils were so choked with sand that it could scarcely breathe. I made the *Ābdār*[3] carry it till we reached the shrine. Not having enough food for the hawks, I bought a fat young sucking-lamb,[4] and killed it. The liver and heart were given to the vulture, which, when the wind subsided, was duly released.

I could have captured gazelle by the same method had it not been for their sense of smell.

---

[1] *Sa'd-i kūfī* is a tall sweet-smelling grass used in medicine. The scientific name is said to be Cyperus Scariosus. The Hindi name is, I think, *nāgar moth*.

"The dale
Was seen far inland and the yellow down
Border'd with palm, and many a winding vale
And meadow, set with slender galingale."
—*Lotus Eaters.*

[2] *Dāl-i murdār-khwār.*

[3] *Ab-dār*, a servant in charge of the drinks, tea-things, etc. He would of course be mounted, probably on a mule.

[4] *Barra-yi shīr-mast.*

CHAPTER XXII

THE MERLIN

THIS little falcon is beyond all praise. There are three varieties, the dark, the light, and the yellow, the first being the best. No Persian falconer has yet found the nest of the merlin, nor is it known in what country it breeds. All I know is that, about two months after the beginning of Autumn, it is spread over the face of the land, and is then caught in nets by the bird-catchers.

Like the *bālābān* there are three kinds, the *Ḥurr Ṣāfī*, the *Aḥmar Shāmī*,[1] and the *Lafīf*. The dark variety, which is the *Lafīf* and has cheek-stripes,[2] is better than the *Ḥurr Ṣāfī*. Unlike the Saker, this falcon is somewhat forgetful by nature.

If you want to train a "cast"[3] of merlins to fly larks,[4] train them quickly, luring them three times or four times a day to a lure made of pigeons' wings.[5] Now get a live lark, and for three days, —after the merlin has been made hot and excited by being called to the lure—tie the lark to the end of a long stick, and fly the hawk at that, making it stoop four or five times.[6] Then let the hawk take, and eat half of the lark. Do this three times a day, flying it after it has digested its meal.[7]

After the merlins are well entered to the lark at the end of the stick,[8] go out into the open country. Show them, by hand, a good lark, unruffled and strong on the wing; then let it fly, casting off both merlins after it.[9] They will stoop at it and take it. When they do, feed them up together. Do this for three or four days.

Now go into the open country and fly them at a wild lark, choosing some spot free from wells or gardens: for, if your hawk

---

1 *Vide* note 4, page 52.

2 *Madāmi'*, pl. of *madma'*, *vide* p. 50, note 2.

3 "'Cast,' *s.*, a 'cast of hawks,' *i.e.*, two; not necessarily a pair."—*Harting*.

4 *Kākulī* P., which elsewhere the author says is called *qumburah* by the Arabs; it is the Crested Lark.

5 A lure made of pigeons' wings is not very durable.

6 The lark at the end of the stick will be in the *air* the whole time, and the merlin, though raw, will not therefore sit on the ground.

7 *Ba'd az burdun-i gūsht.* A merlin will eat in a day, two sparrows or larks.

8 *Kākulī-yi mīkh-band.*

9 *Har du rā juft bi-yandāz.*

chases a lark into a well, it will probably get destroyed; if it chases it into a garden, it will not only lose the lark, but lose itself. You require a clear open plain.

The quicker you train these little falcons the better, but with other hawks the contrary holds good: in training the latter, use deliberation.

METHOD OF SNARING LARKS.—I am certain the reader has been saying to himself, "Where am I to get all these live larks? Surely the author is wrong somewhere." No, my friend, it is *you* that are wrong. Now listen to me while I tell you how to snare larks.

Get a long, light pole,[1] about eleven feet long, and bind to the end of it, a horse-hair noose[2] (of white horse-hair for choice) made of a single hair, and use white thread for the binding.[3] As soon as your merlin is keen on the lure, go out into the open country with an assistant. When you come across a lark, give the merlin to your assistant, and then move aside ten or fifteen paces. Now, alongside of the lark, lure the merlin to your fist. As soon as the lark spies the hawk, it will crouch on the ground, its eyes glued on the hawk. Now hand over the hawk to your assistant. Make him hold his hand high, and by lowering it and raising it cause the hawk to extend and flutter its wings, so that the attention of the lark may remain engrossed on it. Tell your man to go to the left of the lark and to stand about ten paces from it, making the hawk flutter all the time. Do you go to its right, and, advancing very slowly, extend the pole, slip the horse-hair noose on to the poor lark's neck, and draw it to you, and—there is your "train." This device is the invention of your humble servant. It is most successful in the Autumn and Winter months.

A lark, before a cast of merlins, gives a very pretty ringing flight. In the Spring, however, and even on warm days in the Winter,[4] they will not ring up.

---

[1] In the Dera Ismail Khan district, in the Panjab, the common desert lark called *chandūr* used to be snared in this fashion, the wand used being a stalk of the grass called *kānā*.

[2] *Ḥalqa-yi mū-yi dum-i asp.*

[3] The surface of the desert ground would be whitish in colouration.

[4] Not clear whether the author means that it is the larks or the hawks that will not ring up, or both.

A very good female merlin will take "chukor," "seesee,"[1] quail, woodcock,[2] and other small quarry.

DEFECT OF MERLINS.—Merlins are inveterate "carriers,"[3] a great defect in their character, and should therefore be flown as a "cast," and not singly. Another defect is that, if allowed to get very hungry, they begin to tear their own feet; and if the falconer be inattentive, they will tear away the flesh till they reach the shank bone.[4] Once they learn this vice, the only remedy is to give them their freedom. The falconer must therefore be careful to keep them always in high condition, for otherwise they will not only not "ring up" well, but will also contract the vice just mentioned.

A good, young, merlin may be kept and moulted, but just as is the case of a young passage saker and an "intermewed"[5] one, an intermewed[6] merlin will not ring up as well as a young passage hawk. The young hawk is light in body, and ignorant as well; but after the moult it becomes not only heavy, but cunning also, and will give up the moment it sees that the lark it is chasing is very strong on the wing. A "haggard" *bālābān*,[7] however, will, in the hands of a skilful falconer, ring up better than a young passage *bālābān*.

There are two varieties of merlin. In one variety the immature and mature plumage are, even after many moults, the same. In the other, the plumage of the back, after the first moult, becomes blue-grey, while the cere and legs become bright yellow like amber. I have never been able to discriminate which kind it is that will remain the same, and which kind will assume the blue plumage and yellow cere.

---

[1] *Kabk*, the Red-legged Partridge of India: *tīhū*, the See-see of India.

[2] *Yalva*, T., is a name of the woodcock, but it is probably a name given also to some species of rail. One Persian Turk tells me that it is called by the Persians *khurūsak*, and "is of a reddish brown colour, has a long bill, yellow legs, and frequents damp or marshy ground."

[3] "'Carry.' *v.*, to fly away with the quarry."—*Harting.*

[4] *Qalam.*

[5] "'Intermewed'.—A hawk that has been moulted in confinement." —*Lascelles.*

[6] *Khāna-ṭūlak.*

[7] "Haggard," a hawk that has moulted in a wild condition. The author here calls this *dāsh-ṭūlak* T. "moulted outside."

XI

HOBBY WITH SEELED EYES

CHAPTER XXIII

THE HOBBY[1]

The hobby resembles the merlin somewhat, but is larger, darker in colouring, and prettier in appearance. It has long broad wings, dark in colouring. Its feet are small and yellow. In a wild state it kills larks and such-like small quarry, hunting well, like the merlin, but it is evil-natured and cowardly.[2] In the *Shamīrānāt* and in *Māzandarān*[3] it nests in the gardens.[4] Nestlings, however, are useless. The female is about the size of a shahin tiercel. It can be trained, but with much trouble. You can, however, train one easily to fly in company with a merlin, and make it kill by means of the merlin's assistance. More than this is not to be expected of it.[5] If, as I say, you get a fine female passage-falcon, call it to the lure and fly it at "trains" and wild quarry, in company with a merlin, but never bother yourself with an eyess.

---

[1] *Layl*, "The Hobby."

[2] A hobby is too cowardly to be caught by a common quail as a bait. I have frequently tried and failed, but on substituting a sparrow have succeeded instantly. Lieut.-Colonel E. Delmé Radcliffe in his pamphlet on Falconry states that the European Hobby is sometimes trained in India and flown at the Hoopoe and the male at the Diongo-Shrike or "King-crow." I have, however, never met with any Panjabi falconer who had heard of one being trained with success.

[3] For *Shamīrānāt*, *vide* note 4, page 40. Mazenderan is a province on the south coast of the Caspian.

[4] In the desert, the *baghs* or "gardens" are the only places where there are tall trees.

[5] The hobby is not trained in the Panjab. In Albion's *Natural History of Birds* (pub. 1738) it is stated that "The Fowlers, to catch these Hawks, take a Lark and having blinded her and fastened Lime-twigs to her Legs, let her fly where they see the Hobby is, which striking at the Lark is entangled with the Lime-twigs."

XII.

HOBBY WITH SEELED EYES

XIII

HOBBY WITH SEELED EYES

CHAPTER XXIV

THE *SANGAK*[1]

THIS "falcon" closely resembles the Indian Sparrow-Hawk,[2] but the young bird is smaller and darker in colouration. Also it has not the dark stripe under the chin.[3] The only difference between the two is that the *Sangak* is black-eyed while the *Pīqū* is yellow-eyed.[4]

In the jungle it preys chiefly on locusts and frogs, but occasionally kills a small wounded or diseased bird. It haunts "gardens," and, like the hobby, nests in trees. However, it is a bird impotent and unvalued, except for its tail, which can be used for "imping"[5] that of a *pīqū*.

The "intermewed" bird and the nestling are identical in plumage, and cannot be distinguished from each other.

CHAPTER XXV

THE KESTRIL[6]

THERE are two species of kestril. One species is yellowish in colouration and is covered with very pretty spots and markings; the other is yellowish but without markings, whilst its claws are small and *white*.

The first species, the "black-clawed" kestril,[7] kills in a wild

---

1 I am unable to identify this hawk.

2 *Pīqū* or *pīghū*, the *shikra* of India.

3 Usually present in the young as well as in the old *shikra*.

4 *Arzaq-chashm*, properly "blue-eyed." Young shikras have sometimes bluish grey eyes,

5 "Imp to" is to repair broken flight- or tail-feathers by sewing in, "grafting," etc.: for methods *vide* Badminton Library.

6 *Dalīja* or *dalīcha*.

7 *Dalīja-yi nākhūn-siyāh*, the ("Black-clawed") Common Kestril: *dalīja-yi nākhūn safīd*, the ("White-clawed") Lesser Kestril. "Although the two species (the Common Kestril and the Lesser Kestril) are so closely allied, there can be no difficulty in discriminating the eggs, and we found that the Arab boys knew the difference between the two species at once, calling one the black-nailed and the other the white-nailed 'bashîk'."—*Rev. H. B. Tristram's Ornithology of Palestine; Ibis*, 1859.

state, sparrows, quails, starlings[1] and such small quarry, but as it is ill-tempered and slow of flight, falconers care little for it. It, however, serves several purposes.

First: In Bushire and the desert tract of *Fārs*[2] it is caught and trained as the Raven is trained by the Arabs.[3] A raven is caught and so trained to "wait" on, that it will circle above the head for half an hour. A fine cord about forty inches long is fastened to its legs having at the end a bunch of feathers the size of a sparrow. Thus prepared it is cast off to "wait on." From a distance it has the appearance of some bird of prey attempting to seize a small bird, and this, arousing jealousy, attracts *bālābāns* and other birds of prey from a distance. Then, on the arrival of, say, a *bālābān* with the other birds, the raven settles, when the fowler lets fly a pigeon in front of the *bālābān*. The latter fancies this is the quarry the raven was chasing.[4] The moment it seizes the pigeon it is snared. *Bālābāns* are also caught with kestrils trained in this manner.[5]

Second: If you want to take passage sakers with an eyess saker (*charkh*), catch one or two kestrils in a *du-gaza* or sparrow-hawk net,[6] "seel" their eyes and fly them as "trains." Next fly your eyess[7] at a wild *bālābān*: it will certainly not fail to take it.[8]

For an eyess saker that is being trained to take eagles and sakers, kestrils and buzzards[9] are necessary "trains."

When giving a buzzard as a "train" the hind claw must be firmly bound back to the shank. Also for the first three or four

---

[1] *Sār*; I believe this is the common starling.

[2] Bushire is nearly the centre of the coast line of the warm desert tract of Fars.

[3] *Vide* Chapter XV.

[4] Wild ravens in India not only chase house-pigeons but will enter a dove-cot and kill them.

[5] For the use of a peregrine as a decoy *vide* Badminton Library volume; page 264.

[6] The best bait for a kestril is a mole-cricket.

[7] Wild peregrines and sakers will occasionally kill and eat kestrils and *shikras*. Trained hawks will also do so. Under a *lagar's* eyrie, in a cliff, I have found the feathers of quite a number of kestrils. Major C. H. Fisher, in his *Reminiscences of a Falconer* (page 59), mentions that he once took a sparrow-hawk with a trained falcon.

[8] Presumably the birds would "crab," and the eyess being tame would not let go on the approach of the falconer. More than once, had I had a butterfly net, I could have placed it over a wild peregrine that was engrossed in a fight on the ground with a trained hawk.

[9] *Sār*, "buzzard."

times meat must be tied to its back before it is shown to and released for the eyess. When the young hawk takes the "train," she should be fed on freshly-killed pigeon or chicken flesh. It is not, however, necessary to tie back the hind claw of a kestril, as it is too weak to inflict an injury.

Third: the tail, especially that of the moulted and mature bird, is excellent for imping the broken tail-feathers of a sparrow-hawk.

LESSER KESTRIL.—As for the "White-clawed [the Lesser] Kestril" the only useful thing about it is its tail, which can be used for "imping." In a wild state it preys on nothing but locusts and lizards.

In the country of Syria, on the way to Constantinople, I have observed this species nesting inside the rooms of houses, in the niches in the walls, and on the ledges[1] in the rooms. No one molests the birds. They fly in flocks[2] like pigeons. Whenever you see kestrils flying in a flock you may feel assured that they are the "white-clawed" species, for the black-clawed species never flies in flocks.

TRAINING GREYHOUND PUP BY MEANS OF THE COMMON KESTRIL.—The Arabs of *'Unayza* and *Shammar*,[3] as I have myself witnessed, rear the nestling of the Common Kestril, and when it is "hard-penned,"[4] lure it with a lump of meat. As soon as it will somewhat come to this lure, they catch an antelope-rat or jerboa-rat, tie a cord to its leg, and fly the kestril at it. They next tie a long cord of ten or twelve ells in length to a rat's leg, and then fly the kestril

---

[1] Of the Eastern Red-Legged Falcon (*Erythropus vespertinus* of Jerdon, and *E. amurensis* of Blanford), Jerdon writes:—"Although the adult male in its mode of colouration resembles the kestrils, especially the lesser kestril, yet the colours of the young bird and female approach more to that of the Hobbies. . . ."

"Fellowes says that it is very common in Asia Minor, building its nests under the roofs and sometimes even in the interior of houses."

Jerdon also says that the claws are "fleshy."

Dresser, in the *Birds of Europe*, writes:—"In many Turkish villages (as, for instance, Turbali) the place swarms with these hawks (F. *Cenchris*: Lesser Kestril). . . . Its eggs are placed without any nest under the eaves on the clay walls of houses and stables. . . ."

[2] In Kerman, Persia, in the beginning of April, 1902, a flock of Lesser Kestrils roosted for some days in the trees in the Consulate garden.

[3] Two hostile tribes that live in the Syrian desert. They are noted for their breed of horses.

[4] "Hard-penned," *i.e.*, hard-feathered.

at it from a distance. After that they break one leg of a jerboa, and let it go in front of a two months' old greyhound pup, and then cast off the kestril at it. The rat is taken after a few stoops. Next a jerboa is loosed in front of two greyhound pups three or four months old.[1] The pups start in pursuit, and the kestril is then cast off. At one time the pups make a dash, at another the kestril makes a stoop, till at last the rat is taken.

After killing a few rats with broken legs, a sound rat is released, a fine stick, four fingers' breadth in length, having previously been passed cross-ways through the ears. This stick hinders the rat from taking refuge in a hole, for of course two-months-old pups cannot, unaided, overtake and kill a kangaroo-rat in the open country. Well, the rat is let go, and the kestril and the pups give chase. It is exactly like hawking gazelle with a *charkh*. After about thirty or forty stoops and dashes, the rat is taken.

The whole object of this play is to teach the pups, while growing up, to recognize the *charkh*;[2] so that should a hawk be flown at a herd of even a thousand gazelle, the hounds will chase none but the one at which the hawk is stooping. In puppyhood the hound has learnt that without the assistance of the kestril it cannot overtake an antelope-rat, and hence it has learnt to watch the hawk; and gradually it becomes so knowing, that instead of at once starting in pursuit of the gazelle-herd when it is slipped, it will fix its gaze skywards, and wait on the movements of the *charkh*.

---

[1] " . . . When the pups [greyhound] are three or four months old, their education commences. The boys drive out of their holes the jerboa or the rat called " boualal " and set the pups at them. The latter by degrees get excited, dash after them at full speed, bark furiously at their holes, and only give up the pursuit to begin another. At the age of five or six months they are assigned a prey more difficult to catch—the hare. . . ."—*The Horses of the Sahara and the Manners of the Desert*, by E. Daumas. "McMaster says of its agility [the Indian Jerboa-rat or Kangaroo-rat—Gerbillus indicus]: 'I have seen them when released from a trap baffle and elude dogs in the most extraordinary manner by wonderful jumps made over the backs, and apparently into the very teeth of their pursuers'."—*Mammalia of India*; Sterndale.

[2] *Charkh-shinās*, adj.

CHAPTER XXVI

THE SHRIKE

AMONGST the "black-eyed" birds of prey must be classed a small sparrow-like bird, grey and black in colouring. In the Kurdish language it is called *bāzūrī*, and in Persian *ālā güzkina.*[1] In size it is somewhat larger than a sparrow: the wings are dark: the eyes have a dark line of antimony:[2] the claws and beak are black, sharp, and powerful. When trained, it kills with ease sparrows and the small *tisks*[3] found in the wheat and barley, in Spring. It also comes well to the lure from a distance.

There are two species. One grey and black with the antimony line under the eyes, and one yellowish. The former is decidedly the better.[4]

---

[1] This is Turkish, not Persian. Persian Turks call the shrike *ālā güzina* also. In Shaw's Turki Vocabulary (Appendix by Scully), *Lanius Homeyeri*, the Grey Shrike, is said to be called *ālā ghurālāi*, and *Lanius arenarius*, the Desert Shrike, *boz ghurālāi.* The word *ālā* in Turki means "variegated" or "spotted." In *Lahore to Yarkand* (page 182) the Brown Shrike, *Lanius Cristatus*, is said to be called *urulia* in Turki.

[2] *Surma kashīda;* antimony is applied by means of a needle to an Eastern's eye, underneath the lashes of the under lids, and to the outer corners of the eyes.

[3] *Tisk* may be the Short-toed or Social Lark. In Shiraz, however, *tisk* is the name of a warbler like a white-throat, called in Kerman *turnusk*, and also *barādar-i bulbul*, "the nightingale's brother." *Sisk* and *tirnisk* are names that are probably both applied to the same warbler.

[4] The Indian Grey Shrike (Lanius lahtora), called in the Derajat *laṭorā* and *mamālā*, used to be trained in Dera Ismail Khan to catch small birds. A smaller species called *mamālī*—probably the Rufous-backed Shrike, the *harwājī* of Kashmir (Lanius erythronotus)—does not appear to have been trained. Of the former Jerdon writes:—"Mr. Philipps states that he has seen it capture small birds; and that in the North-West, it is occasionally trained to do so. He also relates that it is sometimes picketed to the ground, closely attached to a starling, the neighbouring bushes, twigs, etc., being well smeared with bird-lime. All sorts of birds come to witness the supposed fight and to separate the combatants, and many are captured by the limed branches."

CHAPTER XXVII

MISCELLANEOUS NOTES

I have described to you the chief peculiarities of the "Yellow-Eyed" and the "Black-Eyed" birds of prey. I will now teach you a few matters that will make the masters of the Art of Falconry approve of this poor slave of the Shah—May our souls be his sacrifice!

Term of Natural Life.—Know that the term of natural life of the birds of prey is considerable. In captivity they attain to twenty-five or thirty years at least—provided they remain in the possession of one man, a skilful falconer, and are not constantly changing hands. I myself kept a passage saker for twenty moults, and although it was not as good as it had been, still it continued to take quarry.

To distinguish the Age of a Hawk.—After a hawk has passed its fourth or fifth year, none can tell its age—except God and its owner. However, there are certain signs that mark a hawk of ten or fifteen years. First; it is short-winded.[1] Second; its feet and soles become full of wrinkles. Third; the two outside feathers of the tail, one on each side, called by the Arabs *rudāfa*,[2] are shorter than the remainder, and the older the hawk the shorter these *rudāfa*.[2]

Impossibility of Snaring Long-winged Hawks by Aid of a Lamp.—Never try to snare "black-eyed" hawks by aid of a lamp, for as soon as they see the light they will fly off. The "yellow-eyed," however, with the exception of owls and birds that hunt by night, can be snared by means of a lamp, as will be described later.

Qualifications of a Falconer.—The first requisite in a falconer is patience. The second; that he be a sportsman and have a genuine love for his hawks, and fly them himself. Let him not

---

1 These remarks are presumably meant to apply only to hawks in captivity.

2 *Rudāfa* is the plural of *radīf*. In the text, here and elsewhere, the word is given as *radāni*, but as this is no correct Arabic "form," it is probably a copyist's error for *rudāfa*. *Vide* also note 2, page 52.

say :—"I will take a lot of *chukor*; my master will reward me;" or, "Such and such quarry is unlawful for food (*harām*); I won't fly at it. What is the use of taking ravens and eagles? I'll hawk *chukor* and *seesee*, and take them to my master; he'll have them roasted, and will eat them in front of the fire and will reward me." This ass is an ignoramus, and cares naught for hawks. Does he not know that if a short-winged hawk is flown on level ground, and wedded to large quarry such as ravens and duck and ruddy shieldrake and such like, that it will in the hills with the advantage of gravity fly at the poor *chukor* all the better?[1] His object should not be money and rewards. He must be fond of hawks and hawking; he must know his business; he must be at heart a sportsman. The third; that he be good-tempered, pleasant-spoken, and of a cheerful and cheery countenance, so that the Good God may grant him his daily bread in abundance, and the quarry may come to him of its own accord. Let him be clean of hand, clean in person, and observant of the ordained prayers, so that God, who knows all, may not send him and his hawk home in the evening empty-handed. When mounting, the falconer should repeat the "Four *Qul*" and the "Holy Verse," which is the "Verse of the Throne,"[2] and then exhale the breath on the person, so that the Munificent God may shelter from evil, him and his companions, guard his hawk from the persecutions of eagles, and send him home at night with a full bag and a happy heart. These are the requisites for a sportsman.

If he who made the game be not forgot,
The best of sport will ever be thy lot;
How can He be, in granting sport, unkind
If thou hold fast this fact within thy mind?

Fourth; if you lose your hawk and despair of its recovery, then

[1] The author frequently uses the phrase *māya dāshtan* to indicate the advantage a hawk has when flying downwards from a height, as from the fist of a mounted man, etc. *Chukor* in the hills, and, I think, pheasants too, go down hill when a hawk is after them. At any rate they are beaten for and flown at down-hill, the falconer taking his stand up-hill.

[2] For these four chapters and the "Verse of the Throne," *vide* page 108, note 2. The texts are first repeated and the breath is then exhaled on the breast, shoulders, and hands.

with earnest sincerity repeat three times the *Nād-i 'Alī*,[1] each time exhaling the breath towards the direction you imagine the hawk to be, and saying, "O God! by virtue of these words I adjure Thee to restore to me my lost hawk." There is no doubt but that you will recover her instantly. This is my belief and my practice, and I have now in my possession two or three passage sakers seventeen or eighteen years of age. My son, these are my counsels: give ear to them, and bear them in your mind, and you will experience no ill.

CHAPTER XXVIII

METHOD OF SNARING A WILD GOSHAWK WITH THE AID OF A LAMP

METHOD OF SNARING A GOSHAWK WITH THE AID OF A LAMP.—Should you happen to see a goshawk (*ṭarlān*) settle on a tree towards sunset, keep a careful watch on it from a distance till three or four hours after dusk, and see that it is not disturbed. Then take a long light pole of sufficient length to reach the hawk, and firmly bind to one end a horse-hair noose; a span's distance below the

[1] *Nād-i'Alī* (for the Arabic *Nādi 'Alīyan* ("call on '*Alī*"), a prayer to '*Alī* much used by Shiahs: an amulet on which the following prayer is inscribed, is also so-called:—

"Cry aloud to 'Ali the possessor of wonders!
From him thou wilt find help from trouble!
He quickly removes all grief and anxiety!
By the Mission of Muhammad and his own sanctity!"

Colonel J. P. Hamilton, in his *Reminiscences of an Old Sportsman*, writes: "The following superstitious ceremonies are mentioned in a book on falconry, supposed to be in the time of Edward the Confessor:—After a hawk has been ill and is sufficiently recovered to pursue the game, the owner has this admonition given to him: On the morrow tyde when thou goest out hawking, say, 'In the name of the Lord, the birds of heaven shall be beneath thy feet.' Also if he be hurt by the heron, say, 'The lion of the tribe of Judah, the root of David, has conquered. Hallelujah.' And if he be bitte of any man, say, 'He that the wicked man doth bind, the Lord at his coming shall set free'."

In the middle ages, at the festival of St. Hubert, "dogs and falcons were brought into the church to receive the priest's benediction, to the sound of horn and trumpet: . . . .": *vide Science and Literature in the Middle Ages*, by Paul Lacroix.

noose fasten a lighted wax-candle. Take this pole and proceed alone towards the tree on which the goshawk is sleeping, till within thirty yards of it. Now, with noiseless steps, advance very slowly for ten yards; and then halt for seven or eight minutes: next extinguish the candle and remain in the dark for two or three minutes. Re-light the candle and advance ten yards more, very very slowly; and then halt for some minutes: then extinguish the candle and wait another two or three minutes in the dark. Re-light the candle, and, holding it aloft, advance stealthily to the foot of the tree.

Keep the lighted candle in front of the goshawk's face. Now, my son, pull yourself together and keep your eyes open; let hand and foot be steady; don't get flurried: think not you are after a goshawk. Say to yourself: "It is a leaf of a tree, or a barn-door fowl." Don't let your hand shake. This is the advice I give you: I cannot myself act up to it, nor do I believe that any falconer can. Well, hold the light[1] close to the goshawk's breast. If she is asleep, head under wing, gently, ever so gently, stroke her breast with the horse-hair noose to awaken her, but have a care your nervous hand does not tremble but keeps the pole well away from her breast, or else she is off. Stroke her breast with the noose, ever so gently, till she withdraws her head from under her wing. Then pass the noose on to her neck, and pull her down to you.[2] On the spot, "seel" her eyes with blue[3] thread, using a fine needle,[4] and "mail"[5] her tightly.

---

[1] *Chirāgh* in m.c. is often incorrectly used in the sense of 'light' instead of 'lamp.'

[2] "A praty craft to take an hawke that is brokyn owt of mew. and all maner of fowlys that ſyt in trees if a man wyll.

"Looke Where an hawke perchith for all nyght: in any maner place. and ſofte and layſerly clymbe to her With a ſconce or a lanterne that hath bot oon light. in yowre hande and let the light be towarde the hawke ſo that ſhe ſe not yowr face and ye may take hir by the leggys or oder Wiſe as ye lyſt. and in lyke Wiſe all other maner fowle."—*Boke of St. Albans.*

[3] That is with thread dyed with indigo: indigo is good for wounds.

[4] Hawk-catchers are careless about the manner they "seel" a hawk's eyes: they generally use a coarse, large, needle and not infrequently a thorn.

[5] *Qapāncha kardan*, "To mail" a hawk: *vide* page 59, note 5.

XIV

PERSIAN FALCONER WITH INTERMEWED GOSHAWK (FROM A PHOTOGRAPH BY A PERSIAN).

CHAPTER XXIX

TRAINING THE *ṬARLĀN* OR PASSAGE GOSHAWK

After treating the hawk as described at the end of the last chapter, keep her "mailed"[1] for an hour or two, and furnish her with jesses, leash, and halsband.[2] After two hours or so "un-mail" her, and carry her on the fist for about an hour, gently stroking her breast and wings the while. Then place her on her perch to rest.

Next morning at daybreak take her on the fist, and, as gently as possible stroking her breast and back,[3] carry her till four or five hours after sunrise. Use any device or trick you can to get her to feed; scratch her feet between the digits to induce her to eat. If she will eat, give her a small quantity of meat; but if she won't, let her remain hungry till the afternoon[4] and then try again: if then she will eat, well and good; give her a full meal that she may remember it, and learn to look to you for food. If she won't eat, on no account force meat down her throat, or this will become a habit with her. Again in the evening take her on the fist, her eyes being still seeled, and carry her for five or six hours,[5] stroking her and scratching her feet to induce her to eat. If still she won't eat, it is of no consequence: set her down to rest for the night.

The next morning try her again in the same way: she will probably feed. However, some goshawks will sulk for three days, refusing all food. Don't be alarmed if your hawk does so, for it is of no consequence;[6] she will eat on the fourth day.

A soon as she has learnt to eat freely with seeled eyes, whether on your fist or off it, slightly unseel them, *i.e.*, loosen the seeling

---

[1] *Qapāncha kardan*, "to mail" a hawk: *vide* page 59, note 5.

[2] *Pācha-band*, "jesses." In the Derajat, Panjab, the term is restricted to cotton or silk jesses, fitted with "varvels" (rings); *vide* page 18, note 3. *Shikār-band* "leash;" but in the Derajat the thin leather thong that attaches the swivel to the jesses is so called: *vide* page 18, note 3. For "halsband" *vide* page 3, note 2.

[3] Much stroking on the back is to be avoided, as it removes the oil that makes the back feathers impervious to rain.

[4] *'Asr*, that is two and a half hours before sunset; the time midway between noon and sunset.

[5] In countries under Muslim rule the watch is set daily at sunset, which is 12 o'clock.

[6] If a newly caught goshawk tear off bits of meat and cast them aside, she should be tried with a small bird *with the feathers on.*

XV

INTERMEWED GOSHAWK ON EASTERN PADDED PERCH (FROM A PERSIAN PAINTING)

thread so that she may see a little out of the tops of her eyes,[1] and feed her well, so. The next evening open her eyes a little more. The third evening unseel her eyes completely, and sit near a lamp with your back to the wall that none may pass too and fro behind you. This evening she must be on your fist for four or five hours. After that, carry her into a dark spot and place her on her perch to rest.

Early next morning take her up, and sit, back to the wall, in some quiet spot, where people can be seen at a distance. Near noon, feed her up for the day, and then set her on a perch in a place where people cannot pass to and fro, except at a distance. Two or three hours before sunset, take her on the fist again and carry her till two hours after nightfall, *i.e.*, much less than on the previous night.

In the morning take her up as before. To-day you must feed her twice, giving her less in the morning and more in the evening.

During these few days you must on no account give her feathers or casting, for she will, from fear, retain them in her stomach, and her temperament will be upset.

On the sixth night you must carry her till midnight, stroking her at frequent intervals. By this time she will have become perfectly quiet. Then carry her to her perch, and set her down to rest.

Early next morning take her on the fist, and carry her in a place where no one can pass behind you. Then take her to some quiet, private spot, and place a live chicken or pigeon in her feet, and get her to seize it. Then cut the chicken's throat and give her a little to eat. Try and induce her to step on to your fist, either from the ground or from her perch.

During these few days that you are giving her live birds, feed her while close to a hound,[2] so that she may get accustomed to the presence of such dogs. Tie a long cord to the leash, and placing her on an assistant's fist induce her to fly a few paces to your fist. Do not give her live pigeons and chickens every day or she will learn to come to your fist only for the "pelt,"[3] and that is an error.

---

[1] *Bāla-bīn*, adj.

[2] *Ṭūla, vide* p. 89, note 3.

[3] *Ṭu'ma-yi zinda hama rūz bi-dast-ash na-dihī tā pay-i kushta bi-dast-i tu bi-yāyad:* I think the meaning of the author has been rendered. *Kushta*, the "pelt" or the dead quarry, especially when used as a lure.

Call her rather to plain meat so that, should you in the field not happen to have a live bird about you, she will, the moment you raise your fist, come readily to a meat-lure. There is no harm if you kill in her feet a live bird, say every eight or ten days.

When she is thoroughly trained to the lure, *i.e.*, when she will without a "creance"[1] come with eagerness to your fist, starting without hesitation from any spot where you may place her, cast her on the ground and play with her so as to teach her to run round and round you, so that when, in the field, she puts a quarry into a bush[2] she may run round the bush just as you have taught her to run round you, so that by this means the chukor she has "put in" may not trick her by making off from the far edge of the bush. The object of this instruction on the ground is to teach her to run round the bush and block the quarry after she has "put it in," and then to rise and take up a commanding position on a tree[3] to watch the bush from thence, so that the partridge escape her not.

The more familiar you make your hawk, and the keener you make her on the lure,[4] the better. Now, if you have trained[5] your hawk in less than forty days, you have hurried her training, and "Hurry is of the Devil, but Deliberation is from God."[6] Be not overhasty or you will spoil her. Such and such a falconer is sure to vaunt his skill, boasting that he has trained and flown his hawk in fifteen days. He has erred and blundered: he is not a lover of a hawk but a lover of the pot;[7] he is one who would not sacrifice one

---

1 "Creance," *vide* p. 38, note 8.

2 *Buna*, "bush," is used by the author for the quarry put into the bush. In Urdu *Bāz ne buna kiyā* = "the goshawk has put in the quarry," and *Buna uṭhā,o* = "beat out the quarry that has been put in." A bird has "put in" when it is forced to take refuge in a bush, covert, etc., etc.

3 "Note, uſe to call her from the grounde furst, and that will make her fall at marke in the plaine felde otherwyſe she will to a tree."—*A Perfect Booke for Kepinge of Sparhawkes*: Edited by *Harting*. For "Fall at marke," *vide* p. 92, note 4. For remarks on "taking stand," *vide* "Notes on the Falconidæ used in India in Falconry," by Lieut.-Colonel E. Delmé Radcliffe (pp. 20-1). Natives of the Panjab do not consider "taking stand" a vice.

4 *Garm-i ṭalab.*

5 *Rasānīdan*, Tr.

6 A tradition of the Prophet.

7 *Bāz-dūst nīst; kabk-khwur ast.*

partridge for a hundred goshawks. As for you, your hawk must not be trained[1] in less than forty days.[2]

When your hawk is trained, that is when she is perfect at the lure and accustomed to hounds, horses, and mounted men, go, the day before you intend flying her at wild quarry, into the open country and lure her from a distance with a chicken two or three months old. As soon as she comes, let her take it, and feed her up on it for the day, giving her feathers and bones, that she may throw up her casting[3] early the following morning.

Although it is the custom of many Ostringers[4] to give to a goshawk, the day before she is to be flown, *washed meat*—that is meat cut small, cast into luke-warm water and given with a lot of water—still in my opinion the practice is wrong; for if a hawk be alternately given washed meat one day and flown the next, and habituated to this custom, the custom becomes second nature to her. Now suppose your friends and acquaintances, together with their falconers, some fifty persons in all, have settled to go for a ten days' hawking trip to a certain spot where there is an abundance of *chukor* and other quarry, and have invited you to join them, you ought, during these short ten days, to hawk every day. However, your hawk will only give you five days' sport, for you have habituated her to fly on alternate days, after she has been "set;"[5] she certainly will not now fly every day. Do not therefore teach her this custom. Give her the day before you go hawking, not washed meat but a chicken as I have said, for a chicken's flesh has little nourishment and will "set" her as though she had been given washed meat. By giving her a chicken you will not accustom her to washed meat; and when on that ten days' outing you will not

---

[1] *Rasīdan*, Intr.

[2] Forty days: this is an axiom amongst Indian falconers also, who usually try and make out that the "watching" occupies forty days, and that they must therefore have extra assistants, blankets, oil, etc., etc.

[3] *Ṭu'mah*, Ar. "meat, meal, food, etc.;" this word is frequently used by the author for "casting," *ṭu'ma andākhtan*, P. "to cast." A "casting" is fur, feathers, etc., given to the hawk with its food.

[4] *Shikār-chī-yi zard-chashm*, "Ostringer." "An ostringer or austringer, etc., one who keeps short-winged hawks, especially the Goshawk."—*Harting*. In the *Boke of St. Albans* the term is confined to those that keep "Goſhawkys or Tercellis," while "Those that kepe Sperhawkys and musketys ben called Speruiteris."

[5] *Ishtihā dādan*, "to give an appetite" is by the author always used for giving washed, or rather wetted, meat.

have to stay at home and twiddle your thumbs.[1] Another objection to washed meat is that your hawk gradually loses condition.

To resume. After luring your hawk from a distance and killing the chicken under her and feeding her upon it, set her on the edge of some water: she will perhaps drink and bathe,[2] and oil,[2] and preen her feathers, and so be in fettle for to-morrow's flight. One hour before sunset take her on the fist.

(My son, never, never, go up to a new hawk without meat in your hand.[3] Always approach a new, sitting hawk very, very slowly, and sit down to one side of her. Do not look at the hawk's eyes, for a man's eyes and face have a terrifying effect on hawks, especially when the gazer's head is crowned with a Turcoman cap. Take meat in your hand and get her to jump from the perch to your fist, and let her eat one or two beakfuls: then carry her away. Falconer, listen: should you ever require to go to your hawk in the dark to take her on the fist, having no light with you, talk to yourself in a low tone the while; for she will recognize your voice and not be scared).

In short take her on your fist an hour before sunset, and carry her till an hour after dark. If you ride about with her on a quiet horse, so much the better. After that set her down to rest for the night.

(There should be a light in your hawk's room all night that she may feel secure. It is a mistake to keep a goshawk in the dark, for goshawks are ever fearful.)

Very early next morning take up your own hawk, and be afield before the eagles have begun their daily questing.[4] You must not have with you more than one dog, well-mannered and well-trained. Let your hawk have a beakful or two[5] of meat to whet her appetite

---

1 *Ṣalavāt firistādan*, *i.e.*, pass the time telling the beads while saying "Oh God, bless Muhammad and the family of Muhammad."

2 *Āb-bāzī kardan*, "to bathe." *Rug̲h̲an-kashī kardan*, "to oil the feathers."

3 This was the practice of a certain Panjab falconer who had a great reputation for training goshawks. He never went empty-handed to a goshawk to take her on the fist, even after she was trained: he *always* took with him a bit of meat, about the size of a pea, concealed in his palm.

4 Eagles are late risers and do not leave their roosting places till the sun has warmed the air, that is in the winter not till after eight o'clock. Peregrines leave their roosts while it is still dark.

5 *Ching*, "beak," but *chang*, "claw, talons, fingers, etc.": *ching zadan*, "to strike with the beak, peck, etc."

and make her keen. Now go into a good spot, mark down a *chukor* that will give a fairly easy flight,[1] and, saying "Oh God! my hope is in Thee," cast off your hawk. My son, though falconers and sportsmen do not approve of this, yet I approve it: act as I instruct thee and thou wilt experience no ill.

Give ear to my teaching; my precepts obey:
In the training of hawks I have spent all my day.
A truly-trained bird can see from afar,
And choose for its quarry "Aquilla" the star.
If your hawk to fly rightly you wish and desire,
To God say a prayer, for He is thy Sire.
When the Portal of Hope is open to all[2]
Before God, on thy knees, with reverence fall.
Take care of thy bird, for God made it too,
The earth and the sea, the Heavens and you.

At any rate this hawk of yours has been perfected in every part of her training. Perhaps, too, she is fast. If, as she leaves your fist, she at once take the "chukor" in the air, on no account feed her up: give her only the brain. When by this act of hers you have discovered that she is fast, go and put up another "chukor." If it rise close to you, let it get away a little distance before you cast off your hawk so that the partridge may not be taken, but be "put into" a bush. Now go with a very little meat in your hand, and dismount near the bush. Go very gently and take your hawk on your fist. Set on your dog[3] and make it put up the partridge out of the bush. As soon as the partridge rises, cast off your hawk. However she take it, whether at once in the air, or at a distance before it can "put in," go slowly up to her and cut the "chukor's" throat. If you want to fly your hawk again next day, give her one thigh, the heart, and the liver together with feathers as "casting." If you don't intend to fly her next day, give her in addition one side of the breast.[4] While feeding her, call the dog to your side that she may become accustomed to it.

---

[1] *Kabk-i munāsib-ī;* this is I presume the author's meaning. *Munāsib,* "fitting, suitable," often has the meaning, both in India and in Persia, of "medium-sized, of average size."

[2] At dawn the doors of Heaven are open and the Angels descend to fix each man's daily portion. Morning prayers are accepted by God.

[3] *Ṭūla rā hay zadan.*

[4] *Yak sīna* = the *baghal* of Panjab falconers.

If your hawk be a tiercel,[1] one thigh of the "chukor" with the head and neck and their bones will be a sufficient feed.

Now let us suppose that you are out with your friends on that ten days' hawking expedition and that your hawk has daily killed five or six partridges without misbehaving herself, and that you have duly fed her up after the last flight, at the place she put in; do not suppose that now, after she is thoroughly entered to quarry,[2] you must necessarily during these ten days act so every day. Should you, for instance, now prefer to stay at home one day, lure her from a distance; but should you take the field, then at the last flight, when she has taken her partridge, give her the head and brain to eat. On the spot where she has killed or "put in," place her on a stone and go yourself a long way off, and then lure her to you and feed her up. She has learnt how to kill partridges, and your present action is to prevent her forgetting the lure.

Let us suppose that the first day your new goshawk takes the partridge in the air you feed her up on it. Well, the next time you go out hawking, she will, on the partridge rising, try her best;[3] if she take it in the air, well and good, but if not, she will either return to you or give up; she will not continue to chase the partridge till she puts it in.[4] Many a good hawk have I seen spoilt like this through the gross ignorance of the falconer. A hawk cannot always take a partridge in the air: it should therefore learn to follow and "put in."[4]

Though I have warned you once, I warn you again; do not go hawking chickens and house-pigeons,[5] for this a mistake.

The goshawk falcon[6] is in every respect better than the tiercel. I have proved this by experience. Many falconers say that the tiercel is faster and more adroit, but these do not know that a hundred tiercels cannot do what one "falcon"[6] does. It appears to them that the tiercel is faster, because he is smaller and moves his wings with greater rapidity. But the falcon is larger and longer, and can, from the summits of high hills make a partridge

---

[1] *Jurra qūsh; vide* page 25, note 3.

[2] *Garm shudan.*

[3] *Yak zūr bi-parīdan mi-āvarad.*

[4] *Bi-buna burdan* or—*rasānīdan*

[5] *Vide* note 3, page 80.

[6] *Qūsh-i tavār.* The female of the goshawk used to be dignified by the title "falcon": *vide* also page 25, note 3.

"put in." The tiercel cannot do this; it gives up half way. There is no question but that the falcon is a hundred degrees better than the tiercel,[1] either for quarry as small as the Quail, or for quarry as large as the Common Crane and the Great Bustard.[2]

My son, if you want to be counted by keepers of short-winged hawks a past master in the art, and to reap a full enjoyment from the sport, then train your goshawks,[3] sparrow-hawks, and shikras, etc., as I have described.

You should try to finish your day's hawking before noon, so that you, your horse, your hawk, and your hound, may all rest till the next day. Hawking prolonged into the afternoon[4] is bad, because eagles and other birds of prey are then in search of their evening meal, and they will come down on you even from afar off. Should you lose your hawk in the afternoon, you have little time to search for her and also reach your house before nightfall. Should you not lose her, but manage to add a few more partridges to your bag, it is difficult to know the proper amount of food to give: the Winter nights are long and cold, and if you give her but a small feed she will lose condition;[5] if through fear of the cold you give a full feed, she, tired though she be, will not sleep; or if she sleep, she will not "put over"[6] nor

---

[1] The females of all species of hawks and falcons are, I think, faster and better-winded than the males, though the latter are probably more adroit.

[2] *Tūiṭughlī* T. is explained by the author in more than one marginal note as being the *mīsh-murgh* or "sheep-bird:" *tuiṭuglī, ta,iṭuglī, dūī-dāgh* and *ṭūī* are other forms of the word. (Persians that are not sportsmen often call the Egyptian or White Scavenger Vulture *mīsh-murgh*.)

[3] *Ṭarlān u qizil.*

[4] *'Asr*, the time between noon and sunset.

[5] A hawk in just proper condition, if underfed, will, if the night be very cold, become thin in one night. In the Indian Spring, when the nights are temperate, I have known a saker falcon go up two ounces in weight in *one night*, from a slight overfeed of hubara flesh.

[6] A good Indian falconer would carry his hawk after dark till she had "put over" completely, first allowing her an hour's rest or more. "Carrying," with its constant shifting of position, not only causes a hawk to "put over" quicker, but induces it to digest and empty the bowel: on the fist she will "mute" thrice for every twice on the perch. After a hard day's work, water should be offered her at night, especially if she has been fed on the rich flesh of the hubara: after a feed on hubara flesh, I have known some sakers drink two or three times

digest[1] properly, and next day your friends will start off hawking before your hawk has cast[2] or got her appetite. These are the reasons I do not approve of hawking in the afternoon. If your friends force you to go out hawking with them in the afternoon, feed up your hawk after her first flight.

Do not overfly your hawk. She should fly no more than she can fly with delight to herself. Two or three flights are sufficient, and I consider it unlawful (*ḥarām*) to give her more than five flights.[3] If she be flown only two or three times, she will remain keen on her quarry.[4] This is the way to treat all goshawks and sparrow-hawks. Know that all these sporting-birds are naturally good, and the Wise God has created them all for the pleasure and delight of man; but it rests with the falconer to make or mar them. Except in two particulars, their good or bad points are the result of training. First, the falconer, however good, cannot make slow hawks fast, nor *vice versâ*. Second, he cannot increase the courage of his hawk. Now, although I have seen it stated in works on falconry[5] that to increase a hawk's courage you should feed her for three days

---

between nightfall and midnight. If a hawk has been fed late and is to be flown early next day, it should be taken on the fist before sunrise (a lamp being lit in the room) and "carried," the hawk being made to change its position frequently: this induces it to "cast" earlier than it would otherwise do. When hubara-hawking *all day long* in the desert for ten or fifteen days at a stretch, my falconers would carry the hawks from 3 or 4 a.m. till daybreak, and the hawks (peregrines or sakers) would be ready to fly by 8 a.m. (A hawk "puts over" when it takes down any portion of the meat from its crop into its stomach). "Putting over" quickly is the sign of a good digestion.

[1] *Ṣarf kardan* is properly "to eat," but by it the author evidently means either to "put over," or "to digest," I do not know which. *Qūsh gūsht-ash mī-shikanad* P. and *'aṭīn āpārir* T. are the ordinary expressions for "the hawk is 'putting over'."

[2] *Ṭu'ma andākhtan*, "to cast," *i.e.*, to throw up the casting in the morning. *Vide* page 82, note 3.

[3] It must be recollected that the quarry is the *chukor* partridge which is usually found in the hills, and five flights might represent a lot of work. With the grey partridge of India five flights would be nothing for a good goshawk.

[4] For Falcons—peregrines or sakers—five flights at hubara are sufficient, two in the morning and three in the afternoon: at heron or kite one flight.

[5] *Bāz-Nāma:* many of these Persian MSS. exist both in Persia and India.

on pigeon's flesh steeped in wine,[1] when if she have previously taken only partridges she will now take even cranes, yet this is not the case; the statement is falsehood, pure and unalloyed, for I have tested it: my hawk took no cranes—that was of minor importance—but what she did do was to fall sick. It is God, not the falconer, that bestows swiftness and courage. In these two matters the falconer is powerless.

> God gave the hawk her courage and her speed,
> Can'st thou thyself increase what He Himself decreed?

For instance, if ten horses be trained for a race,[2] one will win, and whenever you race them the same one will win—unless, of course, some accident happen, or the horse is out of sorts. So, too, with greyhounds and other animals. In short, courage and powers of flight have nothing whatever to do with the falconer: for these the Grace of God is necessary.

Now, first you must train your hawk to come eagerly to the fist from any spot where your voice reaches her. Further, you must not encourage her to become so bold and familiar with dogs that she lay hands on them;[3] for it may happen that one day when you have cast her at a partridge, a fox or a jackal crosses her path: if she has acquired a habit of binding to dogs she will fasten on to the fox or jackal, and so suffer instant destruction.

---

1 The *Boke of St. Albans* gives the following "Medecyne for an hawke that has lost here corage":—"Take Oyle of ſpayne and tempere it With clere Wine. and With the yolke of an egge and put therein befe. and thereof geue to youre hawke. v. morcellis. and then ſet hir in the ſonne. and at euen fede hir With an old hote coluer. and if ye fede hir th9 iii tymys that hawke Was neuer ſo luſty nor ſo Joly before. as ſhe Will be after and come to hir owne corege" (page 26). In Bert's *Treatise of Hawks and Hawking*, 1619 (page 101 of Harting's Edition; reprinted by Quaritch) there is a somewhat similar receipt for a "Hawke that hath loſt her courage and ioyeth not, or is lowe in fleſh." For "turning tayle" and "to bring stomake," *A Perfect Booke for Kepinge of Sparhawkes or Goshawkes* (written about 1575 and first printed from the original MS. by J. E. Harting in 1886), says, "ſtepe her meate in claret wyne and the yoke of an egg and nyp it drye and ſo give it, and it will bring her ſtomake."

2 *Sawghān kardan*, "to train for a race."

3 "I haue knowne ſome of them likewiſe that would ſooner catche a dogge in the field then a Partridge, and although ſhe had flown a Partridge very well to marke, and ſat well, yet ſo ſoone as a dog had but come in to the retroue, ſhe would have had him by the face."—*Bert*, Chap. V.

Neither must you allow her to be too bold with small children, lest one day, while you are absent, your small boy come to her on her perch and she seize him, and none be there to hear his cries, and so he be blinded or killed. Both these accidents have happened frequently, *i.e.*, a goshawk has killed a child, and a jackal a goshawk. This evil habit seldom exists in passage hawks,[1] *qizil*, or *ṭarlān*; it is generally the eyess *qizil*[2] that acts like this, and hence falconers are not very fond of the eyess.[2] In short, your hawk should stand somewhat in fear of all dogs except your own hound; it is better for her to remain in fear of strange hounds that might injure her, and of the dogs of the wandering tribes.[3]

Secondly, your hawk should make the partridge "put in" (or take it just as it is going to "put in"),[4] and then after circling round the covert two or three times take stand on the top of the covert till you arrive, when she should leave her perch and come to your fist. She should not fly off and leave the place where the partridge "put in," else by the time you have followed her and recovered her, the partridge will have escaped.

Such is hawking with short-winged hawks in hilly country, that is, hawking "chukor" and "seesee"[5]. As for hawking in flat country, a goshawk will there take duck, geese, common cranes,[6] great bustards, ravens, hubara, stone plovers,[7] saker falcons,[8] and

---

[1] The translator's experience is that passage goshawks are particularly afraid of small children. Indian falconers account for this by saying that the hawk mistakes children for its jungle-enemies the monkeys.

[2] *Qizil-i āshiyānī*, "eyess goshawk:" *qizil* is the local race that breeds in Persia.

[3] *Ṭūla* is a hound, or any sporting dog except a *tāzī* or greyhound: *sag* (gen. term), any ordinary pariah or other breed of dog: *sag-i īlātī*, "a dog of the breed kept by wandering tribes;" it is large and fierce. *Ṭūla* also means "a pup."

[4] The author probably means that the hawk should chase till the partridge puts in; that if she is fast and taught to take quarry quickly in the air, she will acquire the habit of only doing so, and will consequently give up whenever she sees that the quarry is fast enough to take her to a distance.

[5] *Kabk u tīhū.*

[6] In India geese and common cranes are, by means of a stalking bullock, sometimes stalked while feeding, and thus taken by a goshawk.

[7] *Chā<u>kh</u>rūq*, "stone-plover."

[8] *Bālābān*, "passage saker."

even imperial sand-grouse,[1] quail,[2] pin-tailed sand-grouse,[1] and ruddy shieldrakes.[2] All this quarry—(pheasants[3] and black partridges[4] are excepted)—she can take at the first or second dash[5] only, otherwise she will fail in doing so.

If you come across any of this quarry in open country and desire to fly at it, then, if your hawk, by crouching and resting its breast on your hand and becoming rigid,[6] shows that she has a natural inclination for it,[7] be sure you take notice of the direction of the wind. With your hawk's breast towards the wind,[8] gallop your horse towards the quarry. The horse must indeed move, but you must so hold and keep your fist that your hawk does not open her wings; for she must, while the quarry has still a foot on the ground, quit your fist like a bullet; she will then take the quarry in the air before it has got away ten yards. On no account cast your hawk off with her back to the wind, for this is dangerous. First, by casting her off back to the wind, her loins will be strained; and leaving your fist uncollectedly, she will fail to reach the quarry, and your falconer friends will jeer at you and at your action. Should you even manage to cast her off so close that it is as though you are giving the quarry into her hand, she and the quarry, when she "binds"[9] to it, will fall to the ground (*i.e.*, if the wind be at all strong), and the quarry will, breaking away from her, not again be overtaken. Should your hawk even bind so

---

[1] *Vide* page 12, note 2.

[2] *Buldurchīn* T. "The Common Quail." *Anqūd*, "The Ruddy Sheldrake."

[3] *Qarqāvul* (Phaseanus colchicus).

[4] *Durrāj*, the Francolin or Black Partridge of India.

[5] *Bi-yak sar du sar agar girift fa-biha-: sar*, "attack, stoop, etc."

[6] *Māt shudan*, is "to be astonished, perplexed; to become rigid from astonishment:" the author applies this idiom more than once to the goshawk, apparently in the last sense.

[7] Lieut.-Colonel E. Delmé Radcliffe states that a goshawk he owned and sent to a friend afterwards killed grouse on the Scottish moors. He also says that an exceptional goshawk tiercel he once had took "storks, white-necked storks (M. episcopus), bar-headed geese (A. indicus), sheldrakes (C. rutila), kestrels, rollers (C. indica), white-eyed buzzards (Poliornis teesa), on one occasion a merlin (L. chiquera), pigeons and other exceptional quarry without number, and yet was in the constant habit of catching partridges and small quarry;" (page 19).

[8] *Tu sīna-yi qūsh ra bar sīna-yi bād bi-dih.*

[9] "To bind," is to seize and hold on to the quarry, especially in the air, while "to ruff" is to stoop at and hit the quarry, making the feathers fly: 'Vide' *Bibliotheca Accipitraria*, by Harting.

firmly that, on falling, the quarry does not break away, still she will suffer for that folly, and will get injured or fall sick. It is the habit of all birds of prey, when within the distance of five or six spans of their quarry, to cease beating their wings, in order to get ready to seize it. Now if you cast off your hawk, breast to the wind, even though she cease to beat her wings for the last three or four feet of her flight, still by the help of the impetus gained by the cast, by your horse's galloping, and by the beating of her own wings, she will reach and "bind" to the quarry and sportsmen will compliment you and commend your hawk. If, however, you cast her off up-wind of the quarry, the moment when, according to her nature, she ceases beating her wings on nearing the quarry, the wind will strike her loins and overturn her; and she will therefore fail to "bind." Hence it is a law never to fly a hawk with her back to the wind: to do so is botchery. When, however, hawking partridges in the hills with a goshawk, or when hawking gazelles in the plains with a saker, the rule allows of exceptions. In the former case your hawk is cast off from a height, and with the aid of gravity[1] follows the partridge till it "puts in;" in the hills, too, the force of the wind is broken. In the latter case you have no choice but to fly your *charkh* or *bālābān* at gazelle from up-wind, for as soon as the falcon stoops and the greyhound arrives, the gazelle has no choice but to put its nose into the wind and to flee windwards.[2] If the wind is strong, the falcon, flying against the wind, will probably not overtake it; but if she does make sufficient headway to overtake it—which she may do with great difficulty—she will, while stooping and recovering and again rising high, lose ground and fall about a thousand paces behind. In the meantime the greyhounds are too blown[3] to seize the gazelle. For these reasons the gazelle must be flown at from up-wind;[4] this will also be explained later, in the chapter on the *Charkh*.

These observations do not apply to hawking *chukor* and *seesee*, for these "put in." Still, it is better to fly at even these, from up-wind, whether in the hills or in the plains, for then the advantage is with the hawk.

---

[1] *Ṭarlān rā māya-dār az bulandī mī-andāzī.*
[2] *— ki dimāgh-ash rā bi-bād dihad va rū bi-bād farār kunad.*
[3] *Nafas-i tāzī mī-sūzad.*
[4] *Bālā-yi bād.*

When your hawk is thoroughly entered to *chukòr* and *seesee*,[1] and never fails you, you should fly her in the plains at some of the quarry mentioned above; for flying a hawk in the plains, after she has been thoroughly entered to *chukor* and *seesee*, has several special advantages, though these are not commonly known to falconers. Many falconers fancy that if you fly your hawk at large quarry in the plains, thoroughly accustoming her to it, she will not thereafter take *chukor* and *seesee*. This is an error. Now a goshawk can only take duck and hubara and such-like quarry of the plains, at the first or second dash: if not taken at once such quarry will speedily outstrip the hawk. Therefore the hawk must, on level open ground, fly her fastest and strive her utmost at the beginning, and this habit soon becomes second nature. If a man wrestle with a famed wrestler, thereafter novices and ordinary people are to him as nothing.[2] So, too, it is with a hawk flown at large quarry. Even at the commencement, partridges are a mere nothing to her; but when, after acquiring the habit of swift flight by being flown in the plains, she is again flown in the hills with the additional advantage of gravity, her swiftness will astonish you; it will truly be something to see. You must, of course, not weary her by overflying, for by overflying you make her stale.[3] A second advantage derived from flying her in the plains, is that she necessarily sees a large number of buzzards, vultures, kites, eagles, and such-like birds, and so, becoming speedily familiarized to them, ceases to be in terror of them.

A third advantage is, that when she fails to take the quarry and "falls at marke,"[4] she will, on your riding up, readily rise and take stand on your fist, for goshawks have a natural dislike to resting on a flat surface; they love to perch on trees, hillocks, or rocks.

A fourth; your hawk learns to take every quarry at which she is flown: should you fail to find partridges you need not return with an empty bag, tired and cross; for you can fly her at hubara, ravens, stone-plovers, etc., instead.

My son, teach your hawk the habits that I have described.

---

1 *Garm bi-giriftan-i kabk u tīhū shud.*
2 *Miṣl-i āb-khurdan*, "as easy as drinking water."
3 *Sar-i dimāgh būdan*, "to be in the humour for, to be keen on."
4 "To fall at marke," "to alight and there await the owner."

Also accustom her to drink freely;[1] accustom her after each meal to drink a beakful or two. Always, about two hours after dark, offer her water in a cup held close in front of her; try to induce her[2] to take a few beakfuls, as by so doing she will digest easily.[3] Accustom her to drinking at least two or three times a day, either from a cup or from a stream. If she drink only one beakful, it is an advantage, especially at night. Drinking keeps her in health.

Now my son, know that it is the pride and glory of a falconer to train long-winged, not short-winged hawks; for the natural quarry of the former is rats, black-breasted sand-grouse, pigeons, duck, and small birds; but when falcons fall into the hands of a competent falconer, they are required to take common cranes, geese, and gazelles. If the falconer be not skilled, how can such quarry be taken by the falcon? As for goshawks, their natural quarry in the hills is partridges and pigeons, and in the hands of the falconer they do no more than kill partridges: it is merely incumbent on the falconer to familiarize them with horses, dogs and men, so that after "putting in" they may take stand and not make off.

Now I, the slave of the Royal Court, was once in attendance on His Majesty (may our souls be his sacrifice) in the hills of (—— ?)[4] in *Māzandarān*. One day a flight of snow-cock[5] rose suddenly in front of the August Presence of the King of Kings. I had on my fist a female *ṭarlān* of two moults. The moment the covey, consisting of twenty or thirty birds,[6] rose, I cast off my hawk, and she promptly took one cock in the air.[7] I hastily dismounted and gave her the brain only; I did not feed her up. Meanwhile the "*Qibla*[8] of the Universe" dismounted and became busy with his breakfast. I took the snow-cock into the Presence: it was examined and I was complimented. I remounted and rode on a short distance, when three more snow-cock rose in front of me.

---

[1] *Āb-khur kardan.*

[2] With a new hawk it is a good thing to attract her attention by flicking the water in the cup with the finger.

[3] *— tā bi-istirāḥat ṣarf bi-kunad.*

[4] Place illegible.

[5] *Kabk-i darī*, Tetraogallus Caspius.

[6] *— galla-yi kabk-i darī ki bi-qadar-i bīst si dāna būdand.*

[7] *Dast-raw dar havā girift.*

[8] *Qibla* is the point to which Muslims turn in prayer. Applied to the Shah it signifies that he is one to whom all bear their requests.

I flew the same hawk and took one,[1] and the Shah had not finished breakfast when I bore it into the Presence. He applauded me and bestowed on me a shawl, for it is most unusual for a goshawk to succeed in taking a snow-cock. A goshawk may indeed take one straight away, in the air, just as it has risen,[2] but she cannot make one "put in," for a snow-cock will fly for miles.[3]

CHAPTER XXX

"RECLAIMING"[4] THE PASSAGE SAKER

Should a passage falcon with "seeled"[5] eyes come into your possession the first thing is to examine it carefully and classify it. Having decided on the race to which the falcon belongs, fit her with some suitable name such as *Ṣulṭān, Ẓarghām, Fāris, Shabīb, Ḥabīb, Maḥbūb, Shahāb, Badrān,* etc.[6] Next fit her with an old hood that is soft and easy, one that will not, by hurting her eyes, make her hood-shy.[7] Let her eyes remain seeled under the hood for three days. Every day when you feed her, call her name. On the third or fourth day, *i.e.,* as soon as she has learnt to feed freely, which she will show by searching eagerly for food when you mention her name, unseel her eyes about two hours to sunset, and then rehood her. Call her name, and when she bends her hooded head in search of food, give her a mouthful or two. Then stroke her on the breast, the thighs, and the wings, and again remove the hood that she may see daylight, and quickly replace it. Continue this treatment till half an hour before sunset. Then set

---

1 *Yak dāna.*

2 *Agar bi-dast raw qūsh girift fa-bi-hā.*

3 A *farsakh* or *farsang;* "a parasang," about $3\frac{3}{4}$ English miles. The author uses the word merely to signify a long distance.

4 "Reclaim," to make a hawk tame, etc.

5 *Chashm-dūkhta,* "with seeled eyes": *vide* page 14, note 4.

6 *Ẓarghām* is one of the many Arabic words for a "lion": *Shabīb,* "of brilliant youth": *Ḥabīb* and *Maḥbūb,* "loved" and "beloved": *Shahāb,* "meteor": *Badrān,* an old Persian word, seems to mean "wicked." All these names, however, are masculine.

7 *Bad-kulāh,* "hood-shy."

her down and leave her till after the evening prayer.[1] Then again take her on the fist and sit near the lamp, with your back to the wall, so that none may come behind you and your hawk. Again call her name, and when she lowers her head reward her with a mouthful. Stroke her as before. Carry her thus for three or

XVI

ARAB FALCONER WITH YOUNG SAKER ON PADDED AND SPIKED PERCH

four hours. After that, set her on her perch for the night, fastening the hood tight that she may not cast it during the night.

Early next morning, before sunrise, take the hawk on your fist;

[1] The time limit for the evening prayer expires half an hour after sunset.

sit with a few friends near a lamp or a fire sipping your tea or coffee, and perform your prayers. Every now and then remove the hood for about five seconds, and then rehood. For about three days feed her under the hood, calling her name. Now at early sunrise,[1] on the morning of the third or fourth day, take just sufficient meat for one meal; well wet your hawk under her wings,[2] wash her nostrils, letting a little water enter them, and set her perch[3] in a quiet place in the sun where none can disturb you, and seat yourself near on the ground. Now remove the hood and handle her a little, stroking her breast, head, and neck; then slowly carry your fist close to her perch and induce her to step on to the perch of her own accord.[4] Hold the leash in your hand, and occasionally draw it tight gently to induce her to "rouse."[5] She is sure, after one of these rousings, to commence oiling her feathers.[6] When you see that she has carried her beak to the oil bottle[7] near her tail, preparatory to oiling her feathers, you must sit absolutely still; do not pull the leash; keep a guard even over the way you breathe, and let her oil her feathers to her heart's content.

If she oils her feathers very quickly and then rouses, it is a sign she is well-manned.[8] If after oiling and rousing, she a second time applies her beak to her oil-bottle, it is a sign that she is both well-manned and well-plucked.

Let her remain on the perch a little longer while she preens[6]

---

[1] The author is probably writing of October in the vicinity of either Bushire or Baghdad.

[2] Presumably as in India, water would be blown in a spray out of the mouth and with force, the falconer's hand being raised and lowered to make the falcon expand her wings and expose the soft feathers underneath. The outer feathers are so arranged as to be a protection against rain, and it is not easy to soak them.

[3] The perch would probably be of the Arab pattern and consist of a pad on an iron spike; *vide* page 95.

[4] Hawks, even those that have never yet been unhooded since they were caught, know their own perches and have preferences.

[5] "To rouse"; said of a hawk when she makes her feathers stand on end and then shakes herself violently.

[6] *Rūghan-kashī* or *rūghan-gīrī kardan*, "to oil the feathers." *Par-khūn* or *par-kashī kardan*, "to preen and straighten the feathers."

[7] *Mudhun*, "oil-bottle," called in the *Boke of St. Albans* the "note" (nut?).

[8] "To man" a hawk is to make it tame and accustomed to the presence of human beings.

and straightens[1] her feathers and again rouses with vigour. Immediately she rouses, take in your hand the meat you have ready, and calling her name, induce her to step on to your fist, and reward her as before. Do this a third time, but this time try and induce her to jump to your fist the length of her leash or less. Then call her name and reward her by a good feed. Now hood her and place her on the ground. Call her name and strike on the ground with your hand, in front of her.[2] If she advances even two finger breadths towards the sound, it is sufficient. Reward her by letting her pull and eat two or three mouthfuls of meat, and while she is eating pull off the hood and let her finish her meal and enjoy herself. She will by this means learn that no one wishes to harm her, and that being tame is not at all a bad thing. After feeding her take a small piece of wool, or cotton-wool, and clean her nostrils.[3] Then fasten the braces of the hood tight, and set her on her perch in the shade.[4]

---

[1] *Khadang kardan, lit.* "to make straight like an arrow." According to the *Boke of St. Albans* a hawk "reformith" her feathers when she straightens them without oiling them.

[2] In the Kapurthala State, sakers that were to be entered to kite were trained in this manner. The hawk, excited by being fed, was hooded and placed on the ground. Then, the lure being banged on the ground, it was taught to snatch at it (in the dark), and rewarded when it "bound" to the lure. The first live kite given as a "train" was presented to it in this manner, *i.e.*, the hooded hawk was induced to "bind" to it as to the lure and was duly rewarded. The hood was then removed and perhaps a little more meat presented through the kite's feathers. The kite was then forcibly removed and thrown to the distance of one or two feet, and as soon as the hawk bound to it, it was fed up on a fresh warm bird. The eyes of the kite were seeled, its claws tied up, and a string was of course fastened to its leg.

[3] A tame hawk's nostrils get choked up with blood and dust. Eastern falconers are generally particular about keeping the nostrils clean. One of the advantages of "tiring" is that it induces a flow of water that keeps the nostrils clean. "'Tiring,' *s.*, any tough piece (as the leg of a fowl with little on it) given to a hawk when in training to pull at, in order to prolong the meal and exercise the muscles of the back and neck."—*Harting.*

[4] The mid-day sun would be too powerful at that time of the year.

CHAPTER XXXI

ANECDOTES OF A BAGHDAD FALCONER

ANECDOTES OF A BAGHDAD FALCONER.—There is a well-known story of a famous falconer of Baghdad, named *Sayyid Adham.* For a long time he was blessed with no offspring, but at length the Lord of the World bestowed on him one son. At the time of our story, the boy had arrived at the age of two years, and had conceived a great affection and fascination for a certain *bālābān,* the property of his father.

A hawk-catcher[1] had captured a fine *bālābān-i aḥmar-i shāmī,* a young passage falcon, and had carried it as a "present"[2] to *Dā,ūd,* the Pasha of Baghdad.

Sayyid Adham, the Grand Falconer,[3] was summoned and the hawk made over to him with directions to train it to gazelle. He took it to his home, named it "Meteor," and unseeled its eyes on the third day.

In the morning, he was seated at the edge of the sunshine,[4] his new hawk preening her feathers, etc., in the manner I have just described. He was, of course, watchful that his unmanned hawk should not be suddenly scared; for you must know that, should a new hawk be suddenly scared, it is difficult to efface from her memory[5] the remembrance of the fright, and she is perhaps spoilt for ever after. While the hawk was engaged in her preening, *Sayyid Adham* was suddenly horrified to see his small two-year-old son toddling towards him. Quietly intervening himself between the boy and the hawk he beckoned to the former to come to him. As soon as the child came up to him, he deftly took his head under his arm and kept it there till the hawk, having finished her toilet,

[1] *Ṣayyād,* Ar., as comprehensive a word as *shikār-chī*; *vide* page 54, note 2.

[2] *Pīshkash,* "present," a polite word for "sale." The Pasha would give him a "present" in return. Such is the etiquette.

[3] *Qūsh-chī Bāshī.*

[4] *Bar-i āftāb, i.e.,* in the shade (or half in the shade), but close to the sunshine.

[5] ". . . And thereby catch some sudden fear, which at the first you ought to be careful to prevent, for it is hard to work that out again which she is suffered to take at the first, and most commonly she will be subject to it ever after, whether it be good or evil."—*Latham.*

was fed and rehooded. He released his son and found that the poor child had been suffocated :—

To save his hawk from starting in alarm
He seized the child and thrust him 'neath his arm,
And pressing tight and tighter in his dread,
He killed the boy by crushing up his head.

Though I myself never saw the *Sayyid*,[1] I was well acquainted with his immediate descendants. In training *bālābān* to gazelle they had no equal, and were justly proud of their skill. They used to pride themselves on the incident narrated above as being a proof of their father's devotion to sport.

BET WITH THE PASHA.—It is also well known that *Sayyid Adham* once laid a wager with the Pasha of Baghdad that he would, within twelve days, fly at gazelle, with success, a certain newly caught *bālābān*. He did so; on the twelfth day, in the presence of the Pasha, the *bālābān* took its first gazelle in noble style, and the *Sayyid* his wager. Only a falconer knows the difficulty of taking a wild gazelle with a passage falcon *within twelve days of its capture*.[2]

Concerning these two matters God is the Knower[3]—but all the old men[4] of Baghdad bore constant testimony to their truth.

CHAPTER XXXII

TRAINING THE PASSAGE SAKER TO GAZELLE[5]

TRAINING THE PASSAGE SAKER TO GAZELLE.—Procure the head of a freshly-killed gazelle. Excite your hawk's appetite by calling her

---

[1] A Sayyid is a descendant of the Prophet.

[2] Had the falcon been netted (and its eyes seeled) some days before its twelve days' education commenced, the matter would have been much simpler. Even though a hawk be not carried nor handled, the mere fact of having its eyes seeled has a quieting effect. It learns to eat from the fist, becomes accustomed to human voices, and loses a little of its high jungle condition.

[3] *Vide* note 3, page 17.

[4] *Kummalīn*, "old men, elders," double Arabic plural of *kāmil*: inadmissible in Arabic and incorrect in Persian: perhaps a misprint for *akmalīn*.

[5] H.H. the late *Mīr 'Alī Murād* of Sindh used, at one time, to train *lagar* falcons to ravine deer, but with what success I cannot say. He afterwards, for this flight, abandoned *lagars* in favour of passage *charghs*.

name, and then remove her hood that she may instantly jump from your fist to the head. Let her tear off and eat two or three mouthfuls of flesh; then seize the gazelle-head and agitate it, so that the excited and hungry hawk may "bind" the tighter. After this let her feed a little. You must practise her daily in this manner, twice or thrice by day, and twice by night. Each morning set aside the exact amount of meat that she should receive in the twenty-four hours, and feed her from that, otherwise in the irregular feedings you will lose count of the quantity she has eaten, and will in consequence overfeed her. After making her play with the head, and after giving her to eat the quantity fixed for her, remove her, and hood her, and carry her off to the bazar.[1]

In the bazar sit in some spot with your hawk's back to the wall, so that nothing can come behind her. Now remove her hood that, by viewing the varied throng of men and horses, she may rid her of her natural fear. Nay, more than this; you must give your man a bit of meat the size of a pea and let him, as he passes, hand it to her, so that she may look with the eye of expectation at each passer-by and say to herself, "Here comes some one with meat for me." Now hood her and "carry" her. Never for one moment let her be off the fist.[2] The Old Masters have ruled that the falconer may, when seated on the ground, place his hawk on the point of his knee,[3] but that with this exception she must know no other perch than his fist. Great stress have they laid on the observance of this rule: "Break it," they have said, "and let your hawk go wild." Do thou act likewise, my son, and keep thy hawk ever on thy fist. During the twenty-four hours, she will indeed get four or five hours' sleep.[4]

An hour after nightfall, make her as before "play" with the deer's head. Do this by lamp light and while in the company of your friends. Let her eat on the head a little meat, a quantity

---

[1] In Urdu this is called *bāzār kī mār*.

[2] In the East, hawks, even when fully trained, are daily "carried" in the bazar. Keeping hawks unhooded on a block is a western practice that does away with the necessity for a certain amount of carriage. Most hawks, however, even "intermewed" hawks, are the better for much "carriage."

[3] In this Eastern attitude the hawk is nearly on a level with, and is close to, the face of the falconer.

[4] Birds need but little sleep.

XVII

YOUNG GAZELLE

about the size of a filbert. Then take her up and carry her. At one time unhood her and place her on her perch in front of you; at another shake her jesses to arouse her and induce her to "rouse," and look about, and take notice. Now after her preening, hood her and take her on the fist. Anon call her name while she is hooded, and reward her response by a morsel of meat, so that she may thus learn to connect her name with food. In short, you must till four hours after nightfall, keep her on your fist or on your knee, in a crowded room where people come and go continually.[1] Just before you retire for the night take her up, carry her near a lamp and make her play with the gazelle-head, agitating it well. If the head has no meat on it, have a few small bits of other meat ready, and place them on the gazelle's eyes in such a manner that the hawk may of her own accord pull out the meat and eat it. Hood her while she is still "binding" to the head, and draw tight the braces[2] of the hood, so that there is no possibility of the hood coming off during the night; then remove her and replace her on her perch, and leave her for the night. The remembrance of the gazelle-head and of her food will remain in her mind, and keep her keen and excited for another hour. She will not sleep at all, or if she does, it will not be for more than two hours.

Rise at daybreak[3] and take her on your fist, for she must not be allowed to even try to "cast"[4] while her hood is on, and if she be hindered from casting she will fall sick. Hence trouble yourself and relieve her.

> To comfort friends, discomfort do not dread:
> Strive that the good call blessings on thy head.

---

[1] In a Persian *majlis*, servants would constantly be coming and going with pipes and sherbet and coffee in the large bare room. In addition to friends and relations, there would be all the servants of these friends and relations.

[2] The Persian, unlike the Indian, hood, is opened and loosened by straps at the back.

[3] As the hawk was irregularly fed the previous day she would probably "cast" late. As a rule sakers do not "cast" as early as peregrines.

[4] *Ṣafrā*,' Ar. "bile; the 'casting' of a hawk": *ṭa'mah*, *lit.* "food," also means "casting." The Turkish for a "casting" is *tuk-samik*, *i.e.*, *tuk*, "feather," and *samik*, "bone." In a good Indian hood, the beak aperture is so cut away that a hooded hawk can, with a little difficulty, both eat and cast, but in the Persian hood a hawk cannot open its beak sufficiently wide to give exit to the casting.

[The author here cites some copy-book maxims on early rising: these are not translated.] . . . Lastly, by early rising you will be in the field before the eagles are on their prowls.[1]

After she has "cast," proceed to feed her on the head, and to "carry" her in the bazaar, etc., etc., as on the previous day; and continue this treatment till she is thoroughly trained to the gazelle-head.

Now as soon as she thoroughly understands and is keen on the gazelle's head, procure a live fawn and bind firmly to one of its hind[2] legs an iron ring: then take a fine strong cord about twelve yards[3] long, pass one end through this ring and tie it to the opposite foreleg.[2] Next, with fine cord, bind between the fawn's ears a lump of tough meat, one to two pounds[4] in weight.

In the morning call your hawk first to the dead head as before, agitating it well, etc., and hood her on the head. Now produce the live fawn and make it lie down. Call your hawk by name and then remove her hood. In accordance with her daily and nightly teaching she will at once "bind" to the meat on the fawn's head.[5] You must instruct your assistant, who has hold of the fawn's tether, to hold his hand high, so that the fawn cannot toss or shake its head. Let your hawk tear a mouthful or two of meat and then remove her. Let her fly and "bind" to the meat on the fawn's head a second time, and let her eat a little of it. Then hood her and remove her, and handle her, etc. (You must so feed her that she will be fit by the evening to be again flown at the dead head and the live fawn.) Now carry her to the house and wash her nostrils with a little luke-warm water. Remove her hood and let her preen and rouse till evening.

In the evening repeat the morning's lesson and do this for

[1] In the cold weather, eagles are late risers: they do not leave their resting spots till the sun is warm. A peregrine will leave its roosting place before it is light.

[2] *Pā* or *pāy* means any leg, but especially the hind leg. As the fore leg is here called *qalam* (shank), it is concluded the author means, by *pā*, "hind leg."

[3] *Dah zar'*. The Persian *zar'* is about 40 inches.

[4] *Nīm sīr*, *yak sīr*: *vide* page 106, note 5.

[5] In a Persian manuscript written in India, it is stated that a goat may be substituted for the fawn, and that the head should be protected by a piece of leather with two holes for the horns. *Vide* also chapter XXXIV (page 122).

three days. On the second and third day, however, after making the fawn lie down, you must get your assistant to drag it slowly in this position on the ground. Then while it is moving you must fly her at it, at the "crouching" fawn.

On the fourth day you must fly her at the fawn standing. First call her, in the morning, to the dead head and play with it, etc., etc., as on previous occasions. Now place the duly prepared fawn in a standing position in front of you. Fly your hawk at it as before, but instruct your assistant that the moment the hawk "binds" he must pull the cord and cast the fawn. Repeat this lesson in the evening.

You must be careful during these lessons that you do not over-feed your hawk and make her too fat. To avoid such an accident, you must, each morning, weigh and put aside the exact quantity of meat she is to be given during the day. As for the meat on the fawn's head, it must be so tough that your hawk can only, with difficulty and delay, tear off and swallow a small mouthful: on no account must it be the tender meat from the backbone.[1]

In short you must first fly your hawk three days in the manner described, *i.e.*, at the "crouching" gazelle, and then three days at the standing gazelle. Next you must fly her three days at the gazelle in motion, its head being still garnished with meat. The moment the hawk "binds," the cord must be pulled and the gazelle made to fall. Fly her twice in the morning and twice in the evening.

Next, after this nine days' training, you must instruct your assistant to drive the deer in front of him at a quickened pace, he himself running behind. When the gazelle is about twenty paces distant, you must let go your hawk. As soon as the hawk reaches and "binds," your assistant must pull the cord and cast the gazelle as before. Give the hawk a little meat, hood her, remove her, and then fly her a second time from a rather longer distance; feed her on the head, hood and remove her; but you must not give her so much meat that she will not be fit to fly again in the evening. For three days you must fly her at the driven fawn, in the manner just described; but every day increase, by twenty paces, the distance from which she is cast off at the fawn.

---

1 *Gūsht-i pusht-i māza*, P.; this term occurs also in Arabic MSS. on falconry.

Now, during this twelve days' training, you must gradually decrease the size of the lump of meat that is bound on to the live fawn's head, so that at last no meat is visible, *i.e.*, you must bind on the fawn's head only a small bit of dry hard meat the size of a filbert, or a portion of the dried neck of a chicken.

You must next, taking the same poor fawn that you have been using all along as a "train,"[1] go out into the open country. The tether must be removed from the fawn's leg, and the fawn must be in the keeping of your falconer, who should be mounted, and at a distance from you of say a hundred paces. First you must call your hawk to the same old dead and dried gazelle-head, agitating it well as before. While your hawk is "binding" to it in a state of hungry excitement, rehood her. With you there must be a quiet and obedient greyhound. Now order your mounted falconer to release the fawn *with its head to the wind,* and to gallop after it. You, having meanwhile mounted, must now unhood the hawk.

Now at this point there is an accident to be guarded against, an accident that often happens at this stage of the training. A plucky impetuous hawk, suddenly unhooded, may in her excitement bind to the head of the horse[2] on which you are mounted; therefore you must keep your eyes fixed on those of the falcon, and release her only when you perceive that she has spied the fawn and intends flying at it.[3]

As soon as the falcon has ten yards' start of you, slip the greyhound[4] after her. The falcon will arrive, stoop at and bind to

[1] The ordinary word for a "train" (bird or beast) for a greyhound or falcon is *bavlī* or *bāvlī*, in India *bā,ūlī*. The present author also uses *dast-par* for a bird; and for a gazelle given as a "train" *maraj* and *dakl*: the last two words are probably Arab terms; I am, however, unable to trace them.

[2] A young saker the translator had, the first time she was flown at hubara, left his fist and bound to the head of a white pony about twenty yards off. The pony spun round and round, till the rider, an assistant falconer, fell off from giddiness.

[3] A hawk, suddenly and hurriedly unhooded, will leave the fist before she spies anything at all. The hood should be removed quietly without flurry; and if the hawk be raw it is often as well not to release her at her first "bate." From the expression of the hawk's eye it is quite easy to see if she has spied the quarry and means business. Even if she started for the galloping assistant falconer, the saker would spy the fawn on the way and divert her attention.

[4] *i.e.*, of course a trained greyhound; one that would follow the hawk.

the fawn's head, and the greyhound will come up and pull down the fawn. You must make in, secure the fawn's legs, and cut its throat. Let your falcon tear the eyes and tongue a little (for that small bit of dried flesh on the head contains no reward), and then cut the fawn's throat and feed her up.[1] Give her only such a quantity of flesh that at sunset she will still have in her crop[2] a quantity of meat the size of a walnut. Hood your falcon and return home.

The dead gazelle should be tied under the belly of a horse, and while riding home have the horse led in front of you. Twice, on the way, remove the hawk's hood that she may view the gazelle and recognize that that was her quarry, and that from the flesh of that quarry she was fed.[3]

When you reach home, with warm water cleanse your falcon's nostrils from blood, and wash off any blood stains from her feathers. Unhood her and let her "rouse and preen." After her preening, take her up, hood her, and carry her till sunset. (You must now no longer call her in the evening to the dead gazelle's head as on former evenings, for her training is near its completion.) Then set her down[4] and let her rest till the morning.

Now, before dawn, take her up so that she may cast while on your fist. Take a *sīr*[5] or less of good lamb and wash it well in warm water until it becomes bloodless and white. To-day the hawk need not be lured or called: she should be fed on her perch. If your hawk is fat, give her at sunset, as a "casting," a little lamb's wool well wetted: if lean, give her chicken feathers, or a little of the skin and fur of a gazelle. To-night, too, let her rest on her perch.

At dawn take her up, so that she may cast on your fist. About an hour after dawn, go out into the open country, taking with you a couple of quiet trusty greyhounds, as well as a brisk and lively

---

[1] An unnecessary piece of cruelty. There is no reason why the gazelle should not be instantly put out of pain.

[2] *i.e.*, meat not yet "put over."

[3] *Sīr shudan*, *lit.* "satiated." Eastern falconers, however, do not "gorge" their hawks. The author by the term *sīr shudan* merely means to give a hawk the regulation quantity.

[4] Hooded as before.

[5] *Sīr*; one Tabriz *man* equals forty *sīr*; one *sīr* equals twenty *miṣqāl*; and two and a half *miṣqāl* are about equal to an Indian *tolā*. A Tabriz *man* is about $7\frac{1}{2}$ lbs. The Indian *ser* is about 2 lbs., and there are forty *ser* in the *man*. The term *sīr* is used only locally in Persia.

gazelle. As before, call the hawk to the dead gazelle-head, agitating it as on previous occasions, etc., etc. The live gazelle should be released at a distance of five hundred paces, your assistant falconer galloping after it as before. The hawk should next be unhooded and cast off, and when she has flown about ten yards, the greyhounds should be slipped. The hawk will reach the gazelle and make one or two stoops before the greyhounds arrive and pull down the gazelle. You must make in quickly and secure the hind legs of the gazelle, so that the falcon, which will have bound to the gazelle-head, may blood herself well on its head and eyes.[1] Then, cut the gazelle's throat and feed the hawk, giving her just so much food as will leave a quantity the size of a walnut still in her crop[2] at sunset. Her nostrils, etc., must be cleansed as before.

It is no longer necessary to keep the hawk hooded at night. Let her sleep unhooded.

You must now carry the hawk till two hours after nightfall and then set her down to rest.[3]

Take note of your hawk's action when flown at these last two gazelles. If she makes three or four stoops at the head before binding, it is a sign that she has risen too much in condition: if she makes no stoop, but binds immediately on reaching, it is a sign that she is somewhat low in condition: if she makes one stoop only, or two stoops, and then binds, she is in her proper condition. Now if she be too fat, you must, by feeding her for two days on washed meat, lower her condition. If she be too low, you must fly her for two more days at a live gazelle, cast on the ground as on the first day, and as soon as she binds, you must stealthily substitute a freshly-slaughtered white lamb or white kid: or failing these a white chicken, placing the flesh of the chicken's breast over the gazelle's head. Feed up your hawk on the warm flesh. In two days she will regain her condition.

[1] *Vide* note 1, page 106.

[2] *Bi-qadr-i girdū,ī gūsht dar sīna-ash bāshad.*

[3] By that time she would have "put over" the whole of her food: nothing would remain in the crop. A hawk, if carried, puts over more quickly than if resting on the perch. It is an Indian saying that "When carried instead of two mutings it makes three." "Carrying" of course includes frequent unhooding and rehooding and occasional turnings of the hand to induce the hawk to shift her position.

On the following day, again give washed meat[1] in the manner described above. On the day after, fly her at a gazelle that is as stout and brisk as a wild one. For this go into the open country as before, and first call your hawk to the head of the dead gazelle, agitating it as on previous occasions, etc., etc. This time the gazelle must be freed at a distance of a thousand yards, and your assistant must gallop after it. Cast off your hawk, and when she has got a start of ten or fifteen yards, slip the greyhounds, and gallop. Your hawk will make one or two stoops before the greyhounds arrive to pull down the gazelle. Make in, cut the gazelle's throat, feed the hawk, and treat her in other respects as before.

On the day after this she must be keenly "set" by being given well-washed meat. At sunset give her a casting of feathers. On the following morning start from your house about two hours before dawn, and let your hawk throw up her casting while you are on your way to your destination. Repeating the four *Qul* and the verse of the Throne,[2] breathe the sacred words over yourself and over your hawk.

You must early that morning mark down a single half-tame gazelle.[3] After marking it down, call your falcon to the dead gazelle-head and agitate, etc., etc., as before. Then rehood her and go after the wild gazelle. The nearer you get to it the better. Unhood the falcon, and as soon as she spies the gazelle and shows an inclination to give chase, cast her off and shortly after slip the greyhounds.

Most probably you are wondering why you should not first slip the greyhounds and then cast off the falcon behind them. Now in this thought you err, for your falcon is probably full of courage

---

[1] *Ishtihā dādan.*

[2] *i.e.*, chapters 109, 112, 113 and 114 of the Qoran. They are very brief, not containing more than four or five lines, and all commence with the word *Qul* "Say." These chapters are repeated at weddings by the bridegroom, after the *Qāẓī*. Their efficacy is nearly equal to that of the whole Quran. The "Verse of the Throne" is the 256th verse of the 2nd chapter: it commences "God, there is no God but He; the Living, the Abiding; slumber taketh him not nor sleep. His throne reacheth over the heavens and the earth."—*Vide* also page 74.

Āya rā damīdan (*dam karnā* in Urdu): the sacred texts are repeated and the breath is then exhaled on the breast and hands, etc., or over a sick person.

[3] *Yak dānā āhū-yi ārām-i tāk-ī.* Probably *tākī* is a slip for *tak-ī*, "a single one."

and eagerness, and her training has so excited her that she might bind to a greyhound instead of to the gazelle, and so be spoilt for ever. For this reason you must first, *when there is nothing ahead of her but the gazelle*, cast off your hawk; and if it please God, with the help of the hounds, she will take it.

On no account must you, this first day, fly your hawk at two gazelle in company. You must either fly her at a single gazelle or at three together. Doubtless you wonder why you can cast her off at three gazelle but not at two? Let me explain.

Two gazelle together will be either two fawns that have grown up together after their dam has been destroyed by some accident, or else a couple, male and female; or possibly they may be dam and young; in any case domestic affection will prevent them separating. Your hawk, being still raw and inexperienced,[1] or rather quite ignorant,[2] will stoop, first at one and then at the other, while the greyhounds, being trained and experienced, will chop and change, always making for the gazelle at which the hawk stoops. Your hounds, tired out, will fall behind and "get left," and the hawk, without their assistance being unable to take the deer, will get lost. Should you happen to regain sight of her, you will find it difficult to lure her; if successful in luring her, the labour of twenty days will have been lost. However, a single gazelle by itself is the same as the hand-train[3] that you have all along been training her to, and this whether it be a male or a female. If there are three gazelle together, your falcon will single out[4] one and stoop at it; and as soon as she does so, the remaining two will make off together in company, while the greyhounds will only follow the single remaining gazelle at which your hawk is stooping. Now be warned and do as I tell you.

Should the gazelle be taken, feed her up, etc., as on previous occasions and return home. Should, however, any accident happen; should your falcon get tired out and the greyhounds get "left," or should an eagle appear, then act as before; or if you have the carcass of a gazelle with you, cast your falcon at its head

---

1 *Qashm*, Ar., colloquially *ghashīm*, "inexperienced, helpless": though in common use in Baghdad, this word is not used in Persian.

2 *Na-dānam-kār*.

3 *Ahū-yi dastī*.

4 *Sivā kardan*.

and give her a very light meal, together with a "casting" from the skin; feed her so that she will "cast" early the following morning. If it please God she will not fail next morning. Should she, however, be again unsuccessful, you must feed her up well and let her rest for two or for three days.

On the third day, feed her on the head of a live gazelle, giving her only a light meal. On the fourth day, fly her in the open country at a single bright and active[1] gazelle, but so act that she cannot tell that the gazelle is not a wild one. Kill the gazelle under her and act as before.

The next day "set" her by giving her washed meat, and the day after fly her at a wild gazelle. She certainly—please God—will not fail.

CHAPTER XXXIII

TRAINING THE EYESS SAKER TO EAGLES[2]

I WILL now, my pupil, describe to you the method of training the nestling *charkh*[3] to eagles.[4]

In one point the nestling *charkh* excels the rest of the black-eyed race: it can take eagles, the rest cannot.[5]

When you first take the eyess from the eyrie, feed her well, that she may grow fat and stout and strong, and may, by taking her quarry in style, exhibit all her pride and power.

Now when the constellation of Canopus rises,[6] take her up,

---

1 *Ziring* or *zaring*, *i.e.*, not half-starved or crushed in spirit.

2 The Rev. H. B. Tristram writing on the ornithology of North Africa (*Ibis* 1859) mentions "eagles, kites and sand-grouse" as quarry flown at by the Arab Shaikhs. [Elsewhere the same writer says that the Lanner and Barbary falcon are flown at sand-grouse. No Indian falconer, however, has succeeded with the latter quarry: it is too fast, and the hawk and quarry soon disappear from view. The sand-grouse will not let the hawk get above it when the hawk is "waiting on." Mr. Tristram does not mention what device or artifice the Arabs adopt.] The author of the *Land and the Book* (W. M. Thomson, D.D.) says of trained falcons, in chapter XXV, "they will even bring down the largest eagle in the same way. . . ."

3 *Charkh-i āshiyānī.*

4 *Qara-qūsh.*

5 *Vide*, however, page 44.

6 *Vide* page 126, note 5.

hood her and carry her: train her after the manner that falcons are always trained, until she obeys the lure and comes to it readily from any spot where she may be placed.

Now lower her condition a little: let her lose just a little flesh. Procure a young Egyptian vulture[1] and bind some meat on its back. Twice daily, in the cool of the morning and of the evening, show it to her and then let it fly[2] in such a manner that your hawk may take it. If you are unable to procure a young Egyptian vulture, get a "black"[3] buzzard, or failing a black one a "yellow" one, but in any case you must bind the hind claw[4] to the "tarsus."[5] Fly your hawk at this "train," twice in the morning and twice in the evening,[6] and feed her up on it.

Should you be able to procure a second "train" of any of the three birds mentioned, then on the third day cut the throat of the first "train." Be careful, however, to conceal its head, for your hawk must learn to bind only to the back. After killing the "train" and feeding your hawk on the meat that is tied to its back, cut open the back, and let your hawk eat a little of the exposed flesh.[7] She must not see the flesh of any other part except the back. During these days that you are entering your hawk to the "hand-train,"[8] as you increase the distance at which you release the train, you must decrease the amount of meat that is tied to its back, till at last no meat at all is left and your hawk binds to the ungarnished back of the "train."

---

[1] *Kachal charkas* (or *karkas*), *lit.* "the scald-headed vulture." The young of this species is brown and not white.

[2] *Parānīdan*, "to cause to fly." The author always uses this word for showing a train to a hawk and then letting it fly. In the preliminary lesson or lessons, one or two flight-feathers would probably be tied together to make the train fly as slowly as possible, and a creance would be fastened to a leg. *Vide* note 2, page 97.

[3] *Vide* chapter XII.

[4] *Qullāb* or "hook" (for Ar. *kullāb*); the "talons" of old falconers.

[5] The "stalke" of old authors.

[6] After the first flight the hawk would be given only a beakful or two of meat.

[7] From the back she would get little more than a taste of warm blood.

[8] *Dast-par.* It must be recollected that *sakers* are not easily spoilt by being given numerous trains, as are peregrines.

The two[1] uppermost flight feathers in each wing of the birds mentioned above—the feathers called *yār māliq* by the Turks[1]—are broad and large. Take these feathers, two on each side, and placing them on top of each other bind the garnishing meat to them, so that the meat will be conspicuous during flight.

After you have killed the train and fed the hawk, you must, by giving her washed meat,[2] "set" her as previously described. Then go out into the open country and find a *young* Egyptian vulture, which in colouration resembles a young eagle, and fly your hawk at it. She will surely take it.[3] Kill it and feed your hawk well.[4]

"Set" your hawk the next day; and the day after that, go out and find a *būq khura*,[5] which has before been described as the most ignoble of the eagles. Get close to it, and so cast off your hawk that by the time the eagle has risen from the ground, your *charkh* will have reached it and bound to its back. With all haste make in and secure the *būq khura*, and, killing a dark-coloured chicken, present its flesh from underneath the wing of the *būq-khura*, and so feed your hawk; but feed her sparingly. Release the *būq-khura*[6] from the claws of the *charkh* and keep it by you alive.

On the morrow when your hawk is hungry, go out into the open country. Bind the hind claw of the *būq-khura* to its shank, and let it fly, giving it a long start. Then unhood[7] and cast off

---

[1] On page 168, chap. LII, it is stated that there are *three* feathers in each wing so named, and that it is the *Kurds* who call these feathers *yār māliq*. *Vide* also chap. LX.

[2] *Ishtihā dādan.*

[3] The Egyptian vulture is frequently found sitting on the ground and will let a horseman or footman approach within a few feet. It rises slowly, and as it does not shift from the stoop it is at once taken. It does not seem to have any means of defence—except its odour.

[4] Of course on other flesh.

[5] On page 31 the *būq-khura* is described as an eagle always found on marshes and reed beds. It eats frogs, dead fish, etc., and occasionally a wounded duck.

[6] This should be done stealthily at the time the chicken is substituted, or after the hawk has been re-hooded; for the hawk must be induced to believe that it has eaten the quarry it captured. With a thoroughly-made hawk no great stealth need be observed.

[7] *Rihā kardan*, "to release." The author uses this word to signify setting free a train secretly while the hawk is still hooded. *Vide* note 2, page 111.

your hawk. She will certainly take it. Kill the *būq-khura* and feed the hawk.

Now again "set" your hawk and fly her at a wild *būq-khura*, feeding her up when she takes it. This you must do three or four times.[1]

Of one thing you must be careful: during these seven or eight days that you are flying your hawk and feeding her on warm flesh, take care that she does not become fat and get above herself.

After taking with her four or five *būq-khura*, fly her at one of the black eagles that have no spots or markings.[2] Next fly her at a spotted *ā,īna-lī* eagle. After she has taken one of the latter, you can fly her at any species you choose. Should the eagle you are going to fly her at be of a large species (such as the *karlak*, or the *kūjīkān*, or the "moon-tailed eagle," all three of which are the largest of the eagle species), it can, by the cries and shouts of your horsemen, be made so to lose its head as to become incapable of defending itself.

Supposing, for instance, you spy an eagle seated on the ground in a good open plain where there are neither small water-courses nor hillocks[3]—a spot where you can gallop without caution or delay—make the eagle face the wind[4] and gallop on to it,[5] and placing your trust on Almighty God, cast off your *charkh*. The eagle will see the hawk making for it but will not conceive the possibility of the hawk's attacking it, for, poor thing, it is ignorant of the trickery of man. Calmly and leisurely it will spread its wings saying to itself, "This *charkh*, whose dog is it that it should approach me?"

If the eagle be a large strong female, it will certainly carry the *charkh* for about a thousand[6] paces, but if a weak tiercel it will not

---

1 The "train" should not be allowed to get ragged. It should each time be given a longer start. If it settles on the ground, it should be allowed to look about it till it regains heart and takes wing of its own accord. It is also well to go to a different spot each time.

2 Apparently the black eagle described on page 31.

3 *Māhūr*, any up and down ground.

4 *Sīna-yi qara-qūsh rā bi-bād bi-dih*, "give the eagle's breast to the wind"; the author's meaning is not quite clear. Presumably the eagle would be sitting with its breast to the wind.

5 From behind.

6 The distance is probably exaggerated.

drag it more than half that distance. You must gallop hard and keep close up to or under the eagle, until it tires and settles on the ground. It will then run, flapping and trailing its wings like a hunted chicken that is tired out. You must all pursue it with shouts and cries.

As soon as the eagle takes to running like a chicken, one horseman must detach himself and intercept it in front. Now when that son of a dog[1] sees that it cannot fly, that its path is blocked in front, and that shouts and yells arise on all sides of it, it will have no recollection of the *charkh* that has fastened on to its back: from rage and bewilderment it will drive its talons into the ground. Now, my pupil, on no account must you treat this son of a dog like other quarry. Do not in your excitement cast yourself upon it. On no account! on no account do so—unless you seek your own destruction. As soon as the eagle has convulsively clutched the ground, you must dismount in all haste, and approaching it from behind firmly place your long boot on its back just between the shoulders, and so render it defenceless. Then cautiously advance your further hand from behind it and firmly grasp its legs, keeping one leg on the eagle the while. Then cut its throat, split open its breast, bring out the heart, and feed your hawk. You must know that the flesh of eagles is greasy and indigestible, so do not overfeed your hawk or she will fall ill.[2] You must not imagine that an eagle's flesh is the same as a pigeon's; so feed her lightly:—

> If eagle's flesh as pigeon's ere appears
> Then must you match the lion's with the deer's.
> So when two eagle's thighs have passed her beak,
> Enough!—unless you her destruction seek.

The next time you go out, fly your hawk at any species of eagle you like.

Now you must understand that although the hawk *does*, temporarily, cripple the eagle, yet it is owing to the screams and yells of the riding party that the eagle loses its wits and gets taken. If you want to test this, fly your hawk at an eagle as

---

[1] *Pidar-sag*, a common term of abuse: used in much the same way that b——y is by Thomas Atkins.

[2] *Tuʻma-zada mī-shavad*: does this simply mean indigestion or does it mean that the hawk will cast her gorge?

though you were flying a goshawk at a partridge, and ride slowly and quietly after the quarry. Note how the eagle will with its foot sweep the hawk off its back while exclaiming :—

"Thus does wise heaven grant sustenance to fools
That countless wise are filled thereat with wonder."[1]

The awe and fear inspired by man is greater than that inspired by any animal, and especially terrifying is the human voice. God has given to all his creatures, birds, beasts, etc., a weapon of defence for their safety, and man's weapons are his voice and the dread his presence inspires ; every thing that creeps, or crawls, or flies, even the lion, flees from the sound[2] and terror of man—how much more so the eagle. The eagle is captured only by the artifice of the falconer : for what sort of a dog is the *charkh* to master the eagle ?

The falconer by art and skill can show
That feeble *charkhs* can lay great eagles low.
Untrained, untried, how could a falcon fight—
Fight and prevail against an eagle's might ?

This sport with the *charkh* and eagle must be pursued in the plains : in hilly country it is impossible.

Eyess Shahin and Eagles.—The eyess shahin is capable of being trained to eagles, but as it is small and delicate, it is not employed for this quarry.

CHAPTER XXXIV

EYESS SAKER AND GAZELLE[3]

The system of training the nestling *charkh*[4] to gazelle differs from that previously described for the passage saker.[5]

---

[1] From the *Gulistān* : Chapter I, St. 40.

[2] *Kavāzha*, in modern colloquial, "clamour."

[3] The late Sirdār Sher 'Alī, the exiled *Wālī* of Qandahar, told the translator that in Afghanistan he used to fly eyess *charkhs* at gazelle, and he considered those nestlings the best that were taken from nests either on the ground or close to the ground. His theory was that only bold birds dared to build close to the ground, and that their nestlings were, from the egg, accustomed to the sight of jackals and foxes.

[4] *Charkh-i āshiyānī.*

[5] *Bālābān-i tūrī : tūrī* from *tūr*, "net"

In the beginning of the Autumn you must, with your eyess, take a large number of hubara bustard so that she may become adroit and lose her rawness. As your hawk is a nestling and hence without any experience whatever, you must, after getting her to kill one or two domestic fowls, enter her by a train of a live hubara.[1]

You must first seel the hubara's eyes, so that it may not puff itself up and drive away the young hawk,[2] which might thereafter conceive a permanent dread of this quarry. "Seel" the eyes of the train and let it run[3] for about forty paces, and then cast off your *charkh*. She will approach it stealthily[4] and seize it. As soon as she seizes it, give her a small quantity of meat; remove her and rehood her.

In the evening *slightly* loosen the thread with which the hubara's eyes are seeled, so that it can just see out of the top of its eyes.[5] When the *charkh* flies towards the hubara, the latter, spying her out of the tops of its eyes, will puff itself out for the attack; but when the hawk arrives close and drops to the ground, she will no longer be visible, and the hubara will therefore not charge her. When the hawk seizes the hubara, again give her a small quantity of meat.

On the next day unseel *half* of the hubara's eyes, so that at one time it may puff itself out ready for attack, and at another lose sight of its enemy. Let the hubara get some distance, and then unhood the hawk and let her go. As soon as she binds to the hubara, cut its throat and feed up the hawk.

On the next day give another "train" of hubara, but this time with unseeled eyes. Let it get a long distance off before you unhood your hawk. Kill it, and feed up the hawk on its flesh.

---

[1] Passage sakers rarely, if ever, require to be given a "train" for this quarry, as they kill it in a wild state.

[2] *Bād kardan.* An hubara will not hesitate to attack a hawk on the ground, puffing itself up like a turkey cock and striking forwards with its feet. Sometimes several will combine in showing front to the enemy.

[3] The hubara will of course have a few flight-feathers plucked out or tied, to prevent it flying. If many feathers are plucked out it will not look formidable when it puffs itself out. *Vide* note 1, page 117.

[4] *Bi-duzda raftan.*

[5] *Chashm rā bālā-bīn kardan.*

Although it is no feat for a falconer to take hubara[1] (for any inferior hawk will kill this quarry), still in the training of the eyess saker that is destined for gazelle, it has a special place, as will be mentioned later. This remark, however, does not apply to the netted passage falcon,[2] which has killed hubara for itself in a wild state.

From the wild falcon,[3] an hubara, however stout and strong, cannot possibly escape[4]; for what is the flight of an hubara compared

XVIII

YOUNG PASSAGE SAKER (LIGHT VARIETY) ON HUBARA

to that of the wild saker? Until the wild saker overtakes the hubara, she will never relinquish the chase.

If, however, you fly a *trained* passage falcon at an hubara, it is quite a different matter; for the falcon will not be in the same high

[1] Though the hubara is a large and powerful bird the wild saker preys on it largely. The hubara is not a high-flying bird, and its flesh is palatable. After killing one or two, the most cowardly *char<u>kh</u>* becomes wedded to this quarry. When giving a "train," it is preferable, in some cases imperative, to give a flying one. The saker, however, takes to the hubara with little or no entering.

[2] *Bālābān-i tūrī.*

[3] *Bālābān-i ṣaḥrā,ī.*

[4] The author means by open flight, for the hubara frequently escapes by doubling and hiding. It will squat on a perfectly open plain, the pursuing hawk alighting within five or six feet of it utterly puzzled as to what has become of its quarry. On the ground, an hubara does not at first seem afraid of a single saker or peregrine.

condition she was in when wild, and so, if the quarry breaks away from her [1] and rises high, she will not be able to overtake it quickly: neither will she be so thin that she will give up all desire and hope of killing, and remain tamely seated on the ground. She will certainly commence a stern-chase [2] and soon be lost to view. God knows where she will overtake the hubara, whether two *farsakh* off or three.[3] Now in the first place you should not fly a passage saker at hubara.[4] If, however, you must do so, tie together four of the flight-feathers of one wing so that it shall fly clumsily, hugging the ground. The hubara will certainly stand up to do battle and the hawk will also certainly bind to it on the ground.[5] If the hubara

---

1 *Agar hubara jilav-i ū shikast va buland shud.*

2 *Lābud hubara rā dar jilo andākhta 'aqab mī-kunad.*

3 Sakers are passionately fond of the hubara as a quarry: they will never relinquish a chase as long as there is any chance of success: they will fly the hubara even when they are not very hungry. The hubara, when put up with a hawk just behind it, flies faster than is commonly supposed, especially in the Spring when it is fat and in high condition. A passage saker intended for this quarry should not, I think, weigh *less* than 2 lbs. 4 oz. and should have been brought into hard condition by being exercised twice daily at the lure; twenty-five stoops at each exercise are sufficient. A wild saker seldom exceeds 2 lbs. 8 oz. in weight. A haggard of the editor's that weighed when caught 2 lbs. 9½ oz., when killing hubara weighed 2 lbs. 6½ oz. (For kite 2 lbs. 3 oz. will be found a sufficient, and generally a suitable weight. For hare a weight of 2 lbs. is *sufficient*. Beginners should note these weights and so spare themselves much disappointment.)

4 Only passage sakers are, in India, flown at hubara. They are usually flown out of the hood, but in districts full of ravines they are trained to "wait on." The author, like most natives of India also, seems to think that hubara can be killed only on the ground. As already mentioned in the above note, to fly houbara successfully sakers must be in high condition, *i.e.*, they must be kept well exercised and well fed, a simple fact that most Eastern falconers forget. I have seen Arab falconers stuffing their newly caught sakers with *suet* and skin. In *Arabia Deserta* by C. M. Doughty we read, "The Gate Arabs had robbed more than a dozen young falcons. . . Their diet was small desert vermin, lizards, rats, insects. . . on finding naught they maintain them with a little dough; in the nomad life they pluck for them those monstrous bluish blood-sucker ticks which cleave to the breasts of their camels." The translator once gave a school-boy a trained *lagar*: when pocket-money and meat failed, the boy fed it on boiled rice. Even after this treatment it flew and killed a wild raven.

5 Wild hawks seldom if ever kill on the ground. They stoop at the hubara, knock it about and put it up. Many trained hawks even will not, when in high condition, bind to an hubara on the ground but stoop at it till the falconer flushes the quarry.

takes to flight, the hawk will follow only for a few yards, and seeing itself utterly outpaced will give up and sit on the ground.

The nature of the eyess, however, is different. I have had many that would take two or three eagles in a day, that would take crane and gazelle, and were yet afraid of hubara. The reason of this was that I omitted to seel the eyes of an hubara given as a "train": the hubara puffed itself up on seeing the *charkh* coming towards it and got ready for the attack; the *charkh* hesitated and sat on the ground; and the hubara seeing its hesitation became like a spitting[1] cat, charged and put the *charkh* to

XIX

YOUNG PASSAGE SAKER (DARK VARIETY) ON HUBARA

flight. God the All-knowing, has bestowed on the hubara as a weapon of defence a peculiar kind of "mutes;"[2] and although these are nothing in reality yet they have a certain awe.

> When the timid lamb-natured hubára's enraged,
> She becomes, in attack, like a lion uncaged.

---

[1] *Burrāq shuda*. *Burrāq* is the long-haired "Persian" cat; *gurba* is the general term for a cat.

[2] *Chalqūz* or *chalghūz*; excrement of birds only. "Mutes," the technical term for the droppings of hawks. When the hubara is feeding on certain juicy crops, its excrement is thin and glutinous and has an offensive odour. Though the excrement is ejected through fear, it is a very effective weapon. A hawk that is smeared, is unable to fly properly, possibly because the wind strikes cold through the damp feathers. Some of the best hubara hawks, peregrines and sakers, always bind to the wing, and so escape being buffeted or befouled.

If an eyess *charkh* has once been frightened on the ground and driven off by an hubara, nothing will ever induce her to take this quarry on the ground. But a skilful falconer may cast off the *charkh* so expertly that she takes the quarry in the air within a few yards' distance.[1]

In short, as soon as your hawk is so thoroughly entered to hubara that she will take six or seven in a day, you must go out and fly her at as many hubara as you can, but do not feed her: even though you fly her thirty times[2] with success, do not feed her. Go on flying her till she is utterly disgusted and will not attempt even to follow the quarry. As soon as you see this, bring up a gazelle fawn with meat tied on its head, as previously described in the chapter on training the passage saker. As soon as the *charkh* binds to the gazelle's head, kill a fowl or a white pigeon, and feed her up so that she may learn the pleasure to be derived from taking a gazelle.

You must proceed with the training of the eyess as you did with the passage saker, but there are two or three points of difference. First: if the passage hawk binds at the first or second entering, she must be fed up; but the eyess must not be fed up, otherwise she will contract a habit and will always have to be fed up. Second: if the eyess follows the gazelle and works well but the greyhounds go wrong, she will certainly, when worn out, sit down;[3] you must then and there lure her and feed her up. Third: if the eyess works hard several times but is disappointed, and so no longer follows gazelle with her former zest, you must cure her as follows. Go and take two or three hubara with her, one a day, and feed her up on them. On the third or fourth day fly her at all the hubara you can without feeding her, till she is worn out or disgusted. Then, as on the first day, fly her at the gazelle's head, feeding her up. After that let her rest for a day or two. Next, take into the open country a gazelle fawn that is quick and active, and secretly release it at a distance. After it set a dog, or a young greyhound too slow to overtake it. When the gazelle fawn gets to some distance, gallop after it and slip the greyhounds

---

1 *Agar dast-i ustād-i khūb bāshad dūr nīst dast-raw biyandāzī dar havā bi-gīrad.*

2 *Sī dast.*

3 *Az khastagī rū-yi rū nishasta ast:* exact meaning doubtful.

as you do when hawking wild gazelle,[1] and cast off the *charkh*. When the gazelle is taken, feed up the hawk as before, that she may learn the advantage to be derived from taking this quarry and return to a liking for it. The object of entering a *charkh* to hubara is as has been stated.

You may think to yourself, "I will fly my eyess at hare as has been described for the passage hawk!"[2] Now, my pupil, on no account must you do this; fly her not at hare, for this is error. First, the nature of the passage hawk is noble, while the nature of the eyess is ignoble. If, after the disappointment that your eyess

XX

HUBARA SUNNING ITSELF

has experienced at gazelle, you fly her at hare with success, you must of necessity feed her up; and as the gazelle and the hare are both ground-game[3] and akin, your hawk will say to herself, "Why should I not henceforth fly only the easier quarry? No stamped bond have I given to the Court to wrestle[4] with that other kind of

[1] *Ahū-yi ṣaḥrā,ī.*

[2] The author has not mentioned this flight.

[3] *Charanda, lit.* "grazers."

[4] *Du chār u du-lashma bi-shavam*: *lashm* P.= smooth-bodied: *du-lashma shudan* is properly to wrestle together without either opponent getting a good grip.

jackass!"[1] The hubara, on the contrary, is not ground-game,[2] nor has the eyess in a wild state preyed on it as has the passage hawk. By taking one or two hubara, the eyess recovers her keenness and pluck, but, on the third or fourth day, when she is overflown at hubara and unrewarded, she gets disgusted with that particular quarry; being then flown at a gazelle's head and rewarded, she re-transfers her attention to that quarry, and by being afterwards given an easy bagged fawn, her affection for the quarry is cemented.

The system of training the *charkh* and the *bālābān* to gazelle is this that has been described, and it is the system of the falconers of Baghdad and of the Nomad Arabs, who are masters of this particular sport. But the people of Turkistan and Khurasan and Buzhnurd,[3] being unskilled, have a different system, and that, too, for the eyess only; for they are quite unable to train the passage saker to take even *one* gazelle.

Another System of Training the "*Charkh*" to Gazelle.—Their system is this. First they dig a dry canal about three or four ells[4] deep, and four hundred or five hundred paces long. At the end, a recess or chamber is constructed, sufficiently large to contain a gazelle that is brought and confined there. A rope is tied to the gazelle's leg, and the gazelle is, step by step, driven and beaten so that it flees to take refuge in this chamber at the farther end. This treatment is continued till the beginning of Autumn, when the people commence giving "trains"[5] to their eyess sakers.

The gazelle's head is protected from the hawk's claws[6] by a piece of leather that has two holes to admit the horns, and on this leather the meat is securely fastened. The gazelle, released in the canal at the required distance from the chamber according to the progress the young hawk has made, is obliged to run straight and take refuge in its accustomed retreat. If, during the run, the

---

[1] *Bā hamchu narra khar-ī.*

[2] *Az sinkh-i charanda nīst: sinkh* in m. c.=*qism.*

[3] *Buzhnurd*, the capital of a district of the same name, is about 180 miles from the river Atrek, which flows into the south-east corner of the Caspian.

[4] *Si chār yak zara'* (m. c.) "about 3 or 4 ells"; *zara'* (Pers. for Ar. *zirā'*) is the Persian ell of about 40 inches.

[5] — *ki binā-yi marj u būlī kardan-i charkhā-yi shān ast.* The word *būlī* is also *bolī*, *bawlī*, *bavlī* and *bāvlī*. *Vide* also note 1, page 123.

[6] *Mikhlab.*

charkh binds to the meat on its head, the rope is pulled and the *charkh* fed up on the "train's" head. One gazelle can act as a "train"[1] for twenty *charkh*.

As soon as these people have in this manner completed the training and have killed the gazelle under the hawk, they, owing to their lack of understanding, cast off four or five *charkh* at a wild gazelle, and slip five or six greyhounds. God knows whether they ever kill anything. If they do, it is not skill; if they do not, it is utter bungling.

> If the hawks take the quarry no credit is due;
> Their failure we must as incompetence view.
> If you look at the methods of sport of these Turks
> In everything bungling and botchery lurks.

Now the system of the falconers of *Baghdād, Cha'b*[2] and *Mu'ammara*[3] (in which places this ancient flight with the eyess or passage saker was first "invented") is wholly distinct and apart from that of the Turkistānīs and Khurāsānīs; for the former, even at a herd of two hundred gazelle, fly only a single *bālābān* succoured by a couple of greyhounds[4]; but so well trained and intelligent are the hounds that even if a thousand gazelles come in front of them, they will seize only that one at which the hawk is stooping.

The skill of these latter people, however, is confined to training *charkh* and *bālābān* to gazelle, hubara, and hare, and they practise no other flight. Skill is shown by practising every form of sport.[5]

---

[1] *Dakl u bolī*, "train"; in note 5 on page 122 *marj u bolī*. The author in a marginal note (page 117 of the text) gives *dast-par* as an equivalent for *dakl*. *Dast-par* or "hand-flight" can, however, refer only to a bird. *Bā,ūlī* is, in India, a train given either to a hawk or a greyhound, etc., etc.; it has a general application. *Vide* also page 141, note 4.

[2] The *Cha'b* (properly *Ka'b*) Arabs are a tribe inhabiting the southern portion of *Khuzistān*.

[3] *Mu'ammara*: the writer must mean *Muḥammarah* in Khuzistān, 26 miles below *Baṣrah*: it is ruled by an Arab Sheikh.

[4] *Tāzi-yi qūsh-shinās*, a greyhound trained to hunt in company with a hawk. *'Ārif*, "knowing, intelligent."

[5] An ambiguous sentence in the original: it may mean "flying at every kind of quarry."

CHAPTER XXXV

ANOTHER METHOD OF TRAINING THE EYESS AND P SSAGE SAKERS TO GAZELLE

ANOTHER METHOD OF TRAINING *Charkh* AND *Bālābān* TO GAZELLE.—The people of the *Fārs* desert train the *charkh* and *bālābān* to gazelle by another method. In the early Autumn when the passage sakers are caught, they tame[1] one and lure it with the gazelle's head. When thoroughly entered to this lure,[2] they tie it up in a dark place till its bones get set and strong, and its marrow becomes black,[3] and the bird itself fills out and grows stout and vigorous. Twenty days before the *Naw-rūz*[4] they take it up, and every morning and every evening lure it,[5] etc., with the gazelle head. Now in the hot climate of this desert, young gazelles are born from between ten to fifteen days before the *Naw-rūz* to ten to fifteen days after it. A "train"[6] of a small fawn is given, and the hawk is then flown in the desert at young fawns, which on account of their small size[7] are easily taken, and she is so flown till the young fawns begin to go about with their dams. After the *bālābān* has taken seven or eight fawns, she will readily single out the young fawn from the dam. When in this manner she has singled out and taken seven or eight[8] fawn at foot, it is considered sufficient; the weather, too, has grown too hot to go out into the country: the hawks are therefore of necessity set down to moult.

After being taken up out of the moult, they are, next season, given two or three "trains"[9] before being flown at a large wild gazelle.

If the falconer has the patience, this last method is, for the following reasons, the best. First; the hawk, when taken out of the

---

[1] *Rām kardan*, "to tame, to man."

[2] *Ba'd az garm-i ṭalab shudan.*

[3] —*ṭā inki maghz-i ustukhwān-ash siyāh bi-shavad;* an unusual idiom.

[4] *Naw-rūz*, the Persian New Year's Day about the 21st March.

[5] "And make it play with the head:" *bāzī mī-dihand.*

[6] *Dakl.*

[7] I know of two instances in India of a saker trained to hare taking a very small fawn of a "black buck."

[8] The author (*vide* next paragraph but one) means seven or eight altogether.

[9] *Bi-qānūn-i mazkūr du si āhū barā-yash mī-kushand.*

moult, having not forgotten the six or seven fawns she killed in the Spring, will, when flown in the Autumn, single out the smallest quarry. Second; the long rest will have set and hardened her young bones so that she will not be liable to get swollen feet.[1] Third; she will have become domesticated, will have learnt wisdom, and will not be liable to get lost.

Do not be in the least afraid that your hawk, having been entered to fawns, will not tackle a horned buck[2] or a full-grown gazelle. If she is keen, you can fly her at two or three bucks that happen to be together without a female. These three bucks have not been cast in one mould: one is certain to be rather smaller than the others, and this one your hawk will single out. If you find a *single* buck, let it be even as big as the foal of an ass, she will tackle it all right. But if, one day, you fly her at an old buck, and the hounds not arriving she wears herself out and gets jostled or injured, you may rest assured that in the second moult she will not tackle an *old buck*. She will still, however, take does, or small young bucks that are only one or two years old.

A *bālābān* that has been trained by this last method is certainly better than one trained by either of the preceding methods.

CHAPTER XXXVI

TRAINING THE "*SHĀHĪN*"[3]

Now, my son, let me instruct thee in the training of the *Shāhīn* so that thy falcon may in the field excel those of other sportsmen, and thou thyself be acknowledged a master. First, thou must thyself be a *shāhīn*, and thy horse, too, must be like one.

Falconers have compared the *Shāhīn* to a rifle bullet, and what an expert marksman expects from his weapon you must expect from your falcon; she must not miss when cast at quarry within her compass.

---

[1] *Mīkhak* (*vide* chap. LVI), *i.e.*, bruised and swollen soles from stooping at the hard head of the antelope. A hawk may get swollen feet from a variety of causes.

[2] *Narra āhū-yi shākh-dār.*

[3] *Vide* note 3, page 42 regarding the confusion of the term *shāhīn*.

Now know that the nature of the *Shāhīn* somewhat resembles that of the Goshawks; it does not require many "hand-birds" and "trains."[1] Amongst falcons[2] it is the hero.

Should a young[3] *shāhīn* come into your possession, set her on a perch, and feed and fatten her[4] up till the rising of Canopus.[5] Then slightly reduce her food for a day or two, just enough to induce her to step off her perch on to your fist. About half an hour after dark, fit her with a soft part-worn hood[6] that cannot, by hurting her, make her hood-shy; for hood-shyness, in a *shāhīn*, is a vice that can, by no manner of means, be cured.[7] If the back of the hood be too tight, her ears will be hurt, and she will develop the incurable disease of "ear-ache."

Every half hour or so, unhood her near the lamp, stroke her on the head and breast, and then replace her on the perch. Then again take her up and hood her, and continue doing this for three or four hours. After that remove her hood and place her on her perch in the place that she is accustomed to sleep in every night. Early next morning take her up, hood her, and give her a small quantity of meat washed in warm water, and then set her on her perch till midday. After mid-day take her on the fist and carry her in the shade. At sun-down give her a few pigeon's or chicken's feathers washed in warm water, so that she may "cast" early and rid herself of glut and slime.[8] As soon as she has lost some flesh,

---

[1] *Dast-par va būlī.*

[2] *Siyāh-chashm*, "the black-eyed."

[3] *Shāhīn-i yūrī. Yūrī* or *yawrī*, E. Turkish, is the young of any animal; but I think only before it has begun to fend for itself.

[4] Orientals do not fly hawks at "hack." "'Hack.'—A state of liberty in which young eyesses are kept for some weeks to enable them to gain power of wing."—*Lascelles.*

[5] In Teheran about 15th September. In Baghdad about two days later.

[6] The hood used in Persia and in the regions around *Baṣrah* and *Baghdād* is quite unlike the Indian hood. It is, in fact, little else than a bag of soft leather with two straps at the back to tighten it. It is nearly the same pattern as one depicted in *Falconry in the British Isles.*

[7] *Bad-kulāh*, "hood-shy." I have *heard* of sakers being cured of "hood-shyness," but real hood-shyness is, I believe, a vice impossible to cure. Let a hawk sit barefaced during the moult for six months, and two days after she is taken up she will be as "hood-shy" as ever. A hawk is "hood-shy" that has, owing to bad handling, conceived a terror or hatred for the hood, and "bates" when it is shown to her.

[8] *Ṣafrā*, *lit.* "bile" (one of the four humours of the body).

procure a lure made of the wings of a common crane, and firmly bind a piece of meat on to it. If she jumps to this from the falconer's fist, even the length of her jesses, it is sufficient.

It is not necessary to teach the *shāhīn* or the eyess saker to recognize its name.[1] Especially is such teaching improper in the case of the passage *shāhīn ;* for if you have taught the latter to know its name like a passage saker, and should call her by it when she is hooded, she will make her carrier impotent by tearing at his glove,[2] or by "bating," or hanging head downwards with her claws

XXI

STONE-PLOVER

convulsively fixed in his glove. It is sufficient to teach the *shāhīn* to come to the luring cry of *coo coo.*[3]

Now as soon as she is thoroughly trained to the lure of crane's

[1] Hawks quickly learn to associate any particular and peculiar sound with food.

[2] *Dast-kash,* in modern Persian "a glove," is in India "an assistant falconer," or one who "strokes with the hand."

[3] Eastern falconers use the voice freely in training hawks. The luring cry throughout the East seems to be *coo coo.* The translator remembers more than one old-fashioned Panjabi falconer who prided himself on his "*coo.*"

wings, *i.e.*, as soon as she will come eagerly and unhesitatingly to it from the falconer's fist the moment that it is swung, you must, in the following manner, give her one or two live chickens on the lure. As soon as the hawk binds to the lure, insert the head and neck of the chicken through the wings of the lure, and let the hawk grasp it in her claws. Then, cut the chicken's throat and feed up the hawk. Give her several chickens in this manner, one in the morning and one in the evening. In the morning, take care that your hawk eats no feathers with her meat, but in the evening give her a "casting" of feathers. Recollect, too, that the higher the condition in which you train and enter a *shāhīn* the better.

The next step is to fly your *shāhīn* at a blue rock[1] with eyes partially "seeled" so that it can see out of the top only of the eyes. Go out into the open country; show the pigeon to the hawk and then let it fly. When the pigeon has got away a little distance, cast off your *shāhīn* so that she may take the pigeon in the air. Cut the pigeon's throat and feed up the hawk, giving her sufficient food to last her for twenty-four hours. Then carry her home, and with warm water wash away any blood stains, and also carefully cleanse her nostrils from congealed blood. Give her two or three pigeons in this manner.

You must now mark down a "little-owl"[2] somewhere in open country where there are no wells near. Unhood your hawk and walk up towards the owl. As soon as it is on the wing and your hawk shows an inclination to give chase, let her go. If she takes the owl, feed her up. If, however, the owl gets into a hole, quickly cast the lure to your hawk and let her take it: *on no account let her settle on the ground*, for settling on the ground is in a *shāhīn* an odious vice.

> If the *Shāhīn* when settled on the ground
> Be gorged with delicate and dainty fare
> 'Twere surely then beyond all reason's bound,
> To hope she'll take a quarry in the air.

---

1 *Kabūtar-i chāhī*, *lit.* "well-pigeon": blue rocks in certain districts inhabit and breed in old wells.

2 *Chughd* or *būya-qūsh*, the species already mentioned in Chapter VIII as inhabiting ruins and being useful for a preliminary flight for a *shāhīn* that is to be entered to stone-plover. Panjabi falconers call the spotted owlet (*Athene Brama*) *chughd*. This species is not uncommon in Persia, being often found in holes in garden walls. The flight is feeble and slow, and it is easily taken by any hawk. The flesh is palatable to hawks.

Hood the hawk on the lure and feed her. Now go and pull the owl out of its hiding place and put it in your falconer's bag for the evening. In the evening—provided your hawk has not been given too much food in the morning—mount your horse and go out into the open plain, to a place where there are neither holes nor wells. Unhood the *shāhīn;* let her see the owl and then let the owl fly. When it has flown about twenty yards, cast off the hawk. She is certain to take it. Kill the owl and feed up the hawk. You must now fly and kill with her two or three of these "little-owls."

XXII

HERON STRUCK DOWN BY PEREGRINE (PHOTO TAKEN JUST BEFORE THE HERON TOUCHED THE GROUND)

The next thing to do is to fly her at a stone-plover.[1] You must cast her off with her breast to the wind, and then cut off the plover so that it squats on the ground.[2] If she takes it, feed her up on other food, saving the plover alive for another day in case of

[1] *Chākhrūq*, T. Lane, in a note to Chapter xx, Vol. III, of his incomparable translation of the *Arabian Nights*, says that the stone-plover or *karawān* is a favourite cage-bird with the Turks and Egyptians.

[2] *Pas dawr-i chākhrūq bi-gīr tā bi-khwābad:* the author's meaning is not clear.

accident, for you must not let your hawk's success make you over-confident. If she fail to take it, lure her and feed her.

If you have a made hawk, it is better to unhood her at the plover first, to show the youngster the way.

Here let me give you a word of caution. Should your *shāhīn* fail to kill, on no account must you in luring her back release the bagged plover as she comes towards you: do so only twice and she will never after be really good at the lure; she will contract a habit of "waiting on" in expectation of a live bird being thrown out for her, and will ignore the dead lure; then, if you have no live bird by you with which to lure her without delay, some eagle will be attracted to the spot, and she will to a certainty be lost.

Now a properly trained *shāhīn* should be obedient to the dead lure; she should not require live "hand-birds"[1] to call her down.

To resume; you must first take two or three stone-plover with her, and then two or three hubara.[2] After that, three or four mallard,[3] then a wild goose,[4] and then two or three common heron.[5] Fly her at this quarry in the order mentioned, for a *shāhīn* improves by degrees[6] and does not require to be entered to large quarry by "hand-trains."[7] Should you, however, be in a district where all this quarry is not to be found, you must of necessity have recourse to "trains." Next fly her at a raven.[8] If she take it, give her only a little meat and save the raven alive. On the morrow fly her at this raven from a good long distance: as soon as she takes it, cut the raven's throat and let her just taste the blood, but feed her up on the flesh of a pigeon or of a chicken, for the flesh of the raven is not a suitable food for hawks.

On the following day take your hawk and go to some spot where only two or three half-tame undisturbed cranes[9] are accus-

---

1 *Dastī*, adj.

2 *Hūbara* or *āhūbara*, Per.; and *ḥubāra*, Ar.

3 *Murghābī-yi sar-sabz*, P.; *murghābī-yi shil bāsh*, P.T.; *shil*, for T. *yeshil*, "green."

4 *Qāz*.

5 *Ḥuqār* (for *'uqār*); *vide* page 136, note 1.

6 *Pilla pilla bālā mī-ravad: pilla* (m. c.) is the rung of a ladder, a step, etc.

7 *Dast-par*.

8 *Kulāgh-i quzqūn*.

9 *Du si durnā-yi nazdīk-i ārām va amīn. Durnā*, P., or *ṭurnā*, T., is the common crane; also called *kulank* or *kulang*—the "coolan" of Anglo-Indians.

XXIII

YOUNG PEREGRINE (ENGLISH BLOCK AND INDIAN HOOD)

tomed to feed. Get close up to them and cast off your hawk. If your *shāhīn* "bind" to the quarry, get in as quick as you can and secure the crane's wings;[1] cut its throat, rip open its breast, and feed your hawk.

If the *shāhīn* bind to the head of the quarry but let it go again after a slight struggle, call her to the lure and quickly feed her up on the warm flesh of a pigeon or of a chicken, and, on the morrow, she will not fail you.

If the *shāhīn* approach the crane close, but neither strike it nor stoop at it, act in the same way, *i.e.*, lure her and feed her on warm flesh; for amongst falconers it is accepted as a fact that, if a *shāhīn* chase the quarry at which she is unhooded, only for the length of her leash, and be then *quickly fed on warm palatable* flesh, she will, on the morrow, chase the same quarry for double that distance.

Fly her, I say, on the morrow, and if she again chases and again fails, lure her and feed her up on warm flesh.

If you have patience and act as directed, she is certain, at the third or fourth flight, to take the quarry.

Recollect that a *shāhīn* differs in disposition from all other hawks; in disposition it is the most noble. An eyess *charkh* on the contrary, if lured and fed after she has turned tail, will, from the ignobleness[2] of her nature, contract this habit of turning tail. Not so the *shāhīn*, for if *she* be rewarded on the lure after a chase of ten yards, she will on the second day chase for fifty yards; and will, on the third day, either take the quarry, or else make such an earnest stoop that she may be considered to have taken it.

If your *shāhīn* binds to the crane high up in the air, seizing it by the head, and then, when nearing the earth, unbinds and strikes it to the ground, you must be close up to render assistance by seizing the crane to prevent it, if not disabled, from escaping. You should, too, have with you an old made hawk, *shāhīn* or *charkh*, ready to fly at a quarry that is perhaps only partially disabled; for it is the habit of most *shāhīns* to unbind and

---

[1] The common crane has a very sharp claw, which it uses in defence. Even if the falconer make in at once, the hawk may suffer a permanent injury before he arrives to her assistance.

[2] *Dila va past-fiṭrat*, "ignoble": *dila*, apparently here the diminutive of *dil*, "of small heart."

altogether release the quarry before touching the earth.[1] A second made hawk is therefore necessary to secure the partially disabled quarry.

Should your *shāhīn* be buffeted by the crane and in consequence turn tail, you should fly her for a few days at crane just at sunset. Should this expedient fail, try the following remedy :—

Call her to the lure of crane's wings for a day or two (flying her at no quarry), and kill for her under the lure some live bird.

XXIV

INTERMEWED PEREGRINES (FROM A PHOTOGRAPH BY LIEUT.-COL. S. BIDDULPH)

After that mount your horse, go out into the open country and fly her at a raven, an hubara, or a stone-plover, or, failing these three, at a little-owl.[2] Take one of these three with her and feed her on the warm flesh. Next evening fly her at a crane and she

[1] "Haggards" will often unbind to avoid the concussion on striking the ground and then rebind. The translator had a haggard saker trained to kite, which never failed to unbind; he cannot, however, recollect a case of a young passage hawk, peregrine or saker, unbinding either from heron or kite. The Persian author is here writing either of the eyess or of the young *shāhīn*, captured some time before September.

[2] *Chughd* or *bāya-qūsh*.

will not fail you, but will return to her former excellence. For a *shāhīn* that has been buffeted by a crane and therefore turns tail, there is no medicine like a flight at a raven or a stone-plover. Don't, my son, think that you will remake her by flying her at a heron; for on the contrary, you will, by so doing, mar her for crane. Often have I seen a crane-hawk so spoilt.

You may argue that a heron closely resembles a crane in colour and in shape, while a raven does not. Quite so—but a heron is, compared to a crane, a small and feeble[1] quarry, one that your hawk will easily take.[2] Flown at a heron she will say to herself, "Hallo! there are two kinds of crane, one suitable and the other unsuitable; the former is the game for me; no more of the latter." The raven and the stone-plover, however, have no resemblance to the crane; a successful flight at either, duly rewarded by warm flesh, strengthens a *shāhīn's* courage.

> If your *shāhīn* that slays the long-legged crane,
> Fly at her prey, and haply fly in vain,
> An your heart wish her to resume the chase,
> On raven or stone-plover try her pace.
> Then, when at length at crane she may be cast,
> You'll find this flight will far surpass the last.
> But let her kill a heron—then goodbye!
> For naught but easy quarry will she try:
> She'll say, "No strong tenacious crane for me!
> So long as easy crane like *this* I see."

Another remedy for a crane hawk that has turned tail is to fly her several times with[3] a made hawk, giving the latter a goodish start. When the "cast" has taken one or two cranes in this

---

[1] *Bī-jān-tar va kūchak-tar va maflūk-tar.*

[2] In Europe the heron was justly considered a difficult quarry. Its powers of flight, however, have been greatly over-rated. A heron, even "on the passage,"* is an easy *flight* to a good passage hawk. But hawks, at any rate after the first flight or two, fly at this quarry with great deliberation, and stoop at it with some caution, for the heron when high up makes half-hearted dabs with its beak at the hawk. An experienced hawk generally knocks about the heron by stooping several times at the shoulder or point of the wing. I have known a "haggard" break the heron's wing by a stoop. Some hawks bind to the heron's feet sticking out behind, and so drag it down close to earth, out of range of its beak; they then close, on the ground.

[3] *Bā-ham janāḥ andākhtan.*

* "On the passage," *i.e.*, on its regular flight to or from its feeding ground.

manner, reverse the process, that is, cast off, first the hawk that turned tail and then a little later the made hawk.

A *shāhīn* differs from other falcons.[1] Don't fancy you can give her ten flights in a day without spoiling her. If you work her like this, she will become stale and will be spoilt. One to three flights with a *shāhīn* are permissible; more are unlawful.[2]

GOOD HAWKING DISTRICTS.—Possibly you are wondering to yourself what district will produce for your *shāhīn* all this varied quarry. Let me tell you that there is first *Sulaymāniyah* in *Kurdistān*;[3] next, the province of *Baghdād*, which has within a radius of two or three *farsakh* all the quarry you want; and lastly, the district of *Shīrāz*. These are the only three places I have ever come across in my life where all quarry suitable for a *shāhīn* is to be found.[4]

"WAITING ON."—For "waiting-on" flights, the peregrine[5] or the passage shahin[6] is better than the eyess shahin.[7] If you train your *shāhīn*[8] to "wait on" she will never take large quarry such as wild goose, common crane, ruddy shieldrake, common heron, etc.; but she will, however, show you excellent sport with small quarry. The beauty of the *shāhīn* lies in this, that when you gallop on to large quarry, unhooding her at it, she is off your fist like a bullet, to seize it. That his hawk should take unusual quarry that she does not kill in her wild state is the pride of a falconer, and it is in this he exhibits his skill. Pigeons, plover, duck and so on are, in a hawk's wild state, her natural prey; these she takes without the falconer's teaching.

---

[1] *Siyāh-chashm*, "black-eyed."

[2] *Ḥarām*, "prohibited; that which is unlawful."

[3] *Kurdistān*, in Turkey in Asia, N.E. of Mesopotamia.

[4] The black ibis, a favourite quarry in India for the peregrine, is not found in Persia, Baghdad, etc. Gulls are found in the vicinity of Shiraz, notably in the open ground round the "*Takht-i Jamshīd*" or Persepolis.

[5] *Baḥrī*.

[6] *Shāhīn-i ṭūrī*, *lit.* a netted shahin: *ṭūrī* for *tūrī*.

[7] *Shāhīn-i āshiyānī*.

[8] By "*shāhīn*" here the author presumably refers to the eyess.

CHAPTER XXXVII

TRAINING THE PASSAGE SAKER TO COMMON HERON[1]

To train the *bālābān* to heron, she must first be trained, as already described, to a lure[2] made of the wings of a common crane.

When she knows the lure well, get a live chicken and tie it by the leg to the lure, with a string about twenty inches long. Lure the hawk from a long distance, casting into the air, two or three times, the lure garnished with the chicken, so that the hawk may come with force and eagerness and seize the chicken. Cut the chicken's throat and feed up the hawk. Let her kill two or three fowls in this manner, so that she may come with eagerness to the lure.

Now go out into the open country and find a night-heron,[3] get close to it and cast off your hawk at it. * * *.[4]

If you find a night-heron on the edge of a small stream, cast off your hawk, and should she take it, feed her up.[5] If, however, she will not fly it, you must take one with a shahin or with a goshawk and in the morning give it to her alive as a flying train: if she will not take it, bind a little meat on its back. Fly her at this same "train" again in the evening. When she will readily take the "train," you must fly her at one or two wild night-herons and at one or two purple herons. * * *.[6]

---

[1] *Ḥuqār*, corrup. of the Arabic *ʿuqār*, which is possibly also the name of the white egret. In some parts of Persia and in the Kapurthala State in the Panjab, the common heron is called *būtīmār*. Sakers are not as easily entered to heron as they are to hubara or to hare.

[2] *Ṭabla*, P., "a lure": in India *dalba*, corrup. of *ṭalba*. In Basra and Baghdad the lure is called *baftara*, but in Kwet and Bahrain Island *milwā,iḥ*, root unknown.

[3] *Vāq*, "night-heron"; in some parts of the Panjab *wāqwāq*; in the Kapurthala State *awānk*.

[4] A short description by the Author, of the night-heron, being unnecessary, is here omitted.

[5] Sakers as a rule do not fly this quarry unless entered by trains. The flesh of the night heron is not injurious to sakers, *vide* page 137, note 6.

[6] *Jarda*, evidently the purple heron. A few lines describing this species are omitted. The purple heron on the wing looks nearly as large as the common heron. It is, however, a feeble quarry; it is very slow in flight and is unable to shift from a stoop. The flesh is not as coarse or fishy as that of the common heron.

Now procure a bagged common heron[1] and on its broad *yār mālīq*[2] feathers tie a piece of meat *very firmly* so that there is no possible chance of your hawk being able to disengage it and go off with it. Hold the heron by one wing, and get your assistant to stand some distance off with the hawk. When the *bālābān* binds to the meat, let her pull and eat a little: then remove her. You must now seel the heron's eyes so that it may not suddenly ring up[3]—better still, bind two or three of its flight-feathers together so that it may run on the ground and extend its wings.[4] As soon as the hawk takes the train feed her up.

On the morrow, again tie meat on to the heron's back, but unbind the flight-feathers so that it may fly well. Release the heron, and when it has flown ten or twelve paces unhood and cast off your hawk. As soon as she takes it, give her only a little meat and fly her again in the evening in the same way. Do this for several days, gradually reducing the quantity of meat on the heron's back.[5] As soon as your hawk flies the heron in style, seizing it by the neck without regarding the meat, cut the heron's throat and feed her up.[6] Next day procure a fresh heron but tie no meat on its back. Let it fly, and when it has flown a good distance unhood and

---

[1] A saker that kills purple heron will kill common heron. In any case a saker that has killed night-heron will take a *train* of the common heron without the back being garnished with meat.

[2] *Vide* note 1, page 112.

[3] It is very rarely indeed that a bagged heron will attempt to ring up. If once taken by a hawk, it will generally, when the hawk gets close to it, drop to the ground.

[4] It is always advisable to give "trains" flying, especially to sakers. Sakers do not, however, require flying trains of hubara.

[5] It is not necessary to tie meat on the heron's back even for a saker, and most certainly not necessary when the hawk has already been flown at purple herons or night-herons. However, sakers are not spoilt by being given many trains as are peregrines: they do not easily become what Indians call *bā,ūlī-band* or "train-bound." No matter how or where a train is given, hawks at once recognize that it is not an ordinary wild bird.

[6] A saker (unlike a peregrine) should not get a full feed of heron's flesh, nor, generally speaking, of any water-bird's flesh. Some sakers after a full meal of duck or heron will cast their gorge, sicken, and die. For some reason the flesh of the night-heron and of the purple heron is not injurious—at least I have never lost a saker by feeding one on the flesh of these birds. When entering a hawk to a difficult quarry, it is always advisable to kill at least one "train" under her, and to let her plume the feathers a *little* and eat some of the flesh: pigeons' flesh may then be substituted. *Vide* page 188, note 5.

cast off your hawk. When she takes the heron, feed her up. Withdraw the dead heron from her grasp and cast it to a distance of ten or twelve yards that she may know that that is her dead quarry;[1] then let her go and settle on it and take two or three beakfuls. Again withdraw and cast the dead heron to a little distance, but do not let the hawk go: let her "bate" towards it once or twice and then hood her. Wash off any blood spots and clean the "nares".[2]

Now procure another heron, one strong of flight, that will ring up. Get an assistant to mount some high place—a place about a hundred ell high[3]—and release the heron. You must be mounted, and, hawk on fist, take stand below this spot. Remove the hood of the hawk and let her discover the heron above her. She will have to exert herself to get above it, and if, after getting above it, she makes two or three stoops at it[4] before binding, what better? Feed her up.

Next day, go and find a wild heron in an easy and suitable spot, but have with you as a "make-hawk"[5] a *bālābān* that is fully trained to this flight. First cast off your young hawk. She will, of course, make four or five stoops at the heron, but should the heron commence to "ring" and the hawk show signs of slackening, then at once cast off the "make-hawk," so that the jealousy of the young hawk may be excited and they may together take the quarry. Feed up the young hawk *well*, so that you may give her washed meat[6] the day following.

As long as your hawk, while ringing up with the heron, keeps beating[7] her wings quickly, it is a sign that she is trying to get

---

[1] Indian falconers also do this.

[2] "Nares," a hawk's nostrils.

[3] An exaggeration: an ell is 40 inches.

[4] *Sar zadan*, "to stoop"; in some districts *lagad zadan*, *lit.* "to kick." It is very seldom that an experienced hawk will bind to a wild heron at the first stoop. Herons in the air try to use their beaks, and hawks prefer to knock about a heron first, by striking it on the point of the shoulder, and then to seize an opportunity for closing. Once, after binding to a heron in the air, as both birds were falling, the heron seized a hawk of the translator's by the wing and made it scream.

[5] *Bālābān-i ustād*, "make-hawk," *i.e.*, an old experienced hawk to lead and "make" the youngster.

[6] *Ishtihā dādan*, *lit.* "to give an appetite to"; by this expression the author always means washed meat.

[7] *Bāl-ash rā bar ham mī-zanad*, "to beat the wings."

above it; but the moment she ceases to beat, and begins to sail,[1] she has given up. In this case, at once call her down to the lure of crane's wings, and as soon as she comes reward her by killing, under the lure, either a chicken or a pigeon, feeding her up well; for in the opinion of falconers this dropping from a height to the lure is better than taking ten herons: she is now your property; up till now she has been merely a loan.

Next day[2] go and find a heron in an easy place, and first cast off your young hawk at it. As soon as she has made one or two stoops, cast off the "make-hawk" (before the heron commences to ring) so that they may stoop at it alternately and the two may take it together.

On the following day feed her lightly;[3] and on the day following that, again fly her at a heron. If she is in her proper condition[4] and not too fat, and is also hungry, it is impossible for her to fail, even if the heron ring up into the Seventh Heaven[5] —unless, of course, an eagle interferes or the heron drops into a broad stream that can~~not~~ be crossed. Should either of these mishaps occur, lure her without delay, ~~and feed her~~ *well.* In the latter case, you may consider she has taken this heron: it is as though she had done so. On the morrow, please God, she will not fail.

If your hawk has had a hard flight after a heron, she should be fed up on it, and not flown a second time that day. If, however, she kills very quickly and without exertion, there is no harm in giving her a second flight.

If you want your saker to fly heron well, you should keep her for this flight alone and not fly her at anything else.

A young passage saker in the first or immature plumage,[6] is far better for this flight that the "intermewed" hawk,[7] for, after the moult, a hawk becomes heavy, and cannot ring up after a

[1] *Bāl-ash rā dar havā nigāh mī-dārad,* "to sail."

[2] The author must mean the third day, as he has said above that the hawk is to be given washed meat on the day following. *Vide* note 6, page 138.

[3] *Gurisna-ash bi-kun, lit.* "make her hungry."

[4] *Agar bi-gūsht-i khud-ash ast.*

[5] The Seventh Heaven, which is Abraham's, is the highest: it is under the Throne of God.

[6] *Bālābān-i buzyūrī* = *chūz* of India.

[7] *Ṯūlakī,* "moulted": *ṯūlak subs.,* "moult."

heron. For one or two moults a hawk will indeed kill heron in a sort of fashion,[1] but after three or four moults she is useless for this flight;[2] you must procure a young *bālābān*[3] for it.

CHAPTER XXXVIII

TRAINING THE PASSAGE SAKER TO COMMON CRANE

You must know that it is the pride and glory of a falconer that his *bālābān* should take common crane with dash and resolution, *i.e.*, that she should stoop quickly and bind soon, not letting the crane get away any distance; then your mounted friends can watch the sport closely, and applaud the exploits of both falcon and falconer.

There are, in hawking, only two forms of the sport that can be shared by a crowd; firstly, crane-hawking with the *bālābān*, and secondly, heron-hawking with the *bālābān*: hundreds of sportsmen can together witness and enjoy these two flights. In all other flights, whether with long-winged or short-winged hawks,[4] the smaller the party the better.

Though training a *bālābān* to common heron is more tedious and troublesome than training it to any other quarry,[5] still the trouble is repaid.

Now if you want to indulge in the sport properly, you must have with you five or six active mounted men, two or three trained and keen *bālābāns*, two or three keen *shāhīns* and two *charkhs* trained to eagle; for hawk makes hawk: if you want a "make-hawk" it is there, and if you want a live train it is there, or if you want a dead crane it is there. If you have not all this equipment

---

[1] *Bi-murdan murdan kār-ī mī-kunad.*

[2] There is no reason why she should be useless. I have had an intermewed saker of twelve or more moults that was still a first-class hubara hawk, and intermewed peregrines of ten moults that seldom failed to kill either heron or hubara.

[3] *Bālābān-i farkh*: *farkh*, pl. *afrākh*, A., often means a nestling, but also, as here, (a hawk) in the immature plumage.

[4] *Lit.* "black-eyed or yellow-eyed"; *siyāh-chashm* and *zard-chashm*.

[5] In India the common kite is considered the most difficult quarry of all for the saker: only the saker is flown at it. The kite is very rare in Persia, except near Bushire.

yourself, you must join forces with some sporting friend or friends, otherwise it will not be possible for you to train your hawk to eagles.

Before entering your passage saker to common crane, you must train her and fly her at common heron as already described. On most days, too, when other hawks take crane, you must give her one, in her feet,[1] to make her keen and plucky.

From the beginning of Autumn to the beginning of Spring, the immature passage saker[2] is what the Arabs call "ignorant,"[3] *i.e.*, it is "mad": it will take a train[4] of anything that is given it, except an eagle;—for in its wild state it has experienced the tyranny of the eagle and has learnt its might.

Well, from the beginning of Autumn till ten days before the *Naw-rūz* Festival, you must fly your "ignoramus" at common heron. You must then get a live uninjured crane with unshortened wings,[5] and tying meat on its back make it run and flap its wings, and then fly your hawk at it. If she seizes the crane by the head, it is a sign that she has a big heart and is well-plucked, but if she binds to the meat she is only middling. In either case, fly her thus, once in the morning, and once in the evening.

The next day show her the crane and let it fly a little,[6] and then fly your hawk at it: do this twice as on the previous day.

---

[1] *Bāsh-qanāt dādan: bāsh*, T., "head," and *qanat*, T., "wing." This consists in holding a live bagged bird in the hand and getting the hawk to "bind" to it from the distance of a foot or so, or getting the hooded hawk to bind to it and then unhooding her: the hawk is of course rewarded either by a pigeon's wing stealthily inserted under the train's wing, or the train is killed and the hawk allowed to eat a little.

[2] *Bālābān-i buzyūr.*

[3] *Majhūl.*

[4] *Dakl u būlī.* In a note the author says *dakl* means *dast-par*, but as he elsewhere, page 123, note 1, uses *dakl* for "train" of a deer, this rendering appears inaccurate.

[5] The crane should not be dishevelled. In any case hawks quickly recognize a "train." I had a young peregrine that, on taking its first wild heron, was badly injured by another hawk, and in consequence refused even to look at a wild heron. It would, however, always take bagged heron released in the jungle before the hood was removed. It also took a bagged common crane.

[6] Probably one or two flight-feathers would have to be tied together to impede its flight. The common crane has a sharp and powerful claw that it can use with effect after the hawk binds. This should be blunted. A hawk of the translator's once had its wing ripped up by a common crane.

On the third day, if the crane will fly, well and good; but if not, it must be cast off a mound or from some high place—the meat as before being bound on its back—so that the hawk may bind to it in the air, and both birds come to the ground together. If you find that she binds to the crane's head and pays no attention to the meat, you should, if possible, cut the crane's throat, and feed up your "ignoramus"—it being of course understood that you have plenty of bagged cranes or the means of obtaining them. If, however, you have but this one "train," you must stealthily introduce under the crane's wing a blue-rock or any pigeon coloured like the crane, and feed the hawk on it; or else introduce a chicken under the wing, and putting its head into the hawk's foot, so cut the throat that the hawk may not hear the chicken's cries.

On the following day fly the hawk at the crane from a longer distance.

Now when you see that your hawk thoroughly recognizes a crane, and will resolutely fly at any train first shown to it and then released from the hand, you must proceed as follows:—

Get a crane, and as before tie meat on to its back. Cut its sharp front claw—a claw as sharp and deadly as a hawk's—and insert a string through the nostrils; then bind the two mandibles together, so that the crane may in no way frighten or injure the hawk, neither with its feet nor with its beak. Now seel the eyes and drive it off ten or twenty yards, and fly your hawk at it while it is on the move. Continue this practice, increasing the distance, but lessening the meat till no meat remains, and until your hawk, rising from your fist without hesitation, will make straight for the crane, and after one or two stoops bind to its head.

On the morrow, if you have a fresh crane that will fly, you should unhood the hawk and fly her at that, after it is put on the wing; but, if the crane will not fly, you must get an assistant to carry it to a distance and there release it. He must then either lie flat on the ground, or conceal himself behind some cover, so that he may be near to render speedy assistance to the hawk by seizing the crane's legs as soon as the hawk binds to its head.

For a few days, too, you should release two cranes and three cranes in company, so that your hawk may single out one.

If, in the district where you are, there are still cranes to be found, *i.e.*, if they have not yet migrated out of the country, go out into the open country and take with you a made-hawk too, and somehow or other with the latter take a crane. Then, as soon as possible, let this freshly caught crane fly, and when it has flown about a hundred yards, unhood and cast off your young hawk. She is sure to take the crane. Cut the crane's throat, and feed up the hawk, giving her the heart; give her, too, some of the small neck feathers as a "casting."

Next take your hawk out into the country, and if you happen to find a solitary crane put your trust in God and fly her at it. If, however, you find a flock of ten or twenty, on no account fly her; do not even *think* of doing so. If you fail to find a solitary crane, you must with your made hawks take a crane, and at once give it to your young hawk as a flying "train"—as you did yesterday.

On the next day, again go out hawking, and if you find a solitary crane, fly her at it. Have by you a "make-hawk," but if your falconer's knowledge tells you that your young hawk is master of the situation, do nothing: if, however, you see that the young hawk is not flying with resolution, then without loss of time cast off the "make-hawk" to her assistance. When the crane is taken, feed up the young hawk on it.

If during this Spring she takes one or two cranes, return thanks to God, and fly her at nothing else; set her down in the "mew"[1] to moult[2] and act as will be explained later. Leave her in the "mew" till all your hawks are moulted. When she comes out of the moult, you must treat her again exactly as you did when she was "ignorant."[3] As soon as you have re-made her to the lure, go and fly her at a common heron. If she takes it, nothing can be better: feed her up. If she has no inclination for it, or if she does not work well, give her a good active heron as a "train," releasing it at a distance. If to-day she takes the "train," to-morrow she will take a wild heron. After she has taken one or two common herons, you must turn your attention to cranes.

Take a crane with your old "make-hawk," show it to her and let it fly, and then feed her up on it. Next, give her two more

---

[1] *Ṯūlak-k͟hāna.* [2] *Bi-ṯūlak bastan.* [3] *Vide* page 141.

"trains" of common crane released secretly: these should have meat tied on their backs. As soon as she takes the "train" feed her up.

Now go out and find a half-tame[1] crane; stalk it, and get as close as possible to it; then, placing your reliance on God, fly your young hawk at it. The nearer you get to the crane the better. As soon as your young hawk has got a short distance, cast off an old "make-hawk" to her assistance. The first hawk will make a stoop or two; the "make-hawk" will then arrive, and will keep the crane engaged and overpowered till your mounted assistant, arriving in all haste, secures it and prevents it doing an injury to the hawk. Feed up your young hawk on the crane. She is now well on the road to being quite made.

Should this tame crane take wing when you get close to it, on no account be tempted to fly your hawk at it, for the crane may get away a long distance before your hawk binds to it; and a second crane then joining in the fray to assist its fellow, both birds may so buffet and injure your hawk that she will be useless for further sport, or else so frighten her that she will ignore the lure and be lost. In either case the labour of two years will be lost.

Hawks,[2] whether long-winged or short-winged, are of two kinds; those that the falconer must assist, and those that assist the falconer. A hawk that is mettled, high-spirited, and valiant, if given but one "train," is made: such a hawk gives assistance *to* the falconer. Another requires ten "trains" and bagged birds; such a hawk demands assistance *from* the falconer.

Well, for five or six days you must fly your hawk secretly[3] as described above.

Now listen attentively to what I am going to say. When you

---

[1] *Amīn*, "tame, quiet," probably means one that by feeding in crops near a village has come to disregard the presence of men. From what he says later, the author apparently intends the crane to be taken on the ground while feeding. The hawk will recognize that it was not a bagged one.

[2] *Ṭuyūr-i shikārī.*

[3] *Salaf* a word explained by the author in a marginal note to mean *bi-duzda*, "secretly." Apparently by this term the author means that a solitary half-tame crane must be stalked when feeding and the hawk allowed to bind to it on the ground.

are stalking this solitary half-tame crane—or it may be two cranes—should they become alert and seem ready to take wing, hood your hawk and move off to a little distance that they may settle down and again busy themselves with grazing. Should they take wing and settle again, follow them up, or else find others, one, or two, or three—not more. As soon as they settle down to their walking about and picking up grain, unhood your hawk even though the distance be somewhat more, and when your hawk sights the crane, place your trust in God and cast her off. You must judge the distance, and when your hawk is twenty or thirty yards from the crane, you and all your mounted men[1] must suddenly burst into a gallop, *i.e.*, you must so time matters that just as the crane is forced to take wing the hawk reaches it. At the first stoop all three cranes are sure to fall and sit on the ground. You and your falconers will then reach them and they will again rise. Your hawk, however, will be in the air and will command all three. If you see that your hawk is slack, then without hesitation cast off an old "make-hawk" to her assistance.

Whate'er the aim I have in view,
Whate'er the deed I try to do,
Success, I'm certain, will be mine
With Thee to help me, Lord Divine!

Whether the young hawk takes the crane herself, or whether after a few stoops the make-hawk arrives and first binds to the crane, matters not in the least.

On no account must you this season, *i.e.*, up to Spring, fly your hawk at a large flock of crane, for the combination of cranes is like that of no other living thing, and your hawk is only in her second year.

In the opinion of the author, a young falcon in the first year is better than an "intermewed" one of one moult,[2] for the young hawk[3] is "ignorant" and "mad"; it will obey any order that is given her and will fly any "train" that is shown to her. After one moult, however, she has learnt a few falconer's stratagems and

---

[1] The whole party would probably be mounted: a dismounted falconer would be the exception.

[2] *Buzyār-ī bihtar az farkh-i ṭūlak ast.*

[3] *Farkh.*

is not easily deluded: if she has not yet learnt *all* there is to know, she will have done so by the time she is past her second moult.[1]

Now if you fly your valuable passage hawk (of one moult) at a large flock of crane, say a flock consisting of thirty or forty, more or less, she, being plucky and keen on this quarry, will single out and "bind" to one. If you and your mounted companions are up in time, all is well; but if not, the flock will so buffet and bang the hawk that she may be completely cowed. If by nature high-spirited, she will become cunning;[2] if not naturally plucky she will be spoilt beyond re-making. If such an accident does happen, and your hawk suffers, the remedy is to fly her, ten or fifteen times, with a good make-hawk, and then, somehow or other, to manage to take with her alone in the Spring two or three more cranes. However, there is a great risk in flying a passage saker in the Spring[3] whether she be a young hawk or whether an "intermewed"[4] one of one moult; therefore be content with taking only two or three cranes. If one day your passage falcon works hard in the heat[5] and fails to kill, you will hardly succeed in recovering her: she will depart. For this reason you must not be impatient but be satisfied with only two or three cranes. When your hawk has so killed, feed her up well, place your trust in God, and set her down to moult. After the second moult she is your obedient bond-slave, and she has learnt, too, all there is to know of her business.

When you take her out of this second moult, you must, by some means or other, manage to take with her, first a common heron. Next you must, with an old hawk, take a common crane, and on the spot give it as a "train," flying the hawk at it in such a way that she thinks it is a wild one. Now, in this third season, your hawk is thoroughly and completely trained.

---

[1] The author's meaning is not at all clear. He appears to contradict himself. There is probably a copyist's error somewhere.

[2] *Duzd*, *lit.* "thief."

[3] Sakers leave India in February, *i.e.*, much earlier than Peregrines, and the migrating instinct seems to be more powerful. When the Spring stirs in their blood and the migration restlessness is on them, they will sometimes when unhooded look up skywards, and call. One sign of their becoming *mast* is bobbing before rousing. Possibly, too, sakers nest earlier than other falcons.

[4] "Intermewed," *i.e.*, moulted in captivity.

[5] That is the heat of Spring.

To guard against accidents,[1] you should every year keep a good young passage-saker and train her to the flight of the common heron, so that should any accident happen to one of your crane-hawks, you will have by you a youngster all ready for being entered to crane. If you omit to take this precaution, you will some year lose a whole season's sport. Your "mews" should contain hawks trained to various quarry, whether your hawks are sakers or *shāhīns*.

As soon as your passage saker singles out and binds to one crane, out of a flock of say thirty or forty, all its companions will attack her and release their comrade. If the hawk knows her business, she will at once release the crane, and waiting on above the flock will not lose sight of the particular crane to which she bound[2] until you arrive on the spot and again put up the cranes. She will then again stoop at her selected quarry, when again all the cranes will attack her and release the captured bird. You must all gallop as hard as you can; neither pit, nor well, nor stream must hinder you. You must not draw rein till you are right in the midst of the fray, when every sportsman should unhood and cast off his saker or peregrine at the quarry that is nearest to him. I myself have often, out of a flock of five, taken four; often, too, have we knocked over birds with sticks and clubs. As for shooting them, that is quite easy.

There is no bird to equal the common crane in valour and a fine sense of honour; when your *bālābān* takes one, if there are a hundred others in the air, they will one and all drop from the sky like a stooping *shāhīn*, attack your hawk, and perhaps kill her: till they release their captured comrade they will not again take the air. This is how it is that five, or six, or seven, cranes out of a "herd" can be secured or killed. Ah! had a sovereign but five thousand cavalry possessed of the valour and resolution of the cammon crane, he could conquer the world. Well, as I said, you and your men must gallop hard, not funking wells, and streams, and holes.

[1] *Baray-i yadagī u iḥtiyāṭ.*

[2] A good saker flown at kite in cantonments will single out and stick to one bird, even when the air is black with kites. Indian falconers generally select a young female kite at which to unhood the hawk. Whether, if the hawk were unhooded at an old bird, she would not be tempted to abandon it for the feebler flight of a young one, is a question.

You must know that there is no sport more difficult than that of the saker and crane, but there is also none better; none, except that of the lion with a buffalo, and the cheetah with a gazelle.[1] I have hunted many a lion and seen trouble therefrom, for the sport is inauspicious; for the lion is the King of Beasts, and His Highness the Commander of the Faithful[2] (on whom be peace) is styled the Lion of God. Hence the sport of the lion is baleful, and he that follows it will certainly see no good; still it's a fine sport; I have tried it—but my advice to you is on no account to do so, else you will regret it, for no benefit accrues therefrom.

CHAPTER XXXIX

ON MANAGEMENT DURING THE MOULT

Now let me say a few words concerning the management of hawks in the moult. The more hawks of any kind are flown at quarry and the better they are protected from the severity of heat and cold, the better and quicker will they moult. Hawks moult cleaner and quicker in the hot regions of Persia than in the cold.[3] Further you must pay the greatest attention to the flesh you give them, not feeding them on one kind of meat only, for if you do, they will certainly fall sick.

Now if you wish to moult your hawks in a hot region, such as Baghdad, you must construct out of split-cane a "mew" of a size proportionate to the number of your hawks, building it on the river bank where the *Shimāl*[4] wind can constantly be felt. In front of this house or room, enclose an open space with a wall.[5] Inside

[1] It is not clear what the author means by "lion with a buffalo." The hunting leopard is trained in other countries besides India to take antelope and gazelle.

[2] By this title the *Shi'ahs* refer to *'Alī*. The writer was undoubtedly a *Shi'ah*. The *Sunnis* of the present day, but not the *Shi'ahs*, style the Sultan of Turkey "Commander of the Faithful."

[3] *Garm-sīr va sard-sīr*, "hot regions and cold." *Tabrīz*, *Ṭihrān* and parts of *Iṣfahān* are *sard-sīr*. The city of *Iṣfahān* and of *Shīrāz* are "middling."

[4] *Shimāl*, "North," is the name given to the prevalent wind in Baghdad and in the Persian Gulf.

[5] The wall would naturally be of mud or of sun-dried bricks and would cost little.

the room, construct at a distance of forty inches from the wall, as many hollow mud platforms as you have hawks.[1] Fill in the top of the platforms with sand and fine gravel, and spread the floor of the room also to the depth of a span with sand and gravel. On the platforms intended for short-winged hawks, spread leaves of willow, or wild mint, fresh and green, or any other kind of greenery, so that the hawks may lie down and rest on it. Next, in front of each platform, construct in the ground a small bathing tank lined with red clay. Every morning early, you must sprinkle the inside of the mew with water, and every evening as soon as the sun has set, you must take out your hawks, short-winged and long-winged, and "weather"[2] them in the open-air enclosure that is in front of their room. In the outside enclosure, too, there must be, dug out of the ground, small tanks, which should be lined with clay. Doubtless you are saying to yourself, "Why can't I substitute a copper or an earthen basin?" Now, were you to substitute a copper or an earthen basin, there would be a danger that while splashing about in the water, the moulting hawk might strike the half-grown wing- or tail-quills that are full of blood against the hard substance of the basin, and that the injury might cause the blood to dry up in the quills, which would thereby become "strangled," and would eventually drop out. Now with a tank of beaten clay and sand there is no such danger. In short, every hawk in this outside enclosure also, must have its own bathing-pool.

"RANGLE."—In front of each long-winged hawk there should be a handful of pebbles ranging from a size smaller than a pea to a size larger than a bean; for it is the habit of all falcons[3] in the mew to swallow small stones on most afternoons before they are fed, and to cast them up again with a great deal of "bile."[4] Should a hawk have stones in her stomach when you feed her, she will

---

[1] *Sakū* is a "wooden bench, a garden seat"; or as here a "mud platform."

The author has not expressed himself at all clearly or else there are omissions in the text. The passage might mean that the platforms should be forty inches apart or be forty inches high.

[2] "Weathering" is placing hawks, usually unhooded, in the open air on blocks. Eastern falconers do not "weather" their hawks, as during the hawking season the hawks are on their fists in the open air many hours.

[3] I have never seen a saker eat stones.

[4] *Ṣafrā*, "yellow bile," one of the four humours of the body.

retain the meat in her feet and wait a little till she has cast up the stones. Not till then will she feed.

SHORT-WINGED HAWKS DO NOT EAT "RANGLE."—Goshawks and other short-winged hawks do not eat stones in the moult.

During the moult you must feed your hawk twice a day, once in the morning and once in the evening, letting her eat as much as she pleases, so that she be gorged.[1]

If the "mew" be in a "cool-region," every short-winged hawk, from a common sparrow-hawk to a white goshawk, should have a room to itself, proportionate to its size. A few air-holes should be made on the north side. In this room, two or three perches of varying thickness should be erected, and the perches themselves should *not* be turned to a uniform thickness, so that the hawk may have a choice and select a perch that suits its fancy at the time. A roomy bathing-pool must also be constructed in the ground. Next, place in the room a piece of matting [made of split cane] to the centre of which a cord is attached. At first you must feed the hawk twice a day, till she is fat. As soon as she is fat, the amount of her food must be a fixed quantity, and this should be bound on to the centre of the matting and left, so that she may feed when she feels inclined.

It is not advisable to keep falcons loose like this in a room; in fact, it is injurious to do so.[2]

---

[1] In the plains of India, hawks during the moult should not be so gorged, at least not during the four or five months of hot weather. Hawks that are kept too fat will not moult properly. Further they should be fed only once in the day, and that in the morning. If gorged in the evening, their rest is affected, and they do not get the benefit of the slight coolness of the night.

[2] I one year, in Kohat, India, tried moulting a young (*chūz*) peregrine in a large outhouse, high and roomy. The hawk did not moult at all, and frequently got so fat and heavy that she was unable to fly up to her perch until her food was reduced for a day or two. However, falconers in England recommend keeping a moulting hawk loose in a loft.

CHAPTER XL

REMEDIES FOR SLOW MOULTING

MOULTING hawks are of two kinds; the one "generous," the other "miserly." The "generous" are those that moult quickly; the "miserly" those that positively refuse to part with their feathers. Should you happen to have a hawk of the latter description and wish to make it moult quickly, then :—

Receipt: procure a snake; hold its head and tail together in one hand, and then chop off, with one blow, about four fingers' breadth of its extremities; skin it, and give your hawk a little of its flesh.[1] *Item*: feed your hawk a few days on the flesh of the hoopoe.[2] *Item*: give your hawk daily, concealed in a thin slice of meat, one ant-lion with three of the saliva-glands of sheep.[3] *Item*: dry and grind up some hornets,[4] and for three alternate days sprinkle this powder on your hawk's meat. *Item*: reduce your hawk's food for three or four days, so that she may lose a little flesh. Grind[5] up the skin of a snake, and twice a day give some of this to her with her meat. She will quickly cast her feathers.[6] *Item*: dry, in the shade, several saliva-glands taken from the necks of sheep. Grind one before feeding and mix it with her meat. She will soon cast her feathers. *Item*: during the space of six days, feed her thrice on the flesh of a nine- or ten-day-old puppy. She will quickly cast and renew her feathers. This receipt is

---

1 "Now I ſhall tell yow verray true medeeynes for to mewe an hawke haſtyly that ye ſhall beleue for trowthe and ye Will assay them. Ther be in Woddys or in hedgis Wormys calde edders that ben Redde of nature. and he is calde vepa. and also ther be ſnakys of the ſame kynde. and they be verri bitter. Take ii or iii of them and ſmyte of their hedes and thendys of theyr taylis. Then take a new erthen pot: that Was neuer used. and cut hem ito ſmall gobettys * * *."—*Boke of St. Albans.*

2 *Hudhud*, the "Bird of Solomon" is the hoopoe, and not the lapwing as supposed by some translators of the Quran.

3 *Ghadūd* or *qadūd*; found in the neck of animals.

4 According to the old-fashioned theory of medicine, derived from the Greeks, hornets are "hot." In India wasp-grubs are cooked in butter with spices, and the butter is then spread on the meat.

5 *i.e.*, grind by rubbing on a stone as Indians do curry spices.

6 During the Indian hot weather, a fat hawk will sometimes start moulting, if merely reduced in condition.

specially beneficial in the case of long-winged hawks, particularly so in the case of the peregrine, which moults better than any other kind of hawk, for it moults quite two months earlier than other hawks.[1]

CHAPTER XLI

ON FEEDING ON JERBOAS DURING THE MOULT

You must know that during the moult there is no food so good, for both short-winged and long-winged hawks, as the flesh of the two-legged rat, called by the Arabs *jarbū'*[2] (jerboa). In the absence of these rats you must catch house-mice.[3]

Let your hawk eat her fill of the antelope-rat,
For where is the food that is better than that?

The flesh is particularly good about two or three months before Autumn,[4] that is, when your hawks are half-moulted, having three to four flight-feathers of each wing uncast. At this season the jerboa is very fat, and hawks find its flesh palatable.

The properties of the jerboa's flesh are:—First: it keeps your hawks in perfect health; for, though the weather is hot, the flesh of the jerboa is cold. Rip open the belly of one newly killed and put your fingers inside; you will find that, unlike all other beasts and birds, which, when newly killed, are hot inside, the jerboa is cold. Second: every feather of your hawk that draws its nourishment from the flesh of the jerboa will be strong and pliant, and will last till the next moult without fear of breaking; for such feathers have the pliability of a spring. I say this from experience; for I once saw a gazelle, when the *bālābān* bound to its head, trip and fall, and roll over and over with the hawk for twenty or thirty

---

[1] This is not the experience of Indian falconers. In a wild state peregrines moult late; doubtless the duties of maternity retard moulting. I have twice caught healthy haggard peregrine "falcons" at Christmas that still had an unshed flight-feather.

[2] Properly *yarbū'*.

[3] *Mūsh-i khānagī*: *mūsh* is either a rat or a mouse; however, rats, except field rats (jerboas, etc.) are not found in Persia. (Doubtless ship rats are found in the *ports*.)

[4] The Persian Autumn is supposed to commence in the end of September.

paces. The hawk's wing- and tail-feathers were badly bent and bruised.[1] However, I restored them all with the help of warm water; not one was broken. Third: the fur makes your hawk cast twice daily. (If you can feed your hawk twice daily, morning and afternoon, on the jerboa with its fur, so much the better; if not, feed her on this flesh once, in the afternoon). Fourth: at the end of the moult there is a very fine and powdery bloom on the feathers; it is as though a delicate powder had been sprinkled on them. Fifth: it is an excellent tonic for a sick hawk, as, please God, I will explain later on.

CHAPTER XLII

ON FEELING THE PULSE, AND ON THE SIGNS OF HEALTH

My son, though life and death are in the hands of the Creator, still the physician is for the relief of the sick. Such remedies and treatments as I have by my own experience proved beneficial, I will here set down, so that they may remain on record.

Now, you must know that the pulse of birds lies in the second joint of the wing, and that the heat and the moisture of their temperament is known by holding the wing and feeling the pulse in it.

Know, that the pulse of a man in perfect health (that is a man in whom the four humours are balanced, no one humour preponderating over another), has seventy-five pulsations to the minute. If humidity preponderate, it beats less; if heat, more. In birds of prey, however, on account of their natural heat, the pulse beats from 135 to 140.[2] If the bird be fevered, it beats more; but if humidity preponderate, then less.

The signs of health in a short-winged hawk are these: she should be bright and ever on the look-out for food, and never mournful nor moping. The morning casting should be firm. When she mutes, she should do so quickly, and the mutes should be cast

[1] *Mānda*, "bruised, crushed"; an unusual expression.

[2] Later on, under "Hectic Fever or Phthisis," the author states that the pulse of a hawk in health is 120 to 130.

clear away to a distance:[1] the white of the mutes should be very white, with the dark portion somewhat firmer. She should drink regularly, and should bathe. After feeding, the stomach[2] should be quickly filled. When in the evening you place the hawk on her perch,[3] she should not sleep in the centre of it, but should move to one side to do so. A hawk that does all this is in robust health; but if out of sorts these conditions will not be found in her.

CHAPTER XLIII

ON DISEASES OF THE HEAD AND EYES

It may happen that a cataract form on your hawk's eye. If so:—*Remedy:* should it arise from humidity of temperament, feed her for three days on larks and sparrows, giving her the feathers so that she may cast in the morning. Should she not recover, then brand her with log-wood[4] between the eye and the nostril on both sides, making two small brands the size of a peppercorn. *Item:* take a tamarisk stick and put one end in the fire. Then take a piece of twisted cotton-wool and apply the oozing sap, quite hot, to the cataract. Give her also one small dose of manna,[5] so that she be "moved"[6] a few times. *Item:* remove the fine film with scissors.

Should your hawk's eye become white, so much so that the pupil is covered, then, if the disease arises from excessive cold or from the effects of snow, treat as follows. *Remedy:* steam with snow,[7] and should this fail foment[8] with water. Should she not then be cured, foment with curds.

Should the defect be due to cold and snow, it will be removed

---

[1] "Slice" said of a hawk, "When she mewteth a good distance from her."—*Gentleman's Recreation*, ii, 63.

[2] *Khizāna*, the "pannel."

[3] ". . . ye shall say cast yowre hawke to the perch. and not fet youre hawke upon the perch."—*Boke of St. Albans.*

[4] *i.e.*, with a stick of log-wood (*baqam*) burnt in the fire.

[5] *Shīr-khisht*, a species of manna collected from certain trees.

[6] *Iṭlāq shudan*, a medical term.

[7] *Bukhūr bā barf kardan:* snow is placed in a basin and a red-hot stone or iron cast into it.

[8] *Bukhūr bā āb dādan* is either to foment or to steam with hot water.

by these remedies, but should it arise from a blow, then the cure is as follows. *Remedy:* draw a stick of lunar caustic twice across the eye, and she shall be whole. Should she not be whole, then procure a white cock and slay it according to ordinance, and remove its gall. (You must be in a state of ceremonial purity and must have performed the fixed ablutions.) Then cast and "mail" your hawk, and stand facing the *Qibla*.[1] With a pure heart and single faith, doubting not that the whiteness will disappear from your hawk's eye, cry aloud, "O Holy God! Thou who canst melt the rocks of the mountains, remove this whiteness from my hawk's eye.

O Thou who makes the eye both black and white
Change this white spot; restore my hawk to sight."

Saying this, squeeze the cock's gall into your hawk's afflicted eye.

Should a cure not be effected the first time, repeat the remedy, using the same observances but a fresh cock-gall.[2] Please God she will recover, for this is a *proved* remedy.

CHAPTER XLIV

ON DISEASES OF THE MOUTH

SHOULD your hawk's[3] mouth become ulcerated, or break out in an eruption so that she is unable to eat,[4] then:—

Remedy: first bind a piece of cotton cloth on your finger,

---

[1] *Qibla* the direction of prayer, that is, towards Mecca.

[2] The cock's crow is, *Zikr Ullah Zikr Ullah, yā ghāfilīn!* "Praise the Lord, Praise the Lord, oh ye slothful!"

[3] *Qūsh:* a term applied to any large bird of prey, and especially to the goshawk.

[4] This disease is "the frounce i the mouth" of old English falconers. It is said to resemble thrush in children and to proceed from damp. The *Boke of St. Albans* tells us that "The frounce commyth when a man fedith his hawke withe porke or cattif flesh iiij days to geyder." In India this disease, though not uncommon amongst the short-winged hawks, does not seem to attack the long-winged hawks. I have never seen or heard of any falcon being afflicted with it. Bert, however (page 82, Harting's edition), says that the long-winged hawk is more susceptible to it than the short-winged.

which then introduce into the hawk's mouth, and rub the eruption till the blood comes. Take sumac and gall-apple, pounded and mixed, and apply them with the finger protected as before. You must insert your finger right up to her throat, for the disease is sure to have spread thus far. *Item:* treat in the same way, substituting syrup of pomegranates. Then, for a few days, give her, when feeding, the bones and feathers of the neck of the birds she eats, but of a size that she can swallow them, only with difficulty. Should any excrescence remain in her throat, it will be carried down by the bones, and next morning the throat is again scraped and cleansed by the casting. *Item:* make a twist of cotton cloth, three or four fingers' breadth in length. Grind barberries with their stones, and mix a little juice of willow leaves, and apply this freely with the cloth, which must be inserted as far as the crop.[1] Then withdraw the cloth, and if God pleases that ailment will be removed.

SWOLLEN PALATE.—If your hawk's palate becomes swollen—and I have seen a hawk's palate so swollen that she could not close her beak—then :—*Treatment:* cast your hawk and examine her mouth. If the swelling is red, brand it lengthways, in two places, with a packing needle, so that pus[2] may form and she may be cured. If the swelling is white and hard, it is an indication that it is of long standing, although it may hitherto have escaped your notice. You must make a long slit in the swelling and then remove the congealed white substance from its inside. After that rub the wound with black pepper, that it may not refill with matter. You must further feed the hawk on the hot lights[3] of a hare, and let her eat this flesh with the blood. Once a day wash out her mouth with either sumac juice or pomegranate syrup.

---

1 *Ḥawṣala*, "crop."

2 *Jarāḥat*, "wound," in m.c. is "pus, or matter from an *open* wound": *mādda* is pus inside a swelling before it is opened.

3 *Jigar-i safīd*, "white liver," *i.e.*, "the lungs, the lights."

CHAPTER XLV

DISEASES OF THE NOSE

Should your hawk be unable to "tire" with force, and should she draw her breath with difficulty and her crop become filled with air, it is a sign that the air passages of her nostrils are blocked. *Treatment:* for one or two days, give her, as "tiring" and food, the tough thigh of a fowl; for the exertion of pulling at this will induce a flow of water from her nostrils. Should this fail, pound some sneeze-wort[1] very fine, and put it in a fine reed; place one end of the reed on the hawk's nostril, and blow into the reed so that the powder enters the nostril. After a few sneezes, there should be a flow of water from the nostrils, and the ailment should disappear. *Item:* mix the juice of coriander seed with the juice of a turnip-radish, and drop this into her nostrils, and she will be cured. *Item:* with a stick of log-wood, brand her skull from the base of the yellow cere of her beak, upwards, for a length of three barley-corns: if the brand be longer than three barley-corns, it will reach the brain-pan and be injurious. This is a last resort; for, as the Arab proverb has it, "The last of remedies is the cautery."

CHAPTER XLVI

ON DISEASES OF THE EAR

Should your hawk get a swelling on the ear, which afterwards produces pus, the chances are that she will become deaf: if this disease does nothing more, it will at least render her useless for sport. This ailment is found in the long-winged, rarely in the short-winged, hawks, for it arises from an ill-fitting hood; that is to say, a hawk is fitted with a hood too large for her, which she consequently casts repeatedly; the irritated falconer then ties

[1] *Kundush*, Ar., a sternutatory plant, said to be identical with the *nak-chhiknī* of the Hindus.

a knot in the strap, and this knot, pressing on the ear, results in a wound[1] which refuses to heal. For this there is no cure.

I once had an excellent gazelle-saker that became afflicted with this disease. In spite of this ailment, however, she used to take daily, one, or two, or three gazelle. I treated her for two years without effect, and she then died.

If the falconer detects the injury in its initial stage and applies two leeches to the swelling, a cure *may* be effected. If not, no further treatment will avail. You will now understand why I cautioned you, in a previous chapter, against putting a new hood on a newly caught falcon, or on a falcon just taken up from the moult. Let the hood be soft and part-worn, and of a size that fits the head.

CHAPTER XLVII

ON EPILEPSY

If your hawk have epilepsy—and I have owned and seen many epileptic hawks—when you fly her she will perhaps take the quarry, but just before you come up to render her assistance, she will let go, fall on her back, and utter strange cries in an unnatural voice; her wings and tail will be agitated, and there will be a flow of water from her mouth. Unless seized and "mailed," she will not cease from her distressing struggles. In half an hour, perhaps, she will recover.

I once had a passage-saker, a very fine heron-hawk, that was so afflicted. One day in *Qizil Rubāṭ*[2] I flew her at a heron and both birds went ringing up high. Suddenly the fit attacked my hawk, and as though a bullet had struck her she fell to earth, turning over and over. She never recovered from her injuries.

[1] It is difficult to see how the knot would press on the ear. The hood used in Baghdad and in the ports of the Persian Gulf is a soft leather bag with a strap, the eye-coverings being slightly hardened and made to protrude. This pattern differs essentially from the Indian patterns.

[2] *Qizil Rubāṭ* is on the road from *Baghdād* to *Khāniqān* or *Khānijīn*, about seventy-three miles distant from the former and seventeen from the latter: both places are in Turkish territory.

Treatment: pound and mix together half a *misqāl*[1] of sal-ammoniac and half a *misqāl* of sugar-candy, and make into a small round parcel like the little packages of sacred earth.[2] Have *ready by your side* cold water, luke-warm water, a squab, and a chicken-poult, for any delay or negligence is dangerous. In the morning, after sunrise, cast your hawk; make ten or twenty holes with a needle in the paper packet so that the contents may act quickly; put it down the hawk's throat, and then give her a few bits of meat the size of a pea, to induce her to "put over," so that the medicine may reach the lower stomach:[3] then set her on her perch to rest. In half an hour she will vomit. At the first vomit, it sometimes happens that she casts up two or three dead white worms, but this is not always the case. At the second or third vomiting, she will cast up the medicine packet, and also a "purse"[4] of yellow fat. After she has cast up these two things she will vomit no more. Now cast your hawk, and pour a good deal of *tepid* water down her throat,[5] and release her. Wait till she has twice muted and then again cast her, and this time pour *cold* water down her throat. Then set her on her perch. After she has muted once, cut the throat of the squab (or of the poult), and let her eat half of—that is, one side of—the breast,[6] but no feathers. If she is much out of sorts and won't feed, pour the warm blood down her throat as it issues from the cut throat, and, chopping up the heart into bits, put them also down her throat: then after a little, when she has recovered, give her some of the breast. This treatment will cure her epilepsy. *Item:* brand[7] her neck with a line, at the junction of the body, and

---

1 *Misqāl:* 24 *mukhud* = 1 *misqāl* = nearly ⅙ oz. avoirdupois.

2 *Basta-yi turbat* is a small amount of earth from *Qarbalā*, from the grave of *Imām Ḥusayn*: it is tied up in a little bit of cloth and makes a packet about the size of a 12-bore bullet, or less.

3 *Khizāna.*

4 *Kīsa,* "purse": the same word is used by Panjab falconers.

5 About three dessert-spoonfuls should be given. After this, or similar physicing, an Indian falconer fills the hawk's crop with water by inserting a tube (usually the shank-bone of a crane or heron, made smooth at the ends) into the crop, filling his own mouth with water and letting it flow through the tube into the crop. Peregrines and *Shāhīns* will usually drink of their own accord.

6 *Yak sīna,* the *yak baghal* of Panjab falconers.

7 Easterns have a passion for branding things.

vary her food every day, so that she may become as fat and stout[1] as a hawk in the mew. The disease will disappear. *Item:* get a sufficient quantity of olive oil and a little manna. Slay a cockerel, pull off the skin of the thigh whole, and fill the empty skin with the manna, the olive oil, and some old and whitened droppings of a dog. Please God, this will prove a perfect cure.

CHAPTER XLVIII

ON PALPITATION[2]

THIS disease is of three kinds. One arises from smoke and dust and dirt. The symptoms of all three are the same: if the hawk make the slightest exertion, she draws her breath with difficulty, and her body is agitated from the crop to the far end of the "keel bone."[3] When she breathes, her tail and the feathers under the tail[4] heave, and the wings are carried loose and drooping.

Treatment: put the hawk in a dark room and keep her quiet, and fatten her up as much as possible. Give her three doses of castor oil,[5] on three alternate days, before feeding her. Keep water in front of her, that she may bathe and drink. Feed her daily on larks, with the bones and feathers, and on young pigeons. (On no

---

[1] *Chāq u farbih.* *Chāq*, T., means "stout, healthy, well," and of a stallion "ready to cover."

[2] *Khafaqān*, properly "palpitation of the heart." The disease described under this name appears to be identical with the "Teyne" of the *Boke of St. Albans* and with the "Pantas" of other writers. Markham describes the latter as "A dangerous disease in hawks whereof few escape that are afflicted therewith; it proceeds from the lungs being as it were baked by excessive heat, that the hawk cannot draw her breath and when drawn cannot emit it again; and you may judge of the beginning of this evil by the hawk's labouring much in the pannel, moving her train often up and down at each motion of her pannel, and many times she cannot mute nor slice off; if she does, she drops it fast by her. The same distemper is also perceived by the hawk's frequent opening her clap and beak."

[3] *'Aẓm-i zawraqī*, "the sternum."

[4] *Dum-līza:* I do not know whether this is the "Pope's nose," or the feathers under the tail, the "brayles or brayle federis" of the *Boke of St. Albans.*

[5] *Rūghan-i karchak* is in m.c. "castor oil;" *vide* note 3, page 171.

account feed her on pigeons reared on millet, for millet is poison to hawks). Fatten her up till the disease leaves her.

One variety of palpitation arises from moisture of temperament: the hawk pants with the slightest exertion and there is a watery discharge from the mouth, eyes, and nostrils, and she is continually wiping her eyes on her shoulders to clean them; probably she is costive [1] as well. Observe her when she mutes; if she mutes in small quantities at a time, the soft feathers in the region of the vent getting soiled with the mutes, it is a sign that her disease is complicated by costiveness. *Treatment:* make her as fat as you can, feeding her on good meats. Once, or twice, in the manner previously described, give her oil and manna and the whitened droppings of a dog. On alternate days, mix with her food either butter, or almond oil. If she still mute in patches, then:—*Treatment:* take oil of peach-kernels, with oil of filberts, and oil of blanched almonds, and mix a quantity equal to a *sunjad;* [2] then dip the cotton-wool end of the clyster-stick [3] in these three oils, and by its means give her an enema twice a day, once in the morning, once in the afternoon. Feed her, too, on young pigeons, and on larks, and on the flesh of the wild boar and of eagles, and, if it please God, she will recover. *Item:* get some sheep's wool, and removing all burrs, etc. etc. from it, tease it out like carded cotton. Round about the middle or "waist" of this wool, tie a piece of silk of two or three strands in thickness, and about two spans in length. Wash the wool in warm water and bind a little meat to one end of it. Holding the end of the silk, induce the hawk to swallow the wool thus garnished with the meat. As soon as she has swallowed it, show her other meat to excite her cupidity and induce her to "put over" the wool now in her crop. As soon as you have ascertained by touch,[4] that the wool has reached the

[1] *Marẓ-i khuskī*, "dryness," *i.e*, "costiveness."

[2] *Sunjad* or *sinjid*, a sort of red wild plum, oblong in shape like the *'unnab* or jujube.

[3] *Shāf* or *shāfa* is a stick with cotton wool at the end; this is dipped in oil and used as an enema for children.

[4] By feeling the stomach and bowel with the fore-finger it is easy to tell whether the stomach is full or empty. Indian falconers, who have a hawk on the fist for many hours every day, can frequently tell by touch whether the hawk has "cast" or not. The "casting" apparently forms only a short time before being ejected and can be distinctly felt by an educated finger.

lower stomach, pull the silk and withdraw it, and it will bring up with it any impurity there may be in the stomach.

If the hawk be a goshawk, or indeed any short-winged hawk, substitute cotton-wool for the sheep's wool.

If the cotton-wool, or the sheep's wool, be washed in warm water, or in the milk of a young girl or of a donkey, and then given to the hawk soaked with the milk, so much the better.

The third form of palpitation is due to a blow, and those skilled in Avian Pathology have named this, "Contusional and Incurable Palpitation." This disease is probably due to the ill-temper of your falconer. Perhaps the weather has been cold and there has been snow[1] about: the hawk, suffering from the cold, has bated[2] incessantly till the ill-tempered falconer has, in his irritation, buffeted her and boxed her, and then "mailed" her in the skirt of his filthy coat. The result is that some ribs, or small bones, have got broken or injured. Or it may be that the hawk was low in condition and maddened by hunger, and in pursuit of her quarry dashed herself against a stone, or against a branch, and so broke a rib. *Remedy:* send for the falconer and show him the hawk; let him have thirty or forty cuffs over the head;[3] kick him out of your service and see that he does not get a place elsewhere, and set about procuring a new hawk for yourself. For "Contusional Palpitation" there is no treatment but this.

CHAPTER XLIX

THE SICKNESS CALLED *KARAJ*,[4] WHICH IS COSTIVENESS

THE symptoms of this disease are, that the soft feathers under the tail and round the vent are soiled by the mutes; that when muting the hawk raises her tail higher than usual, mutes with difficulty, and is unable to cast the mutes clear to a distance.

Treatment: feed the hawk for some days on the flesh of a

[1] *Būrān*, "a snow-storm," a word not in the dictionaries.

[2] *Parīdan*, "to fly, *i.e.*, to bate."

[3] The usual punishment would, in Persia, be the bastinado. The author probably wrote in Baghdad where the bastinado is not used.

[4] Apparently the "Stoone in the fundement" of the *Boke of St. Albans*.

cockerel, sprinkling the flesh with the juice of the marsh-mallow;[1] feed her thus twice a day. Further, anoint the vent with almond or with olive oil. *Item:* vary her food, giving her pigeons and sparrows, and the larks called by the Arabs *qumbarah*. Apply the clyster-stick as already described, dipping the cotton-wool in oil of peach kernels, apricot kernels, and almonds; administer it before feeding her: give her also a pill of powdered sugar-candy[2] mixed in a pat of cow's butter the size of two filberts. She will, please God, be cured. Keep water ever near her, that she may drink her fill. *Item:* take oil of apricot kernels, and powdered cummin seed,[3] a quantity equal to the size of a walnut. Sprinkle the powdered cummin seed on the vent; then anoint the vent and adjacent parts with the oil. Do this for three days in succession, and she shall be whole. This is the practice of the ancient falconers. *Item:* anoint her vent a few times with a mixture of oil of jasmine, white wax, and pitch.[4] *Item:* take marrow of the shin-bone of a goat and mix it with her food for a few days. If the goat be an old female, so much the better.

CHAPTER L

HECTIC FEVER OR PHTHISIS[5]

As mentioned in a previous chapter, the pulse of a human being in sound health has seventy-five beats to the minute, while a hawk in good health has a pulse of a hundred-and-twenty or a hundred-and-thirty. The pulse of all hawks is, however, not alike; for instance, as the *shāhīn* is faster and more powerful than any hawk, short-winged or long-winged, so, too, it has a faster pulse.

If you are unable to feel the pulse of a hawk in the second joint of her wing, or if after discovering it you find that its beating is too

[1] *Khaṭmī*, the "Persian Hollyhock," and the "Marsh-Mallow." It is the latter that is used in medicine.

[2] Powdered sugar-candy is a simple and harmless purge for hawks. About eighty grains' weight is a suitable dose for a female peregrine in good condition.

[3] There are two kinds of cummin seed, the black and the white: the former is used in cooking, the latter in medicine.

[4] *Zift*, "pitch," and also a kind of ointment said to be made of black damar.

[5] *Tab-i lāzim.*

rapid to be counted, know that this is a symptom of hectic fever. Another symptom is that both by day and by night, she puts her head under her wing at unusual times. Another symptom is an inordinate appetite: she will gorge till the meat appears in her throat, and even then tear at meat and throw it away, there being no more room in her crop; but the more good food she eats, the thinner she gets.

Another symptom is that she is unable to cross her wings, but lets them droop one on each side of her tail, leaving her oil-gland and loins uncovered. Another symptom is that she drinks and bathes more than usual.

If the disease be not of long standing but has reached the first or second stage only, it may admit of cure; but if it has reached the third stage, you may set about procuring a new hawk for yourself, for her case is hopeless.

Now this disease arises from both humidity of temperament, and from heat: if from the former there will be a slight discharge from the eyes and mouth. *Treatment:* feed her twice a day on pigeons, larks, sparrows, black chickens, and pork. *Item:* give her daily one white pepper corn;[1] and if you notice an improvement increase the dose by degrees till you can give as many as five pepper corns. *Item:* roughly crush some ginger and give her daily with her food a small piece the size of a pea. *Item:* grind finely a piece of cinnamon equal in size to a pea, and give it to her in her food. If the disease arises from heat of temperament, change her perch to another room and thus give her a change of air. Feed on jerboa rats, land tortoises, and cockerels. Instead of water, give her to drink the juice of ispaghul,[2] and sprinkle dried ispaghul seed on her afternoon meal, giving her also feathers with her meat. When the heat of her temperament abates, you will find that she will no longer drink the ispaghul juice; you must therefore exert your falconer's skill and get her to take in the morning about two or three *miṡqāl*[3] of the juice with her meat.

---

[1] "White pepper" is prepared by divesting the ripe berry of its skin by maceration in water, after which it is rubbed and finally bleached in the sun. It is occasionally bleached still further by means of chlorine. It is twice as expensive as black pepper, but is in little demand.—*Dict. Econ. Prod.*, Vol. VI, Pt. 1, p. 261.

[2] *Isfarza* or *ispag͟hūl;* said to be the seed of the pea-wort.

[3] *Vide* note 2, p. 165.

If, on account of the abatement of her heat, she will in no wise touch ispaghul juice, you must resort to the device known amongst falconers as *chālma*. Now this is *chālma:* sever the thigh of a cockerel close to its body and draw back the skin to the knee joint, reversing the skin in so doing. Next sever the skin at the knee-joint, and bind up the end firmly with silk. Into this bag put some ispaghul juice and also some of the seed, to the amount of an acorn in quantity, such a quantity in fact as the hawk can swallow with ease. While feeding your hawk, carelessly introduce the loose spare end of the skin bag, and get her to swallow it. If you cannot induce her to swallow it, you must use force. Every morning you must give her the juice of ispaghul, and every afternoon the dried seed; for this will cool her liver. She will cast up the seed every morning with the casting of feathers and bones. The quantity of ispaghul juice may be two or three *misqāl*, but of the dried seed less than half a *misqāl* so that she may find no difficulty in ejecting it with the morning casting. Please God, she will recover.

Item: take juice of long cucumbers and juice of small cucumbers,[1] and give it to her in the same way you would give ispaghul juice. First put down her throat a quarter of a *misqāl* of manna; on the top of that administer the cucumber juice. Wait till she has muted three or four times and then feed her up for the day, giving her a moderate meal. Employ this treatment on three "alternate" days.

> With these drugs, dose her thrice, on alternate days;
> For that's what the book of Greek medicine says.

On no account should you give her manna after feeding her, but she may be allowed to drink as much cucumber juice as she pleases. *Item:* give her daily, if a female goshawk, one *nukhūd*[2] of camphor, and if a male goshawk, half that quantity: to a sparrow-hawk give a quantity proportionate to her size. Fatten up the hawk as much as you can.

---

[1] *Khiyār-i chambar*, a long variety of cucumber: *khiyār-i ābī*, a small variety.

[2] A *nukhūd* is the twenty-fourth part of a *misqāl* and a *misqāl* is equal to about three grains. Camphor has a peculiar effect on hawks, producing intoxication, and later convulsions, according to the dose and the condition of the hawk. Two grains of fresh, strong camphor, given to a saker in fair condition and on an empty stomach, will produce intoxication. A larger dose will generally cause convulsions and possibly death.

CHAPTER LI

ON CANKER OF THE FEATHERS [1]

THIS disease, which is called *qārishqa*,[1] is commoner in Persia than elsewhere. From what I have observed, it arises from taking a moulting hawk out of the mew too soon, that is, while some of her feathers are still in blood. The hawk bates, injuring a young quill, and the blood dries up and putrifies; then the flesh near the root of the quill gets infected, and soon a tiny kind of maggot, similar to the "disease of parasites"[2] that sometimes infests man, is produced, and it eats away the root. The following case, I think, corroborates my opinion:—

I once had a very fine eyess-goshawk, brought to me from an eyrie in Mazenderan, just about a month before Autumn. I noticed that one of the two centre tail feathers, called the *qāpāq* feathers, was broken close to the flesh, too close to admit of "imping." I thought that as it was a young bird I might pull out the feather without fear, and that it would speedily grow again.[3] Accordingly with the utmost care I neatly removed the stump[4] with pincers. On examining it, I found some hundreds of minute insects the size of a poppy seed, wriggling about inside the quill. I examined them under a magnifying glass; they looked just like lice,[5] but were broader. It struck me that these were the cause of canker in quill-feathers. I closed the end of the quill and circulated it for inspection amongst all my sporting friends and acquaintances. These parasites, after attacking and eating one quill, work their way under the flesh to the next, and so on. They have the same passion for feathers that white-ants[6] have for wood. If you examine carefully, with a glass, a feather that has broken off from a hawk afflicted with this disease, you will find that it has a dead appearance; it has not the water of life in it: the

---

[1] *Par-khura* or *par-khuragī*, P.; *qārishqa* appears to be the Turkish name of the disease.

[2] *Da'u 'l-qaml*, *lit.* "disease of lice." By this term the author probably refers to some parasite other than the louse, *i.e.*, other than the common louse.

[3] Flight-feathers that are pulled out never grow again; tail-feathers *sometimes* do; *vide* page 177, note 1.

[4] *Būqa.*

[5] *Qaml*, Ar.

[6] *Rashmīz*, either white-ant or weevil.

marks of erosion will also be apparent. These insects are the cause of feather-rot, and naught else—but God knows best.

Treatment: first give her three doses of manna on alternate days, but give her no more manna than the quantity mentioned previously. Then cast her, and pull out the small feathers from round the diseased spot. If the flesh is black and swollen, it is a sign that the injury arises from a blow. *Treatment:* apply a leech to the injured spot and let it suck out the impure blood. Sprinkle salt on the wound, or apply ice to staunch the bleeding. *Item:* rub the injured spot with powdered stone or brick till the blood is near flowing; then apply the fouling of a tobacco-pipe. After this keep her loose in a room. Do this twice.

If, however, the spot be red, the disease is the second or parasitic kind. The treatment in both cases is the same, with a difference. *Treatment:* prick the red spot with a needle and induce a flow of blood. Mix vinegar and ox-gall, and paint it on the affected spot. *Item:* take carbonate of soda,[1] blue-stone, sal-ammoniac, "yellow aloes,"[2] and long pepper,[3] a grain[4] of each, and three black raisins: pound and mix. Prick the injured spot with a needle, and wash with strong vinegar. Then apply the powder and she will recover. This is the practice of the ancient falconers. *Item:* when the feather falls out, wait till a new one takes its place;[5] then before the stage has arrived when it will fall out, pluck it out by force and do this three times. The fourth time let the feather reach maturity. This, too, is a receipt of the ancient falconers.

[1] *Būra-yi Armanī*, crude carbonate of soda.

[2] *i.e.*, Socotrinæ aloes, which are yellow.

[3] *Dār filfil*, "Piper Longum."

[4] *Dānak-i*, a pea-grain in weight.

[5] The author seems to have confused "false moult" with "feather-canker," but the two diseases are separate. In "false moult" the hawk casts newly grown feathers, and, as it were, recommences a second moult before she is out of the first, and so on. This disease is well known to Indian falconers, but no case has come under my direct notice. In "feather-canker," or in one form of it, the hawk moults well and clean, but when flying to the lure one of its flight-feathers will make a whirring sound as though not set in the wing at the proper angle. In a few days this feather will break off at, or in, the flesh, and there will probably be a trace of blood. One by one every flight feather will break off in this manner. In the only case I have seen, the hawk, a saker, had moulted perfectly and was apparently in the best of health. The disease attacked both wings and she lost every one of her flight-feathers.

CHAPTER LII

LICE [1]

The symptoms of lice are these: the feathers on the back of the neck stand erect, and the hawk is ever scratching her head with her foot and picking at her back and breast, with her beak: she is never at rest. *Treatment:* get some quick-silver and "kill"[2] it with vinegar; then apply it to a thread and cast the thread on the neck of the hawk, and the lice will be destroyed.[3] *Item:* take tobacco-water and mix therein a little salt, and apply the mixture to the back of the neck and to the loins, and she shall be free. *Item:* there is in Mazenderan a grass called *kankarvāsh:* pound some of this very fine and mix therein a little wine, and apply to the back of the neck and under the wings, and to every place where you know the lice collect and hold their councils. Apply this and the lice will instantly fall off. *Item:* place your hawk in the sun, and as soon as she is warmed, the lice will collect on the large broad feathers, three on each side, called by the Kurds *yār māliq.*[4] You can then remove the lice with scissors. *Item:* take Armenian bole,[5] country tobacco-leaf and good cigarette tobacco;[6] grind and mix. By means of a reed, blow this powder on to and into the feathers. Then place the hawk in the sun for a little, and the lice will disappear. *Item:* take some carded cotton-wool and twist it into a roll as thick as your finger, and at night cast it on your hawk's neck and put her in a warm place. All the lice will collect on the wool. In the morning snip off the wool hastily and cast it away.

---

1 *Shipish* or *shupush.*

2 *Bi-kush*, a term of alchemy.

3 Quick-silver is a well-known Indian remedy for lice. Women mix oil with the quick-silver. Indian falconers mix saliva with a little quick-silver in the palm of the hand, and then dab it on at night on the back of the hawk's neck, etc., and under the wings. In the morning not a trace of the vermin will be found. Newly-trained sakers are invariably troubled with lice, but if so treated after they are "manned" (and will preen freely), they generally continue free—unless infected by another hawk. Peregrines in health, that bathe regularly, are rarely if ever troubled with lice.

4 *Vide* note 1, page 112.

5 *Gil-i Armanī* "Armenian bole"; once celebrated as a European medicine; said to be identical with the *gerū* of the Hindus.

6 *Tumbākū*, "tobacco-leaf"; used for smoking in the water pipe: *tutun* is good cigarette tobacco, from Syria.

CHAPTER LIII

WORMS

If your hawk is ever pulling out the feathers from her breast, and thighs, and stomach, and has done so since she was young, and even after moulting has not forsaken the practice, know that the habit has become second nature to her, and is incurable. You must put up with this foulness in her, and fly her as she is. Do not, however, let her ever get too hungry; for in hunger she will pull out her feathers all the more. She is like one who has contracted the habit of always toying with his beard and moustache and pulling out the hairs: some men, too, I have seen who have a habit of ever plucking out the hair from their chests, and their armpits, and their pubes. Your hawk is like one of those and cannot be cured.

If, however, she has newly acquired the habit, it is a symptom of worms in the stomach.[1] *Treatment:* if a long-winged hawk, give her sal-ammoniac and sugar-candy, as previously described; but if a short-winged hawk give her, on alternate days, a few doses of manna. Perhaps the worms will be got rid of by this simple purging. *Item:* give her one *nukhūd* of asafœtida, and by degrees increase the amount daily till you have reached five *nukhūd*, so that she may void the worms either by vomiting or by purging. *Item:* rub gall and tobacco-water on the spots whence she plucks the feathers, and she will be cured :—

> Give your hawk the medicine bitter;
> Then the good result ascribe,
> With a highly sweetened temper,
> To the drug she did imbibe.

Item: pluck out all the feathers from the spot at which she worries, till the bare flesh shows. Mix a little Armenian bole with wine and old vinegar, and apply it. Fatten her up. Please God she will be cured. I myself have proved this receipt.[2]

---

[1] *Khazīna.*

[2] *Vide* Latham's *The Falcon's Lure and Cure*, Book I, Part II, Chap. xlii, for a receipt: "To kill the ranckness and itching that sometimes will be in Hawkes bloody feathers, which is the cause she pulls them forth in that estate." The disease referred to is not uncommon in cage birds that are carelessly tended, but I have never met with it in trained hawks in India.

CHAPTER LIV

HEAT-STROKE [1]

If your hawk mope, and the feathers of her head stand on end, and her mutes, too, be red as though there were drops of blood in them, it is a sign that she is suffering from heat-stroke. *Treatment:* mix a little saffron and sugar-candy and give it to her at meals, concealed in a fold of meat: the quantity of the dose depends on the size and the constitution of the hawk. Feed her on cooling meats, such as cockerels, jerboa-rats, and tortoises. With every meal give her cucumber juice with juice of ispaghul (as previously mentioned under *chālma* [2]), so that her liver may be cooled thereby.

CHAPTER LV

PALSY, ETC.

Akmaja is a disease akin to paralysis, palsy, and epilepsy, but is yet none of these three. The hawk grows thin without any apparent cause, and her tail and wings seem palsied. Sometimes this distressing symptom will so overpower her that she will at one time fall on her face, at another on her back, and be unable to sit on the fist. Sometimes, too, she will cast her "gorge".[3] As a rule this disease, which generally occurs amongst short-winged hawks, is fatal. The cause of it is stale meat [4] (mutton, she-goat, or hare, two or three days old), given her by your ignorant falconer, who has afterwards placed her in a damp room. *Treatment:* at once brand her with a stick of log-wood, branding her four limbs with lines, and branding also her oil-bottle, her forehead, and between her nostrils from the direction of both eyes. Feed her on pigeons. Give her one *nuk͟hūd* of quinine:—

> Quinine cures man in the West and the East;
> 'Tis also good for bird and beast.

[1] *Garmā-zadagī.*
[2] *Vide* page 165.
[3] "Gorge," the crop and also the contents of the crop.
[4] *Gūsht-i du-si-rūza-mānda,* "meat two or three days old." *Tainted* meat kills all trained hawks, even *lagaṛs* and sakers.

Give her that amount of pigeon's flesh that will be digested[1] by two hours before sunset. In the afternoon kill another pigeon and chop up one side of the breast very fine, and mix with it the yolk of an egg, and give it to your hawk. *Item:* pound a little cinnamon[2] and give it to her in a fold of meat and on the top of her meal. *Item:* powder a little ginger very fine, and give it to her as a first mouthful in a fold of meat. Then let her tear at the breast of a pigeon, applying to it, as she does so, a little wine. You must be specially careful about feeding her twice a day and giving her just the right quantity in the morning, so that she may be empty and keen by the time of the afternoon meal. *Item:* give her in the morning one *miṣqāl* of castor-oil.[3] Feed her on minced meat mixed with the yolk of an egg. If you observe any improvement, then two days later give her a second dose of castor-oil. *Item:* give her, before her food, one white peppercorn; and, if you observe any improvement, gradually increase the peppercorns till you can give as many as five. If she be not cured by this, repeat, "Verily to God do we belong: Verily to Him do we return,"[4] and set about procuring another hawk.

> Who is there that can Fate's decree contest;
> Who can complain against Time's ceaseless flight?
> God in his wisdom does what He thinks best;
> Will men presume to guide the Lord aright?

[1] *Ṣarf kardan.*

[2] Such spices do indeed whet a hawk's appetite, but their continued use is very injurious.

[3] *Rūghan-i karchak, lit.* "oil of cotton seed," so-called from an idea that castor-oil was obtained from this seed.

[4] A formula repeated by Muslims in times of distress, especially at death.

CHAPTER LVI

DISEASES OF THE FEET[1]

THE "PINNE"[2] IN THE FEET

KNOW that this disease is of two kinds, and that gazelle-hawks are peculiarly subject to it; for a keen *bālābān* will stoop with force at the hard head of the gazelle, thereby injuring her feet;[3] from the blow a small vein in the sole of the foot gets torn or bruised, and the blood under and on the surface becomes corrupt, and soon black spots appear in the sole: one day the foot is well and one day bad, till the beginning of Spring, when the trees put out new leaves; then the "pinne" too breaks bounds and soon cripples the hawk completely.

The second kind also arises from a bruise: the spot swells, but there is no discolouration, nor any sign of black spots. This kind is called by the Arabs *ḥafā*,[4] and the cure of *ḥafā* is easy. *Treatment of the first form, i.e., "mīkhak"*: the sole is sure to be hot, so make a dough of ispaghul seed and put it on a piece of blue[5] cloth, and at night-fall bind it on your hawk's feet. Watch her for half an hour lest she tear it off before the ispaghul has dried and adhered to the foot. In the morning rip up the cloth, and let your hawk rest, having previously, by spreading cotton-wool seed, prepared a place of rest for her. If she lie down, so much the better. In two or three nights' time the swelling will disappear, but the discolouration will still remain. Continue the treatment nightly till the ispaghul poultice comes away with that blackness adhering to it. *Item:* thread a needle with ten or twelve horse-hairs, and pass it in from the outside[6] of the foot and

---

[1] "When yowre hawkes fete be swollyn she hath the podagre."—*Boke of St. Albans.* "Podager" is said to be gout in the feet (from *pod* "a foot"), but the name was probably applied to the initial stage of the "pinne in the feet" of other writers.

[2] *Mīkhak.*

[3] "Bating" on a hard perch during the moult when the hawk is heavy, will also cause this disease. Also a hard perch when the pressure always falls on the same spot, will produce it. Hawks moulted on sand do not suffer from it.

[4] *Ḥafā*, Ar., is "the sole of the foot of man or beast being chafed or worn down by travel."

[5] *i.e.*, dyed by indigo, which has medicinal properties.

[6] The top?

bring it out at the "blackness" in the foot. Knot the horse-hairs in such a way that you can pull them upwards and downwards. Two or three times daily, pull the hairs to induce a flow of the foul matter. Do this for forty days, or for two months, till the black core moves with the hairs. By the time the upper knot will pass through the foot and come out at the under side of it, she will be cured. *Item :* pierce the discolouration in the sole with a needle, forcing in the needle for the distance of two or three barley-corn lengths. Then stick to the eye of the needle a bit of touch-wood,[1] the size of a filbert; set a light to it and let it burn till it is consumed to ashes; then withdraw the needle and anoint the place with oil of walnuts. In two or three days' time the blackness, together with the core which is the real corn, will come away. Do nothing to the hole that will be left, except anoint it. *Item :* if both feet are affected remove the jess from the worse of the two, and break the tarsus bone.[2] Keep the hawk in a dark room on a bed of cotton-seed, in depth about four fingers' breadth. The room must be so dark that the hawk cannot distinguish night from day. Once a day anoint her leg with clarified wax and mummy-oil.[3] It is not necessary to set or bind the leg. If your hawk is young, say of one or two moults, her leg will set in twenty days. If old, say of ten or fifteen moults, it will take forty days. The younger the hawk the sooner will the leg set. In this respect a hawk resembles man; for the broken bone of a five-year-old child will join in five days, of a ten-year-old child in ten days, of a fifty-year-old man in fifty days, and of a ninety-year-old in ninety days. However, a man of ninety years will, during these ninety days that he is laid up, contract so many other ailments that he will die.

Should an old man break a limb,
Leave him, take no care of him,
Since before his bones can mend
Further ills procure his end.

[1] *Qū*, and colloquially in Turkish *qāv*, "touch wood." *Yābis miṣl' 'l-qāv*, "dry as touch wood," is a common Arab saying in Baghdad.

[2] *Qulam*, the "stalke" of old English falconers.

[3] *Mūmiyā*, "mummy," is a name in Eastern bazaars now applied to several forms of asphalte, mineral pitch, Jew's pitch, and maltha. Formerly the name was applied to Egyptian mummy; and by the vulgar at the present day this mysterious medicine is supposed to be the extract of negro-boy boiled in oil. "Mummy-oil" is made by mixing equal parts of mummy and clarified butter over the fire.

The same rule applies to hawks, too. Now, as soon as you see that when you throw the meat to your hawk she grasps it with her broken leg, change the jess from the sound to the unsound leg, and then break the former as you did the latter. *Item :* (and the best remedy of all) take a broken piece of a mercury-backed mirror, grind it very fine, and sift it through taffeta, so that it is as fine as collyrium of antimony. Then mix with it the gall of a black goat, and make it into the consistency of an ointment. Bind this ointment on to the feet of your hawk in the morning, removing it in the evening. After removing it, let her rest for half an hour. Again bind on this poultice, removing it in the morning. Again, after half an hour, bind on a fresh one and leave it on till sunset. That blackness will by this time have been drawn out and will protrude somewhat. Take hold of the blackness with tweezers and gently pull it. By the dispensation of the Creator the corn will come out by the root.[1] Fill the cavity left, with powdered antimony, and see that the feet are kept quite dry. This cure was invented by the writer and has been proved by experiment. *Item:* take fresh hot cow-dung and add to it double the quantity of salt.[2] Apply the mixture thickly to the perch, and renew twice a day, morning and evening, for a month or forty days. She will be entirely cured. Doubtless you will say that to keep a hooded falcon on such a perch may be easy; but what about an unhooded yellow-eyed hawk? This is my answer: take your hawk, *ṭarlān, qizil,* or sparrow-hawk—or whatever she may be—into a dark room and drive into the wall, as a perch, a wooden peg of proper thickness,[3] but not so round that the cow-dung will not stand on it: the perch should be broad. The hawk should be so tied to this perch that when she bates she will remain hanging. For the first day or two she must be watched by your man, for the heat of the cow-dung and salt will certainly make her "bate." When she "bates," go not near her; let her "bate" till she is exhausted: then, when she is quite still, and has ceased beating

[1] Ordinary poultices or repeated fomentations will produce the same result.

[2] An Indian remedy, whether good or ill, I cannot say, is to keep the hawk on a lump of rock salt instead of on a perch : *vide* page 175, note 5.

[3] In India a sparrow-hawk's perch is usually a wooden peg driven into the mud wall of the living-room.

her wings, raise her and replace her on the perch. Every time she "bates" act in this manner. After a little, she will put up with the burning in her feet, finding it a lesser evil than hanging head downwards. In two or three days her feet will become numbed and she will no longer feel pain in them, and will therefore cease to "bate." You must put on such a quantity of cow-dung that the hawk's feet are buried in it. The fresher and warmer the cow-dung, the more efficacious the effect and the speedier the cure.[1] You should, in fact, tether a cow near the "mew" so as to have a fresh supply of dung ever at hand.

Now as regards the second form of this disease, called *ḥafā*, the symptoms are the same as in *mīkhak*, except that in *ḥafā* the blackness is absent from the sole of the feet. *Treatment:* bind on her feet, a few nights, powdered ispaghul seed as previously described, and she shall be cured. *Item:* pound up a little of the skin or rind of sweet pomegranate,[2] and add thereto a little salt. Apply this a few times to the perch, in the manner described, and the disease will disappear. *Item:* take acorns and gall-apples and pound them together, add camel's urine to make a dough, and bind on to the feet a few times, and she will be cured. *Item:* take camel's urine and green ispaghul,[3] and pound together; boil slightly; remove and place on the ground to cool. When lukewarm, immerse the hawk's feet for half an hour, and the ill will be removed. *Item:* take her on the fist and carry her every day, and lure her. The glove and "carriage"[4] will cure her better than anything else.

If she's ill, let the falconer carry the hawk;
Both man and bird will get good from the walk.

Item: keep her on a rough stone or rock, instead of on a perch.[5]

I have myself tested these remedies for *mīkhak* and *ḥafā*, and I have certainly found them beneficial.

[1] The translator tried this treatment with success, but it was difficult to keep the tail-feathers from being stained a green *khākī* colour.

[2] *Anār-i shīrīn*, "sweet pomegranate," is a particular variety.

[3] *Ispand-i sabz*, "green (or black) *ispand*," is the variety used in medicine: *ispand-i zard* or *isfarza-yi zard*, "yellow *ispand*," is used to keep off the evil-eye. *Ispand* is, I am told by an authority, the seed of Peganum Harmala, one of the rue family.

[4] *Bahla*, "hawking glove": *gardānīdan*, "carrying."

[5] In the *Booke of Kepinge of Sparhawkes*, a cold stone is mentioned as a cure; *vide* also note 2, p. 174.

CHAPTER LVII

ON PARALYSIS OF A TOE

SOMETIMES a hawk loses all power in one of its toes and is quite unable to grasp its food with it. *Treatment:* apply a leech. If this fail, brand the toe lengthways with a needle, taking care that the tendon[1] is not burnt. If these two remedies fail, waste no time in further treatment, and "labour not at beating cold iron." Many a hawk have I seen with this disease, but seldom a cure. The long-winged hawks are more liable to it than the short-winged. Perhaps the injury arises from a strain, by the hawk grasping her food too tight and straining or tearing a tendon. Now a severed tendon will not join. Should such an accident happen to your hawk, God grant that it fall on one of her small toes, for that is not so serious; but if it happen to one of her "hunting talons"[2] she is ruined; she can do no good at all.

O hawk, if of your hand a tendon break
For evermore you must the hunt forsake.

CHAPTER LVIII

FEATHERS PLUCKED OUT BY THE ROOT

SHOULD anyone, out of enmity to you, break the wing- or tail-feathers of your hawk, you must match the broken feathers as far as possible with others, and "imp"[3] them. First "imp" them with a needle; then, if they break again, imp them by inserting a shaft[4] into the hollow quills. If they again break off at the root, close to the flesh, you can do nothing more.

On no account must you pluck out the tail- or flight-feathers by the root. Flight-feathers plucked out will never grow again; but tail-feathers, though they will grow again, will be defective

---

1 *Rag-i pāy-i ū*, "tendon."
2 *Mikhlab-i shikārī.*
3 *Payvand hardan*, "'to imp' a broken feather; to graft a tree."
4 *Lūla-payvand:* I conclude this is the author's meaning.

in two points.[1] First, they will be weak and "withered," and will probably break: possibly, too, some will not grow at all. Second, during the moult, the hawk will experience great difficulty in casting the re-grown feathers, and you may be constrained to pull them out again, and so on, year by year, your hawk being thus rendered foul and disfigured for ever.

If, through personal enmity or by some accident from a gazelle or a crane, it does so happen that a flight-feather gets plucked out, then:—*Treatment:* take the feather that has been plucked out and at once replace it in its socket,[2] and bind it firmly with silk to that primary-covert[3] that impends it. You must foul, with blood, the portion of the quill that goes into the flesh, and see, too, that it is pressed home into its exact place.[4] You must know that by Divine Agency every flight-feather has a short stout feather as a "supporter,"[5] called by Arabs a "key."[3]

Do not after this fly the hawk for two or three days, *i.e.*, not till the feather has set; and do not remove the silk binding for forty days. At the expiration of this period you can, if you like, remove the silk, but it is not necessary to do so. Fly your hawk regularly till the moulting season, but remove the silk before you set her down to moult. She will cast this replanted feather before any other, and the new one that will take its place will be smaller than its fellow in the other wing. In the second moult, however, there will be no difference.

Should the feathers that have been plucked out be lost, or should several days elapse since the injury occurred, then:—*Treatment*: put the hawk in a "sock,"[6] and wet the wing near the seat of injury, so that the down[7] is soaked. Very carefully search out the spot. The hole will have closed somewhat, and be too

---

[1] On a first of October I saw a young passage-saker minus six of its tail-feathers: the clumsy hawk-catcher, in his eagerness, had stepped on the tail. Forty days later these tail-feathers were one-fourth part grown and the falcon was also coming well to the lure. In *Falconry in the British Isles*, by Freeman and Salvin, mention is made of a merlin's tail-feather, which had dropped out, growing again.

[2] The flight-feather of a female peregrine penetrates the flesh for the distance of more than $1\frac{1}{4}$ inches.

[3] *Miftāḥ*, Ar., "a key, or any instrument that opens a door."

[4] The hole in the flesh closes up and is very difficult to find.

[5] *Pas-band;* in chess, "a piece that guards another."

[6] *Vide* "to mail," page 59, note 5.

[7] *Narm-parhā*, "down."

small to admit a full-sized feather; you must, therefore, plant a corresponding feather of a smaller size. Thus, if it is the second flight-feather of a female goshawk that is plucked out, you must plant the second flight-feather of a male; if of a male goshawk, then the corresponding feather of a female sparrow-hawk; if of a female sparrow-hawk, then the feather of a male sparrow-hawk, and so on. Well wet the down with lukewarm water, and place the end of the "artificial" feather in your mouth to soften it. When soaked, act as before, binding the feather to the "key," etc., etc.

The sooner after the accident the artificial feather is planted the better, but the operation can be carried out with successful results even three or four months after the accident, that is, any time before the socket-hole has closed up and the feathers on each side of it have fallen inwards and "blinded" it.[1] This operation was invented by your humble servant, the writer.

Now the flight-feather of a hawk is to be compared to the tooth of a man. If, owing to the chucking of a horse's head, or to a fall, or to other accident, a tooth gets knocked out of the head of a youth of ten or twenty years, if the tooth be at once replaced in its socket and bound to the teeth on each side of it, it will certainly take root again, though it will remain somewhat weaker than its neighbours; and will, on the approach of old age, when the powers decay and the teeth loosen, be the first to come away. Should, however, the tooth of that youth not be replaced, the teeth on either side will fall together inwards and so obliterate the gap that none can tell that there is a tooth missing. Hence the sooner you replace a plucked out feather the better.

---

[1] In *Forty-Five Years of Sport*, by J. H. Corballis, 1891, the author says that if a wing- or tail-feather be accidentally pulled out, the hole should at once be plugged with cotton-wool dipped in grease or honey to keep it open, and that if the plug be kept in its place for a few days a new feather will probably make its appearance. "If a feather should be plucked out, base and all, it is advisable to put some solid grease into the place, to keep it from closing up and preventing the new feather from growing down."—*The Art and Practice of Falconry*, by E. B. Mitchell, page 161. Tail feathers will grow again, but most falconers are agreed that flight-feathers plucked out do not grow again. I once tried the operation mentioned by our Persian author, but no new feathers grew.

CHAPTER LIX

OPERATION OF OPENING THE STOMACH.[1]

Obstruction due to a "Casting."—Now, my son, a casting of bone, or of feathers, or of wool, or of cotton-wool, may get stuck in a hawk's stomach[1] at the end of the sternum,[2] and the hawk be unable to eject it upwards or downwards. *Symptoms*: If you place your finger on the stomach, you will be able to perceive a hard substance the size of a large walnut, and this although you may have given no casting.[3] The hawk will not be able to eat more meat than an amount equal to one sparrow; she will try to, but there will be no room, and gradually she will waste away till she dies. *Treatment*: in the morning, before feeding, give her an emetic, such as the fouling of a tobacco-pipe, or the juice of black raisins;[4] rub these on her tongue and on the inside of her mouth. Watch her till she shows signs of vomiting; then, as she works her neck from side to side "to cast," that obstruction will come up as far as the throat but no farther. You must promptly grasp her by the throat, an assistant holding her firmly by the legs, while with a probe or tweezers or other instrument you somehow or other extract the obstruction, and so cure her. For a few days after this, mix her meat with the yolk of an egg, but beware of giving any feathers or bones or casting of any kind. *Item*: Should she not vomit, or should she not bring up the obstruction, then cut some mutton into small pieces and cast it into warm water, and give her of that an amount equal to a sparrow. Then, after a minute or so, give her a small amount of sal-ammoniac and sugar-candy, in the manner previously explained, and watch her. As soon as she begins to vomit, and the obstruction appears, seize her and remove it as just explained above. *Item*: if this expedient also fail, then cast her and tie her up firmly in some quiet spot protected from wind and draughts. Have by you ready a needle and silk, and yellow aloes powdered and mixed with antimony. Have the hawk's legs separated wide apart. Now, the hawk being on her

[1] *Khazīna.*
[2] *'Azm-i zawraqī*, *lit.* "boat-bone."
[3] *Ṭu'mah*, Ar., "meat, food; lure, etc.," is used by the Persian author both for "food" and for "casting."
[4] *Mavīz*, black raisins with stones.

back with her head away from you and raised, you will find at the root of the thigh and at the end of the sternum a fine skin:[1] pluck out the small feathers[2] from this, so as to lay bare the skin. Then with a sharp pen-knife make a slit lengthways in the skin, two fingers' breadth in length. After the "skin,"[3] you will find a second and a third "fine-skin,"[1] which also slit. Now, with the greatest care, insert two fingers, and lift up and expose the guts to view. Quickly and dexterously open the stomach, replace it in its proper position, and after that sew up, one by one, the three "fine-skins" and lastly the outer "skin." On the outside wound, sprinkle the powdered aloes and antimony, and then free the hawk and let her rest. Feed her every day on the yolks of eggs: if she will not eat them, pound a little meat, about half a sparrow in quantity, and mix it with the yolks of two eggs[4] and give it to her in the morning, and again at noon, and in the afternoon. If she eats this meat and "puts it over," again give her the yolks of two eggs with pounded meat. Feed her thus for two days. On the third day give her minced meat with the yolk of egg, and feed her thus for three days. Then for three days more give her meat, cut up into bits the size of a filbert and mixed with the yolk of an egg. During this period you must on no account let her pull or tear at her food; for the exertion of pulling will burst the stitches, either inside or out, and if the stitches of even one of the skins gives way, she is destroyed. Anyone accustomed to caponize cocks will have no difficulty in performing this operation: the two operations are practically the same.

Obstruction due to a Blow.—There is another form of this disease, which does not arise from a retained "casting": to cure this is an easier operation than that of cutting out the "casting" as above. The symptoms are the same: the hawk, even if a female goshawk, cannot eat more than one sparrow in quantity, and has in its stomach a hard substance the size of a walnut. If you give her her sparrow's portion of meat with feathers, she will cast in the morning but the hard substance will still remain present in the intestine. This disease is generally found in long-winged hawks,

1 *Parda.*
2 *Par-khurda-hā.*
3 *Pūst.*
4 The eggs are half to two-thirds the size of English eggs.

since it generally results from a kick in the guts from a gazelle, or from a buffet by a goose's wing (and a buffet from a goose's wing is worse than a blow from a club), or from an injury from the beak or claws of a crane, or from such an ill-judged stoop at some quarry that the stomach has come in violent contact with the ground.[1] The injury produces an internal hemorrhage, and the blood gradually congeals and fills up the stomach, and so reduces its capacity that it cannot contain its full quantity. The congealed blood gradually becomes converted into a white substance like cheese, day by day growing harder and pressing more on the stomach, till at last the substance petrifies and the bird dies. If the hawk is treated before "petrefaction" has set in, she can be cured. *Treatment:* the operation is the same as in the previous case; the cheese-like substance must be cut out and the stomach freed. The hawk must be fed after the operation in the same way.

After these operations, you must on no account let your hawk bathe till the scab[2] formed by the aloes and antimony drops off of its own accord; for bathing before this may kill your hawk. This is a rule that applies to every kind of wound, whether inflicted by the claw of an eagle or by the foot of a deer. Should your hawk be thirsty, you may, after five or six days have elapsed, offer her water in a cup, letting her drink a few beakfuls, enough to allay her thirst.

CHAPTER LX

ON THE NUMBER OF FEATHERS IN THE WING AND TAIL

In all hawks, whether long-winged or short, seven flight-feathers, by God's creation, show from under the coverts called *yār māliq*,[3] while in the tail there are in all twelve feathers. Very, very rarely, indeed, are eight flight-feathers apparent under the *yār-māliq;* but occasionally fourteen or even sixteen feathers occur in the tail. Birds with the latter number are in no way better than birds with the normal twelve.

---

[1] Even wild hawks make mistakes in stooping and injure themselves, but in this case it is the breast-bone that gets injured.

[2] *Kivla*, "scab."

[3] *Vide* note 1, page 112.

CHAPTER LXI

COUNSELS AND ADMONITIONS[1]

My son, I will now give thee sage counsel: do thou give ear to my advice and store it up in thy mind; for so shalt thou find future salvation and present success.

Monition the First. Be not a liar. Although it is said, and commonly believed, that all sportsmen are liars, still do thou employ no falsehood. Shaykh Sa'dī says:—

> "Truth-speaking God hath high in favour set
> Nor will he e'er the truthful man forget."[2]

Second. Act not perfidiously with thy friends and companions. Should the hawk of a rival "put in" its partridge and "fall at mark," and none see it but thee, conceal not the fact from the enquiring owner; nay, more, go thyself and point out to him the lost hawk, for perhaps some day he may be able to return the favour.

Third. Steal not the hawk or hound of an acquaintance, for theft is one of the vilest qualities in a man. Moreover thou wilt live in dread lest the owner should come along and proclaim thee dog-stealer and hawk-stealer. If thou findest a lost hawk, proclaim it or return it to the owner,[3] so shalt thou lay up great merit for thyself in the world to come, and also prove thy nobility of mind in this. Just think of the enormity of ensnaring a lost hawk and bearing it home, while the anxious and distressed owner wanders in the snow, from peak to peak, calling her and searching for her—you in your snug home the while.

> As noble deeds are recompensed in kind
> So evil acts an ill requital find.

Certainly the Almighty will not be pleased, and before many days elapse, some retaliation[4] will overtake thee. My boy, copulating

---

[1] This chapter has been somewhat abridged.

[2] Eastwick's translation.

[3] In India it was lawful to trap a man's pigeon but not to keep his lost hawk. In India if a hawk is caught the whole village knows it, and the news at once spreads for a radius of thirty miles. I once lost a hawk in Dera Ghazi Khan which was caught in Kapurthala, but the news of its capture soon reached me. Such instances are common.

[4] *Qiṣāṣ*, "exact retaliation"; an eye for an eye.

with the penis of others is poor sport: refrain or you'll fall into evil repute.

Fourth. Should an enemy loose a hawk and the hawk happen to come into thy possession, take it thyself and return it to him; for thy generous action will remove his enmity, and, should it not do so, men will extol thee and revile him: if thou do not act thus, then leave his hawk alone and make as though thou hadst not seen it, for often have I seen an evil man quarrel with his comrades about a single partridge, and the next day the lost hawk of a comrade having by chance fallen into his evil clutches he has killed it and buried it. Do thou avoid such practices, else neither in this world nor the next wilt thou escape punishment.

"Rend'ring evil for evil is easy to do;
If you're manly do good to the man that wrongs you."

CHAPTER LXII

ACCIDENTAL IMMERSION DURING WINTER

If your hawk, in pursuit of a water-fowl, happen to fall into the water in the depth of Winter, she will, if you do not apply remedies, certainly perish.[1] *Treatment:* if the hawk has taken the quarry, give her its warm heart and liver. Then "mail" her, place her in the bosom of a falconer and send him home. He should carry the hawk into the bath[2] or into a warm room and there take her out of his bosom and "unmail" her; and if she have digested the heart and liver he gave her, he should give her a proper meal of warm chicken. *Item:* mail the hawk and light a fire. Place the hawk in your waist-shawl, or in the skirt of your cloak, or in a handkerchief, and hold her some distance from the fire so that she may be gradually

[1] During a Panjab winter, if a hawk falls into water, even late in the evening, she will suffer no harm if fed up on warm flesh—provided, of course, she is in proper flying condition and not too thin. The cold in Persia, however, can be intense, while in the open desert an icy, paralysing wind often springs up and blows with such force that it is difficult to make headway against it.

[2] *Ḥammām:* even the villages in Persia have "Turkish baths," which are used by all. A Persian gentleman usually has a private bath attached to his own house.

warmed through: feed her as described above. *Item:* should you be in a spot where fuel is unobtainable, "mail" your hawk, place her in your horse's nosebag and put the nosebag on the horse's head. Then mount and ride hard for home. The horse's breath will give life to your hawk: it will save her from death. Arrived home, feed her. Though by this expedient the hawk's feathers will get ruffled and perhaps broken, still this is a lesser evil.

CHAPTER LXIII

EXPEDIENT IF MEAT FAIL

SHOULD you be caught in the snow far from your stage and have no means of procuring food for your hawks—a deadly cold wind springing up in your teeth, your hawks will certainly perish, unless fed. *Remedy:* at once dismount and bind the forearm of your horse. With the point of your pen-knife open the vein;[1] hold a cup underneath so that the blood may collect and congeal in it; then give this blood to your hawk that she escape death.

CHAPTER LXIV

RESTORATION AFTER DROWNING

SHOULD your hawk fall into a stream and be swept away,[2] and when recovered be lifeless, the treatment, even though the hawk has been apparently dead for half an hour, is as follows. *Treatment:* light a fire and lay the hawk down by the side of it. Collect the hot ashes under the wings and heap ashes on the back, and as soon as the ashes cool, pile on other ashes, fresh and warm.

[1] Blood is drawn from human beings in two ways; either from between the shoulders by the process called *ḥajāmat*, "cupping;" or, the arm being bound above the elbow, by opening the vein in the inside of the elbow, *faṣd kardan*. The latter operation is attended with some danger.

[2] A hawk that falls into deep *still* water can flap its way to shore—certainly for twenty or thirty yards.

The ashes must not be so hot as to burn the feathers. In a short time, by God's decree, the dead hawk will come to life. This remedy is suitable for a man also, or, indeed, for any beast that has been drowned. It is efficacious even up to half or three quarters of an hour after insensibility. I have several times successfully tried this remedy on man, beast, and bird.

> When a man is half-drowned, and with death is at strife,
> Hot ashes for him are the Water of Life.

CHAPTER LXV

SAGE ADVICE

NEVER forget the advice I will now give you. *First:* borrow nothing from any man, neither one penny nor a million; for if your request be granted, you are under an eternal obligation and must ever carry out the orders of him who hath obliged you.[1] Borrowing hawks, and dogs, and greyhounds, which are instruments of the chase—bad though such borrowing be—does not place you under a very great obligation, and further, should the loan be refused, it is no great slight to you.

Second: Three things you should never lend to any friend or sportsman; your own special horse, your own special gun, and your own special hawk. Lending any one of these is like lending your wife; therefore, my friend, lend none of these; for, if you do, the bands of friendship will be changed for the bonds of enmity. Bestow things freely, if you like, for giving is generosity.

> Lend not at all, or else when thou hast lent
> Seek not again from the recipient:
> Of what they've lent, they seek no restitution
> Such as be men of gen'rous constitution.

"HALSBAND" DANGEROUS IN HILLY OR WOODED COUNTRY.—*Third:* before you go hawking in hilly or woody country, remove the "halsband"[2] from your goshawk's neck, and this for two

[1] This "placing a person under an obligation" is a common Eastern idea. Indian falconers will press their perquisites of old bells, jesses, and hoods, on their friends in order to "mount an obligation on him."

[2] *Chalqū.*

reasons: (1) the "halsband" interferes with her foot-work when she puts in; she perhaps gets her foot entangled in it, and the partridge or pheasant goes out at the other side of the bush; (2) it often happens that a lost hawk is found hanging dead from a branch, suspended by its "halsband." Hence in hilly and woody country the hawk should be freed from what is there an encumbrance.

"HALSBAND" NECESSARY IN THE PLAINS.—In plains, however, a "halsband" is necessary to support the hawk when she is cast off and to prevent a strain to her loins: for, in the plains, you put your horse into a gallop that your hawk may start from the fist with the force of a bullet,[1] and to this impetus you add the force of your arm when casting her. However, when flying at *chukor* and *seesee* in the hills, the flight is down-hill, and the hawk has the advantage of gravity, so it is unnecessary to use hand-force in casting her.

CHAPTER LXVI

CURE FOR THE VICE OF "SOARING"

PERHAPS a goshawk or a sparrow-hawk may come into your possession that is naturally addicted to the vice of soaring;[2] that is, when you cast her at any quarry she will either take it at once, or, failing to do so, will give up and take to soaring and soon disappear from view. With such hawks there are three courses to be pursued, all three of which I have tested and proved.

FIRST DEVICE.—Slightly brand the oil-bottle or oil-gland, to produce inflammation. Then thread a needle with two or three threads of silk, and wax them well to strengthen them. At a distance of three fingers' breadth below the hawk's oil-gland, insert the needle into the first tail-feather, and bring it out at

[1] Considerable skill is necessary to cast off a short-winged hawk so as to really aid her. The difference that skilful casting makes, in the amount of quarry taken, is astonishing.

[2] *Dawr-chī*, "a soarer," *i.e.*, a hawk given to the vice of soaring. *Dawr kardan*, "to soar; also to ring up."

the twelfth; draw it just so tight that when the tail is spread there will be not more than an interval of a finger's breadth between each two feathers. When a hawk "soars," she spreads out her whole tail. Now this silk thread will prevent her spreading her tail to her heart's content: when she feels the unnatural constraint she will settle and give up the attempt to soar.

SECOND DEVICE.—Cut off four of her flight-feathers on one side on a level with the *jarka*[1] feathers, laying the severed feathers aside in a safe place till wanted.[2] If the hawk is a sparrow-hawk, go and fly her at quail: if a goshawk, take her into the field and fly her at quarry from a height (giving her the help of gravity), so that she may know that she has lost pace and is lop-sided. Fly her thus with shortened wings for a few days. Certainly, for two or three days, she will take no quarry. The next time she settles, call her from the ground to your fist and feed her up, and give up all thoughts of the quarry. Treat her like this for a few days. Now, when you see that, on failing to take her quarry, she sits on the ground, after she has done so once or twice, imp one of the cut feathers and again fly her. Fly her for four days in succession, every day carefully imping, with a fine needle, one feather. She will have quite forgotten her inclination to "soar."

> You ask advice, then my prescription try,
> That she forget this soaring in the sky.

THIRD DEVICE.—Pinch her in flesh considerably. If the weather is cold, every now and then give her a "snack" so that her stomach may not be empty and the cold may not cut her and kill her. Fly her from a height with the help of gravity. If she fails to take her quarry on account of her low condition, she will not attempt to soar, but will sit down; then call her to the fist and feed her up. Now gradually bring her back into her

---

[1] *Jarka:* apparently the "coverts," but this is not the word used elsewhere by the author for "coverts."

[2] ". . . When he is at the height of his familiarity, cut out of either wing three of his best flying feathers, and put to his heeles a knocking paire of bels, and so traine him when his want of power will hinder his desire to trauaile further, then you may with ease follow him."—Bert's *Treatise of Hawkes and Hawking* (page 77, Harting's reprint).

proper flying condition.[1] She will have forgotten her vice of soaring.[2]

I once had a very fine young *shikra* sparrow-hawk (*pīqū*), which showed much sport to me and my friends at quail. However, whenever she failed to take her quarry, she used to take to soaring. I cut off four of her flight-feathers, as described above, and for a few days succeeded in taking quail with her merely by the force of my throw,[3] until she quite gave up all thought of soaring: when she failed to take the quarry she sat on the ground. I then imped her four feathers, one by one, in four days. She continued to fly right well, and never again attempted to soar. This device is an invention of your humble servant.

NOTE OF WARNING.—Should your goshawk, when flown at *chukor* or *seesee*, give up the pursuit half way and take to soaring, and should another partridge rise[4] and the hawk then leave its soaring and start in pursuit, either taking the partridge in the air or on its putting it, on no account reward her: give her no food at all, for if you do you will confirm her in the habit of soaring. Had not this second partridge risen, your hawk would certainly have soared away out of view.

It sometimes happens that a *bălăbăn* trained to heron or crane gives up ringing after a heron, or gives up a flight at a crane, and that a duck[5] or an hubara gets up under her and that she comes

---

[1] Such a course would be fatal with a peregrine, for if a peregrine is trained and flown in low condition she will certainly take to soaring when brought into high or proper condition. Sakers, however, are not inclined to soar.

[2] *Dawr kardan va parsa zadan.* A dervish or professional story-teller sends round the hat at the most exciting point of his tale and this is called *parsa zadan;* hence any going round.

[3] *Shikras* are slow, and in India are always held in the hand and thrown like a ball. The hawk is placed on the palm of the right hand and collected, its legs and tail projecting between the thumb and forefinger. A careful falconer uses a small pad, as, from constant grasping, the feathers become soiled and ragged.

[4] *Buland shudan,* "to rise."

[5] Trained sakers will chase duck; but do they kill them in a wild state? A saker if gorged on the flesh of a water-fowl will often vomit. A fine haggard-saker of the translator's got violently sick from eating the flesh of the common heron; its stomach was so upset by the flesh that it could digest no other meat, and died. A small quantity, however, of heron's flesh may do no harm. This objection does not apply so much to the flesh of the purple heron and of the night-heron. *Vide* note 6, p. 137.

down on it and kills it. Go and lift up the hawk and her quarry, and if there be water near, duck both of them well till the hawk lets go. She will not do such a thing a second time.[1]

> When once in Noah's flood her passions cool,
> She ne'er again will play the giddy fool.

CHAPTER LXVII

ON BRANDING THE NOSTRILS BEFORE SETTING DOWN TO MOULT

Before setting down long-winged hawks that have been flown at great quarry, it is necessary to brand their nostrils, and this is especially necessary in the case of gazelle- and crane-hawks; for the orifice of the nose of a long-winged hawk is a pit, and when the throat of a gazelle is cut and the hawk pulls at the spurting throat, her nostrils become filled with blood, which congeals and stops the passage of her breath; the blood cannot be completely removed by washing, for the nostril is like a well. Take a packing needle and make it red-hot and brand the "button"[2] in the centre of the nostril, and with the point of the needle clean out the tube of the nostril shaping it like a spout,[3] so that you may hereafter be able to rinse out the nostril and remove the congealed blood.

For long-winged hawks flown at large quarry, especially for

[1] "But if you will have me grant that which I cannot yeelde unto, that hauing flowne a Partridge to a house, notwithstanding all these kinde courses taken with her, ſhee hath caught a Hen, then let some one in the company, that can tell how to doe it, make haste unto her, taking up both Hawke and Hen, and runne to a pond or pit of water, (there is no dwelling house inhabited, and where hens are, but you shall finde some water) and thereinto ouer-head and taile wash them both together three or foure times. . . . It is not possible there should be a hawke so ill but by this means she will be recouered."—Bert's *Treatise of Hawkes and Hawking* (pages 54-55, Harting's reprint). An Indian device to disgust a hawk with a particular quarry is to rub asafœtida on it. This is said to be effectual. It is, however, not always an easy matter to break a hawk of a quarry at which she flies with zest. The translator once had a young passage-saker trained to and flown only a few times at kite. He took the quarry from her without rewarding her, a dog frightened her, an old woman threw a blanket over her; in fact she suffered every ill a kite-hawk can suffer after taking the quarry, but she was not broken of the quarry.

[2] *Tukma* or *dukma* or *dugma*, T., "a button."

[3] *Miṣl-i nāvdān durust kun;* meaning not clear.

gazelle- and crane-hawks, branding the tube of the nostril is essential. Perhaps you will say, "Why has not the All-knowing God created hawks with noses ready branded?" The reply is that in a wild state these hawks prey on small quarry, such as pigeons and sand-grouse and larks, and, what is more, at their own leisure they first plume the quarry and then eat it, so that only their beaks get defiled by the blood and these are cleaned on the ground after the meal. But the trained hawk is artificially flown at gazelle and crane, and out of her hungry eagerness she buries all her head in the throat of the quarry as soon as it is cut. Now the main artery in a gazelle's throat will send the blood spouting out for ten paces' distance, and so, too, with a crane.

> If a hawk's nostrils with a brand you sear,
> Its wind suffices to pursue the deer.

CHAPTER LXVIII

A HAWK NOT TO BE FED WHEN "BLOWN"

If your hawk has worked hard and taken her quarry and you come up and see that she is blown, that her beak is open and her wings are loose, on no account feed her up, or you will make her ill; or else she will not fly with zest for three or four days. Now the reason is this: from the violence of her exertions the blood and fat in her body have become mixed, and her quarry too, owing to its fear, has exerted its utmost efforts to escape, and in this state you kill it and feed her on it. Now *Ḥāriṣ bin Kilda*, one of the most noted physicians in the time of the Lord of the Prophets[1] (God's peace on Him and his Family) said to *Nūshīravān* the Just, "Eat not when thou art in a state of excitement"; and this maxim appears to be applicable to all living things. Therefore cut the quarry's throat—letting your falcon see you do it—and hood her on her quarry, and remove her. "Carry" her for at least half an hour[2] till she has roused twice or thrice and her beak is closed, and she has collected and crossed her wings, and regained her wind. Then remove her hood close to her quarry and feed her upon it.

---

[1] *i.e., Muḥammad.*

[2] Two or three minutes' rest is really sufficient.

With goshawks, however, and with merlins, too, flown at larks, cut the throat of the quarry and let the hawk "plume"[1] it thoroughly and then eat. As a goshawk has no hood, you cannot treat her as just described for a falcon.

The reason that hawks in a wild state keep in health is, that after taking the quarry, they are forced to wait till they have "plumed" it before eating it; for this is Nature's law. Do thou likewise follow Nature.

> Since the revolving skies, the changing moons,
> The daily sunshine, all are Nature's boons,
> Show her perfections, and her charms display,
> Gaze carefully, my son, and learn her way.

Before you go out hawking, see, before you mount, that you have with you various bird-catching apparatus, such as a sparrow-net, a sparrow-hawk net, and a *du-gaza*; for out hawking you will frequently come across a goshawk, or a sparrow-hawk, or a saker; if you have the necessary apparatus and can prove your skill by catching one of these, just see what pleasure it will give you.[2] I once was flying a favourite passage-saker at a heron, and the falcon had rung up into mid-heaven and was on the point of taking the quarry, when suddenly an eagle[3] appeared and seized my falcon in mid-air and slew her. I and my men galloped after the brute to rescue the falcon, but she was dead. The bastard that had made my liver into roast meat[4] went and settled on a rock, but I had with me only a sparrow-hawk net, and with a sparrow-hawk net it is not possible to catch an eagle; for an eagle will not come to a sparrow-hawk net, or a sparrow-net[5]—or if it does come, it carries it away. I suddenly spied a kestril perched on a stone, and set up my sparrow-hawk *du-gaza*[5] in front of it. The poor bird, through vain greed, fell into the snare and into my clutches. I pulled a few

[1] "'Plume,' *v.*, to pluck the feathers off the quarry."—*Harting*.

[2] There is a peculiar fascination about Eastern devices for bird-catching; the methods are so quaint and so successful, and the "quarry" is so varied.

[3] Eagles are slow in flight, but make up for their slowness by dropping suddenly from a height.

[4] *Kabāb*, "meat cut in little bits and roasted on a skewer," is by a weird metaphor applied to a heart torn by grief, or love.

[5] It *is* possible to catch eagles in an ordinary *du-gaza*, for I have done so. A "sparrow-hawk *du-guza*," however, is sometimes much smaller than an ordinary *du-gaza*. I have caught hobbies in a *du-gaza* about two spans high and about four long, suspended on straws or thorns.

hairs out of my horse's tail and made four or five strong nooses, and I skinned the sparrow.[1] I tied the feathers into the kestril's claws and concealed the nooses amongst the feathers. I then half-seeled the kestril's eyes and cast it into the air, but the murderous eagle was not attracted; it ignored the kestril. Suddenly a buzzard (*sār*) appeared, and, stooping at the feathers in the kestril's claws, got entangled in the nooses. Both birds fell to the ground. I galloped and secured the buzzard. Adding to the feathers, and strengthening the nooses, I half-seeled the buzzard's eyes and treated it as I had treated the kestril. The buzzard rose in the air; the eagle saw it, and rose after it to rob from it those tempting feathers; little it dreamt that the hunter would be hunted. It rose and made a glorious stoop; then, its fingers inside those nooses, it fell to earth along with the buzzard. I murdered the murderer and rejoiced. So great was my exultation you might almost have fancied my falcon had not been slain. Now, you see you should always have with you complete apparatus for all kinds of sport and fowling, even to fishing tackle, for each sport has its own peculiar delight.

Should an eagle slay and devour your hawk before your eyes and then clean its talons in the ground, and should you, having with you a *charkh* trained to eagles, cast it at the eagle and take it, and then execute various mutilating punishments[2] on it—why, what delight can equal this?

CHAPTER LXIX

MISCELLANEOUS NOTES

If wheat be soaked three times in the froth of a *mast* camel and then dried and given to birds to eat, they will fall senseless. Also if beans be boiled in rats-bane,[3] and then scattered in a spot where common cranes, and wild geese, and crows, and choughs collect,

[1] Presumably a sparrow was the bait. For a kestril, however, a mole-cricket is a surer bait.

[2] *Nasaq* is any mutilating (or corporal) punishment, such as cutting off the nose and ears, etc., etc.

[3] *Marg-i mūsh*, P., or *sammu 'l-fār*, Ar. (*lit.* "death to mice") is "white arsenic."

those that eat thereof will fall down in a swoon, and if left alone will become *ḥarām*.[1] When you take these birds, cut their throats and at once rip open the stomach and cast away the contents, so that the poison may not spread to the flesh.[2]

If you lose a hawk when out hawking and do not recover her till the next day or a few days after, know that, whether she be a young hawk of the year or a moulted[3] hawk, she will ever after be a trouble to you, for her nature will have changed for the worse, especially if she has preyed for herself while out. As for me, *I* would not keep her; my friends may please themselves.

Perchance some night your hawk may wanton prove,
And leaving place and keeper seek to rove.
Moreover, oh! my friend, should vagrant prey
Fall to her beak as quarry while astray;
Think not, howe'er you worry, to retain
Your hawk, that she can ever fly again.
Beshrew the jade! I would not have her so,
Not as a gift, though friends might scarce say "No."
When garden trees run riot o'er the wall
The gardener brings his axe and fells them all.
To me, the noblest bird of all is she,
That ever sits on friends' hands willingly.
May this *Bāz-Nāma*, written thus by me,
When I am dust, keep green my memory.

[1] *i.e.*, they will die of their own accord and so be "unlawful" for food.

[2] "If you desire to take *House doves*, *Stock doves*, *Rooks*, *Choughs*, or any other Birds, then take Wheat, Barley, *Fetches*, Tares, or other Grain, and boil them very well with good store of Nux Vomica, in ordinary running water. When they are almost boiled, dry and ready to burst, take them off the Fire and set them by till they be thoroughly cold. Having so done scatter this grain in the Haunts of those Birds you have a mind to take; and as soon as they have tasted thereof, they will fall down in a dead *sound*, and shall not be able to recover themselves in a good while. And as you take these Great Land-fowl with this Drunken Device, so you shall take the middle and smaller Sort of Birds, if you observe to boil with what Food they delight in, a quantity of this Nux Vomica." Further on, the same writer says that "Lees of Wine," can be substituted for Nux Vomica, and also that the grain may be steeped in the "Juice of Hemlock, adding thereto some Henbane seed or poppy seed, causing them to be infused therein four or five days." "HOW TO RECOVER A FOWL THUS ENTRANCED:—If you would restore these entranced Fowl to their former Health, take a quantity of Sallet-oyle, according to the strength and Bigness of the Fowl and drop it down the throat of the Fowl; then chafe the Head with a little strong White-wine-vinegar, and the Fowl will presently recover and be as well as ever."—From the *Gentleman's Recreation*, by Richard Blome.

[3] By "moulted" (*ṭulakī*) the author probably means "intermewed."

I wrote it in the Great Shah's golden days,
The King whose orders Heaven itself obeys;
High Rank and Fortune riding rein to rein,
With honour and with glory swell his train;
The game of courage captive in his noose:
His strength is mighty and his gifts profuse;
His barbéd arrows are God's swift decrees;
His butts the lives of all his enemies.
His strength of arm is such as angels know,
The curvéd sky he uses as his bow.
When Heaven itself to praise the Shah would fail,
What can *Mushtāqī's*[1] humble verse avail?

This book, by the aid of the Munificent King, was finished on the day of Wednesday, in the month of *Zū 'l-Qa'da* the Sacred, in the year 1285[2] of the Flight of the Prophet; and it contains the Views and Experience of *Taymūr Mīrzā*, son of *Ḥusayn 'Alī Mīrzā*, and bearer of the title of Governor of the Province of *Fārs.*

[1] *Mushtāqī*, the author's *takhalluṣ* or poetical *nom de plume.*
[2] Corresponding to A.D. 1868.

PRINTED FOR BERNARD QUARITCH, 11, GRAFTON STREET, LONDON, W.,
BY G. NORMAN AND SON, FLORAL STREET, COVENT GARDEN, LONDON, W.C.

XXV

HUNTING AND HAWKING SCENE